MAKING YOUR CASE: USING *R* FOR PROGRAM EVALUATION

MAKING YOUR CASE: USING *R* FOR PROGRAM EVALUATION

Charles Auerbach

and

Wendy Zeitlin

OXFORD
UNIVERSITY PRESS

OXFORD
UNIVERSITY PRESS

Oxford University Press is a department of the University of Oxford. It furthers the University's objective of excellence in research, scholarship, and education by publishing worldwide.

Oxford New York
Auckland Cape Town Dar es Salaam Hong Kong Karachi
Kuala Lumpur Madrid Melbourne Mexico City Nairobi
New Delhi Shanghai Taipei Toronto

With offices in
Argentina Austria Brazil Chile Czech Republic France Greece
Guatemala Hungary Italy Japan Poland Portugal Singapore
South Korea Switzerland Thailand Turkey Ukraine Vietnam

Published in the United States of America by
Oxford University Press
198 Madison Avenue, New York, NY 10016

Cataloging-in-Publication data is on file at the Library of Congress
ISBN 978–0–19–022808–8

9 8 7 6 5 4 3 2 1
Printed in the United States of America
on acid-free paper

CONTENTS

MAKING YOUR CASE: USING *R* FOR PROGRAM EVALUATION

/// 1 /// INTRODUCTION TO PROGRAM EVALUATION IN SOCIAL SERVICE AGENCIES

INTRODUCTION

A couple of years ago, in our academic travels, we were reintroduced to *R*, an open-source statistical programming language. We wrote a package, *SSD for R*, to analyze single-subject research data with *R*, and we began using *R* with our students in master's-level practice research classes in social work. Eventually, this led to our first book, *SSD for R: An R Package for Analyzing Single-Subject Data.*

In the course of writing that book, we looked at who was using *R* and for what reasons. After all, there are a number of user-friendly, comprehensive statistical packages available, many of which enjoy a sizable market share. We also looked at issues related to organizational research. We discovered that research capacity and organizational challenges are oft-cited barriers to conducting research in practice settings (Auerbach & Zeitlin, 2014). Some of the primary roadblocks to conducting organizational research include a lack of skill, both methodological and statistical, and resources, including both time and money.

There is, however, a growing need for research within practice settings. Increasing competition for funding requires organizations to demonstrate that the funding they are seeking is going toward effective programming. Additionally, the evidence-based practice movement is generally pushing organizations toward research activities, as both producers and consumers.

Within this context, we discovered that *R* is an excellent solution to addressing some of the struggles that organizations currently face in conducting research. First, *R* is both free and open-source. What this means is that there are no financial barriers for individuals or organizations wishing to use it, and it can be installed and used on any platform. It is also constantly being developed, as there is a dedicated community of users who are writing and disseminating packages, which are discrete sets of statistical functions, on the Comprehensive R Archive Network (CRAN).

We have also discovered that, while not menu-driven, *R* is relatively simple to teach and learn. *RStudio*, a free graphical user interface, provides an easy-to-use format for working with *R*, and basic commands are typically just a few words. Because of the size and breadth of the *R* community, there are many resources available to provide support to users of all levels.

THE PURPOSE OF THIS BOOK

There have been many books written about research methodology and data analysis in the helping professions, and many books have been written about using *R* to analyze and present data; however, this book specifically addresses using *R* to evaluate programs in organizational settings.

Why did we write it? As professors, we believe that using *R* to teach research skills is extremely valuable. We have learned through experience that since *R* is freely accessible, students are motivated to download it and use it outside the classroom for homework assignments, class projects, and evaluations. We hope that students eventually use this knowledge to introduce evaluations into the settings in which they work, both as student interns and as professionals.

We also recognize that many organizations would like to do research for some of the reasons described earlier, but the barriers to doing so can be high. Helping staff learn the skills to conduct evaluations in-house using free and reliable software can go a long way in reducing barriers to carrying out these activities. We have noticed that intentionally engaging staff in the research process helps them become invested in the results and implications of research findings. Finally, we have learned that staff can participate in the research process if given some guidance and meaningful context. This book is designed to address all of these.

Throughout the remainder of this chapter, we provide you with an overview of program evaluation in organizational settings. In it, we discuss what evaluation research is and what differentiates it from other forms of research. We provide a rationale for conducting this type of research, and we also discuss issues related to conducting evaluations. The chapter concludes with suggestions for using this book.

It should be noted that we have worked and consulted across the helping professions (e.g., psychology, speech pathology, medicine, education), but our primary background is in social work. Many of the examples in this book come from our own experiences, and we have used generic language with regard to the helping professions and practice settings, wherever possible. In the interests of simplicity, though, we use the term *client* to denote the receiver of some sort of service. We recognize that various practice settings and professions refer to these individuals differently.

WHAT IS EVALUATION RESEARCH?

Evaluation research is practice-based, and it closely looks at one or more aspects of a program. The setting for the research and the population studied are real-life organizations, clients and/or practitioners.

The overall purpose of evaluation research, then, is not to produce findings that are generalizable to larger populations, but rather to assess the effectiveness of distinct interventions with the intention of impacting practice and/or organizational policy (Corcoran & Secret, 2013; Holosko, Thyer, & Danner, 2009). Evaluation research is the most commonly conducted form of research in social work settings (Corcoran & Secret, 2013).

As research designs, in general, are driven by research questions and resources, the most frequently used methods in evaluation research are simple group designs, such as pre-test/post-test, or single-subject designs. In our previous book, we focused on single-subject designs; however, this book focuses on simple group designs.

WHY SHOULD WE CONDUCT EVALUATION RESEARCH?

There are a number of reasons that you might consider engaging in evaluation research. First, evaluation research can help organizations answer important questions, such as the following:

- Who are we helping?
- What is useful to our clients?
- Do our services meet identified goals for those we serve? For our organization?
- Are our services cost-effective?

A major benefit to conducting evaluation research is that you can examine programs or interventions in real-life settings. Because of this, findings are particularly valuable to administrators, board members, practitioners, and other stakeholders who can use the results to, among other things, improve services or apply for funding (Kirk & Reid, 2002).

Once data are analyzed and results interpreted, findings can be used to adapt and improve programs. For example, you could seek to identify the characteristics of clients who may be helped by existing programs, as well as those of clients who are not helped. It may be useful, then, to determine additional strategies to better serve those clients who may not have met their goals (Grinnell, Gabor, & Unrau, 2012). Subsequent evaluations can then be used to determine if program modifications have successfully met the identified objectives.

Practice-based research, in general, can contribute to the advancement of the social work profession by establishing the effectiveness of specific practices. This type of research is helpful to clients, who are consumers of social work services, and in promoting social work as a distinct profession (Epstein, 2010). Sharing research findings at professional conferences and in social work journals can help provide evidence to the efficacy of social work interventions.

WHEN AND HOW OFTEN SHOULD WE EVALUATE OUR PROGRAMS?

Programs should be evaluated periodically to determine to what degree they are meeting stated goals. Sometimes, there is some sort of directive to conduct a program evaluation, such as when an organization is initially applying for funding or to report periodic progress to funders or other stakeholders. The timing of this, of course, is dictated by those mandates.

There are, however, other times when organizations should consider evaluating their services. Any time there is a notable change, either in services or client populations, it may be helpful to consider conducting an evaluation. For example, if a new intervention is introduced into the organization, a plan should be made, based upon the goals of the program, to evaluate it at some point in the future. This plan should consider issues such as the number of individuals served by the program, the specific goals of the program, and when it would be logical to conduct an evaluation. Alternatively, if client populations change, it may be useful to evaluate services in order to determine if these new clients are served with the same level of success as previous clients.

ETHICAL CONSIDERATIONS IN CONDUCTING EVALUATION RESEARCH

One of the first and most serious considerations in program evaluation includes ethical issues. On the one hand, it is clear that professional social workers should engage in practice-based research. The Council Work on Social Work Education, the accrediting body of BSW and MSW (bachelor's and master's degrees in social work) programs in the United States, considers engaging in research-informed practice and practice-informed research one of the core competencies in the development of professional social workers (Council on Social Work Education [CSWE], 2008).

The National Association of Social Workers discusses 16 points related to program evaluation in Section 5.02 of the Code of Ethics. Among other things, social workers should monitor and evaluate programs and practice interventions and should promote research in order to develop knowledge. On the other hand, the Code of Ethics provides firm guidelines with regard to ethics in research of all types, including evaluations. Also in Section 5.02, social workers are warned to take precautions to protect clients who may be the subjects of program evaluations. These precautions include providing informed consent when appropriate. Clients also should not be penalized if they choose not to participate or if they withdraw as research subjects. Additional safeguards include minimizing any type of harm to research participants and assuring the anonymity or confidentiality of participants (National Association of Social Workers, 2008).

Other helping professions, of course, engage in program evaluations as well. The American Evaluation Association, for example, has interest groups that focus on evaluation in a range of sectors. These vary widely and include fields such as higher education, human services, criminal justice, and nonprofit evaluations.

Program evaluations have some unique ethical considerations, as research subjects are often current or former clients. One specific issue arises when active clients are simultaneously consumers of social work services and research subjects. In these cases, it is important that evaluation activities not interfere with social work intervention (Martin Bloom & Orme, 1994). Additionally, extra care needs to be taken to ensure the confidentiality of client/research data (Grinnell et al., 2012; Holosko et al., 2009).

Another ethical issue in evaluation research revolves around informed consent. Depending upon the research design selected, it may be possible to obtain written informed consent, as is typical in social science research. In other cases, informed consent may be built into the initial written arrangement between the client and organization, which may also include Health Insurance Portability and Accountability Act (HIPAA) disclosures and other agreements.

In research that uses existing case records or other forms of retrospective data, it may be difficult, if not impossible, to obtain informed consent from participants (Epstein, 2010; Holosko et al., 2009).

In all of these situations, evaluation research may or may not fall under the auspices of an Institutional Review Board (if one exists within the organization); it may, instead, exist within the realm of quality control or similar committees (Epstein, 2010). It is, however, incumbent upon the evaluators to determine under what umbrella the evaluation falls and to meet all necessary ethical requirements in order to protect clients throughout and after the evaluation process.

ADDITIONAL CONSIDERATIONS IN CONDUCTING EVALUATION RESEARCH

As in any type of research, there are a number of factors to consider in the design and implementation of evaluation projects. These include resources in the form of time, funds, expertise, and computer resources. Other factors to consider include what data you have access to and in what form, what information stakeholders need to receive and in what form, and the complexity of the evaluation.

There are, however, considerations that are unique to evaluation research in practice settings. One of these is the involvement of practitioners and other staff in the research process. In many cases, an evaluation may, at least initially, be perceived negatively, as staff may feel unnecessarily scrutinized, and that the process wastes both their time and efforts. To address this, it may be helpful to get staff involved in various aspects of the research process, and they should also be shown the practical value of the research (Centers for Disease Control and Prevention, 2011; Epstein, 2010; Rock, Auerbach, Kaminsky, & Goldstein, 1993).

Another consideration in evaluation research, which pertains to any type of intervention research, is fidelity to the intervention. That is, when evaluating any type of intervention, it is important to ascertain that services are delivered in the same manner, or substantially in the same manner, across practitioners and settings (Fraser, Richman, Galinsky, & Day, 2009; Samuels, Schudrich, & Altschul, 2008). In some cases, when specific interventions have been clearly defined, fidelity instruments may have been produced by the developer to ensure adherence to the practice. Organizations conducting evaluations may want to consider using existing fidelity measures. Alternatively, agencies could work on developing their own checklists to ensure faithfulness to the intervention model.

HOW THIS BOOK IS ORGANIZED

This book is divided into three sections, each addressing different but related topics regarding the use of *R* to conduct program evaluations. The first section encompasses the first two chapters and deals with background information that is helpful in conducting practice-based research. This first chapter provides a context and rationale for conducting agency-based research and addresses ethical and pragmatic issues encountered in doing so. Chapter 2 discusses issues directly related to program evaluation, including different types of evaluations, developing research questions, various types of research designs, developing measurement plans, and presenting findings. Chapter 2 is only meant as an overview, as there are many excellent texts that address these issues in great detail; the purpose of this chapter, then, is to provide food for thought and to identify issues to consider when planning evaluations.

The second section of the book consists of two chapters that provide necessary background to begin working with *R*. In Chapter 3, we discuss, for example, how to download *R* and *RStudio*, the graphical user interface we mentioned previously. We also talk about navigation, *R* packages, and the most basic of *R* functions. Again, this is an overview chapter, as a great many books and resources already exist that provide general information about *R*. Instead of providing a comprehensive background on *R*, the purpose and structure of this chapter is to provide sufficient information to help readers get started using *R* and to provide sufficient context for the remainder of the book. Chapter 4 talks about the various options for getting data into *R*. These include entering data directly and manually into *R*, but also importing them from popular software programs such as Excel, Google Docs, and Survey Monkey. We also show you how to import data from other statistical package file formats such as SAS, SPSS, and Stata. Finally, we introduce you to our software package, *The Clinical Record*, a free downloadable database that we developed to help small to mid-sized organizations track and record client information. Data from *The Clinical Record* can be downloaded and imported into *R* for evaluations.

The third section of the book consists of six chapters, all of which are designed to teach readers how to use *R* to conduct program evaluations and all of which are based on case studies, which we describe in depth in each chapter. Chapter 5 shows different methods for graphically reporting and displaying data. Chapter 6 provides instruction on summarizing data. Chapters 7, 8, and 9 discuss looking at the relationships between various factors and one or more outcomes. These chapters provide the most technical instruction on determining to what extent program goals and objectives are being met. Chapter 10 provides a comprehensive example of a program evaluation. It includes complete instructions for downloading and using *The Clinical Record*. We then show you how to select and import data from *The Clinical Record* based upon a stated research question. This concluding chapter incorporates concepts from all of the previous chapters to illustrate how the various components of an evaluation come together.

The final section in this book provides additional resources in the form of appendices. As previously stated, there are many resources currently available that address both *R* and research methods, in general, and we provide you with these in Appendix A in the form of an annotated bibliography. Appendix B provides a brief glossary of terms that we use in this book. In Appendix C, we provide a listing of *R* packages used throughout the book and recommend others that we believe you will find helpful in the future. Finally, in Appendix D, we provide a listing of tables that are part of *The Clinical Record* and field names that appear in the application. Throughout this book, we will refer you to one or more appendices when we believe they will serve as a good reference.

While this book and some chapters begin with the title *Making Your Case*, we are using this phrase to describe the reasons that agencies might engage in practice evaluation. A note of caution, however, which is an important consideration in all research: as researchers, we attempt to be as unbiased as possible. Therefore, while the ultimate goal of an agency might be to make a case about something or other, it is our role as researchers to form testable questions that can be empirically answered.

Beginning with Chapter 3, we illustrate functions that are available in various packages. At the beginning of each chapter, we list the packages used in the examples in the chapter. You may choose to install and load these packages early on, and instructions for doing so are in the Packages section of Chapter 3.

USING THIS BOOK

In this book, we tie together organization-based research with data analysis using *R*. We began addressing this topic in our first book, *SSD for R: An R Package for Analyzing Single-Subject Data*, for those looking at single-case designs. In this book, we expand our focus by examining group designs.

One of the unique features of this text is that we provide you with case studies in many of the chapters to illustrate concepts that we are demonstrating. These present real practice scenarios, and we provide you with the data files necessary to work through the examples illustrated in each chapter. These data files can be downloaded free of charge from our website at www.ssdanalysis.com.

The case studies we present are based, in large part, on existing agency records that were gathered and analyzed. We took this as our primary approach for several reasons. First, much of the data needed to conduct program evaluations already exist within agencies, and we wanted to demonstrate how useful this can be. Often data are collected from clients at various points and in different forms, and these can be gathered and analyzed to better understand the impact that programs are having on clients. These data are often meaningful to practitioners, who may be involved in the evaluation process, and they may be easily accessible. Often, collection of these data can be unobtrusive (i.e., it does not interfere with the delivery of services in any way), so many of the ethical issues discussed earlier in this chapter are avoided entirely (Epstein, 2010; Whitaker, 2012).

This book, however, is not a primer on either research methods or *R*. For in-depth information and additional resources on either of these topics, we refer you to the many excellent texts and resources listed in Appendix A. What we attempt to do in this book is to teach and demonstrate the necessary skills in *R* to conduct quantitative program evaluations using group research designs.

A FEW NUTS AND BOLTS AS YOU GO THROUGH THIS BOOK

As you make your way through this book, you will notice that we have written in different fonts in order to clarify what we are demonstrating. When we show syntax that we enter into *RStudio*, which you may want to replicate in order to practice the concepts we are teaching, we begin each command with a prompt displayed like this: >, and the command itself is written in bold in **`this font`**. This duplicates what is actually observed when you enter commands in *RStudio*. Output that is shown from each command `is also displayed in this font, but is not bolded.` IMPORTANT NOTE: As you enter commands yourself, DO NOT enter the prompt that we display. *R* provides you with prompts, and you simply begin entering a command by clicking on the space to the right of the prompt.

As you read through the book, we shorten our notation regarding the use of drop-down menus in *RStudio*. When navigating these menus, we tell you where to begin and then give you the options you should choose by listing them in sequence, each separated from the next with a slash.

When we refer to an *R* command, we specifically refer to an entire instruction that you enter. Commands are made up of primary functions and additional options that are separated from the primary function by a comma in most cases.

You will notice that *R* makes extensive use of parentheses in writing commands. It is important in all cases to have matching parentheses; that is, for each open parenthesis, there must be a matching closing parenthesis. *R* will return an error when these do not match.

Finally, we use the term *observation* throughout this book. This term refers to data for a single unit. Other texts and disciplines may use different terminology to denote to this concept, including *record* or *case*.

/// 2 /// ISSUES IN PROGRAM EVALUATION

In this chapter, we begin expanding on ideas that are unique to evaluating programs in organizational settings. We will describe the various types of program evaluations, but we will quickly narrow our focus to outcome evaluations, which are the emphasis of this book. We will provide you with ideas to consider when you begin your own evaluation. This will include a discussion on identifying the boundaries and functions of the program. We will talk about conditions within a program that make it more favorable for conducting a useful evaluation. Then, we will move on to the more pragmatic topics necessary to consider with all types of research. These include a discussion on developing research questions, selecting an appropriate research design, sampling and data collection, identifying variables, instruments, and presenting findings. Notice that we purposely avoid talking about data analysis in this chapter. That is because the vast majority of this book is devoted to data analysis and interpretation. Therefore, this chapter is dedicated to an overview of the other issues that must be considered when doing an evaluation project.

The topics covered in this chapter are overviews and are meant to provide you with food for thought. Before embarking on your own evaluation, you should thoroughly consider each of these topics. References for additional resources are included in Appendix A.

TYPES OF PROGRAM EVALUATIONS

There are essentially four different types of program evaluations:

1. Needs assessments
2. Process evaluations
3. Efficiency evaluations
4. Outcome evaluations.

Needs assessments are typically used for program planning. Research questions asked in these types of evaluations include inquiries into how many people in the program's catchment area experience the problem the program is aiming to address. What are the sources of these problems? What other needs might these people have? These could include issues related to language proficiency, child-care needs, or transportation. What funding is available to support the program?

Needs assessments may involve some quantitative methods, but more often heavily uses qualitative methods such as in-depth interviews and focus groups. Stakeholders outside the agency may be included in research activities.

Process evaluations are concerned with how well a program operates. The purpose of these is to examine the strengths and weaknesses of the program's performance for the purpose of improvement. Research questions include addressing issues such as the screening of potential clients. How are treatment plans developed? How are they implemented? How faithful to the treatment model are the services that are being delivered? Process evaluations are particularly good for describing the context in which services are delivered. Like needs assessments, process evaluations may rely primarily on qualitative analysis.

Efficiency evaluations assess programs in monetary terms. Efficiency evaluations fall into two broad categories: cost-effectiveness studies and cost-benefit studies. Cost-effectiveness studies examine program costs. For example, a result of a cost-effectiveness study of homeless services could estimate that Program X costs $60 to house a family of four per day, compared to Program Y that costs $45 per family per day. Cost-benefit studies examine not only program costs, but also the financial benefits to society. Using this example, a cost-benefit study would look more closely at the longer-term financial benefits provided by the program. This could include factors such the value of job training and behavioral health services that could help clients remain independent in the community after leaving the shelter.

Outcome evaluations are the focus of this book. These studies look at the degree to which programs achieve their stated goals. The main question that these types of studies answer is, "How well did the program work?" On the face of it, this may seem simple, but it is actually quite complex. For example, in looking at the homeless services discussed earlier, we might ask, "How successful were clients at moving into permanent housing?" But this broad question can spur additional points of inquiry, such as the following:

- Were clients who moved into permanent housing still living in the community six months later? A year later? Two years later? This brings up the question of the duration of program impact, which should influence both your study design and measurement. If we anticipated that clients leaving the shelter were going to remain living in the community a year later, we would need to devise a way to track these individuals and measure to what degree they have retained their housing. We might need to ask questions about income sources, whether they are paying their rent on time, how many times they have moved, and what additional supports they may have obtained after leaving the shelter.

- Were clients who were "successful" different from those who were not? Notice that the word "successful" was put in quotation marks, as how one program defines success may be quite different from how a similar program defines success. However success is ultimately described for the program you are evaluating, a natural follow-up question will be to identify the differences between those who were successful and those who were not, especially when the goal of the evaluation is to improve services for clients. Perhaps at the homeless shelter we find that families who have more than one child are much more likely to become homeless again within a year of leaving the shelter than those with no children or only one child. This finding may lead us to further inquiry in order to answer the question of why this may be, and what the shelter can do to better serve these families.

As you read about the various types of program evaluations, you may begin to realize that these types may not be independent of each other and may overlap depending on an organization's needs for information. For example, the homeless shelter described above could have multiple related questions, including the following:

1. How successful are we in meeting our program goals?
2. How do we get the most "bang for our buck?"
3. What could we do to be more efficient?

Here you could see that one question could lead to another, and findings from one type of evaluation could inform another.

Therefore, another way of looking at program evaluation is whether the evaluation is *formative* or *evaluative*. Formative evaluations focus on looking at issues related to program development and improvement, while summative evaluations look at overall program success (Grinnell et al., 2012).

UNDERSTANDING THE PROGRAM BY BUILDING LOGIC MODELS

Regardless of the type of evaluation you are planning, it is very helpful to begin the research process by documenting key aspects of the program. This will help clarify certain program parameters that will be used during the evaluation. It is important to note that programs that do not have well-articulated goals and objectives are difficult to evaluate, and logic models are one way to detail these key aspects.

Logic models can be used to visually depict features of a program and relationships between those features. While there is not one single method for developing these, logic models may document program resources, activities, and goals and

Draft Logic Model

Program Name: Family Services

Program Vision: To help families gain housing and maintain it in the long-term

Population Served: Parents who enter the shelter with one or more children

Population Needs to be Addressed by Services: We serve homeless families in the tri-state area. Those entering the shelter need help with obtaining and maintaining permanent housing. This includes help with obtaining housing, but also affordable chid care, job training and job obtainment, and behavioral health needs.

**Services	Resources	Outcomes	Indicators	Measurement
Parents are screened for necessary services including parenting skills, chid care arrangements, job skills, interviewing skills, job search strategies, income supports, and health/behavioral health care. Some services are provided on-site at the shelter while others are referred out to other agencies in the community.	Sufficient shelter beds, access to housing through the local housing authority, connections to behavioral/ mental health care providers throughout the tri-state area, meeting space for program components (e.g., job training seminars, AA/NA meetings, child care), MSW-level social workers	Public and private agencies (schools, child development centers, faith-based groups, health departments, etc.) enhance their services to strengthen families.	• Public and private agencies have policies in place that support meaningful partnerships with parents. • Public and private organizations communicate with other he lping agencies to coordinate and enhance family strengthening activities. • Public and private agencies make appropriate referrals to families as needed. • Public and private agencies help parents actively participate in agency decision-making activities. • Agencies assist with chidcare and transportation needs, schedule meetings to accommodate parent's schedules, etc.	• No Tools Selected

		Participants know how to manage family life to promote self-sufficiency, safety, and stability.	• Participants demonstrate knowledge of how to find high-quality, reliable childcare. • Participants demonstrate knowledge of where to go and how to access adult education and job preparation services as needed. • Participants demonstrate knowledge of how to effectively search for employment with livable wages. • Participants demonstrate knowledge of how to develop and manage a household budget. • Participants demonstrate knowledge of how to comparison shop for food, services, and household goods to say within budgets. • Participants demonstrate knowledge of how to obtain safe and affordable housing. • Participants demonstrate knowledge of where they can access clothing, food, medications, and shelter in emergency situvations.	• Multi-Problem Screening Questionnaire (MPSQ) • Family Resource Scale • Family Needs Scale Community Life Skills Scale (CLS) NCAST

****Service Assumptions**: We use a Housing First model, which suggests that many of the underlying issues related to homelessness can be addressed once clients are in permanent housing.

FIGURE 2.1 Logic model of Family Services at the homeless shelter

objectives. They can also record community needs, assessment methods, assumptions, and the vision of the program.

Creating a logic model requires some effort; however, this is time that is well spent, as a well-developed model will help you focus your evaluation. Additionally, individuals who may contribute to the logic model are often valuable resources that you will want to include in additional evaluation efforts.

In the previous section, we talked about various research questions that could be explored at the homeless shelter serving families with children. Figure 2.1 illustrates a logic model that the agency developed. This logic model was built using the Child Welfare Information Gateway's Logic Model Builder, which can be found at https://toolkit.childwelfare.gov/toolkit/.

Notice that this particular logic model does not emphasize all aspects of the organization, but focuses specifically on the Family Services Program. Again, the specific contents and design of a particular logic model should depend upon the particular needs of the organization.

Many of the texts listed in Appendix A provide more detail on developing logic models. Additionally, there are multiple free resources available, including templates, to help you develop your own logic model. These are also provided in Appendix A.

Preparing Your Logic Model to Conduct an Outcome Evaluation

As you develop your logic model, you will want to begin planning for your evaluation. Use the process of creating your logic model to document key aspects of the program that are needed in order to conduct a successful evaluation. In order for outcome evaluations to be useful, programs must have several characteristics (Corcoran & Secret, 2013; Kaufman-Levy & Poulin, 2003; Van Marris & King, 2007).

1. Programs should have a clearly defined target population, program participants, and a program environment. You should be able to describe *who* your program aims to serve and *where* you serve them.
2. There should be a process for recruiting, enrolling, and engaging clients in services. Who are you actually serving? Where are you finding these people? What draws them to your program?
3. The program must be a sufficient size. How many people have been served in the past? How many people are being served now? If the program is too small, group research designs may not be helpful and alternative methods, such as a series of single-subject designs, should be explored.
4. Interventions should be clearly defined. In what activities does the program actually engage? Are services consistent across providers?
5. Outcomes should be specific and measurable. Whatever you are hoping to achieve with clients should be able to be described and measured in some

way. In the sample logic model illustrated in Figure 2.1, agency administrators documented desired outcomes for the Family Services program, but they also noted "Indicators" and "Measurement," which show how the program will assess the degree to which outcomes were achieved and how each outcome will be measured. Notice that for the first outcome, no measurements were listed. Through the process of developing the logic model, the agency administrators have learned that they will need to develop some sort of measurement tool in order to assess progress toward achieving that outcome.

6. The program must have the ability to collect and maintain data. How are you going to gather the information needed to do this evaluation? What resources do you need? While this quality may not seem directly related to program activities, without this capability it is impossible to do an effective evaluation. Luckily, the resources provided in this book can help you achieve this. You will learn how to download the freely accessible software we developed, *The Clinical Record,* which can be used to collect and store client data. We will also teach you how to use *R* to effectively analyze your data.

As we proceed through this chapter, we will be bringing up a variety of topics: defining research questions, research designs, sampling and data collection methods, and instrument construction. These topics, although discussed separately, are interrelated. You may, for example, write a terrific, robust research question, but then discover that you do not have access to your ideal sample, or you cannot answer the question with the measurement tools that are available to you. In these cases, you may need to adjust your research question or design to fit the situation within the organization. Notice how we refer to other topics discussed, as they cannot truly be discussed independently in a practice-research setting.

As stated earlier, the discussion of each of these topics is in no way exhaustive. We refer you to Appendix A for a variety of resources that cover each of these in greater depth.

DEFINING THE RESEARCH QUESTION

As with all types of research, your research question will help shape the overall approach to your research activities, so it is advisable to begin your research by formulating an answerable question. After all, the remainder of your research activities will be aimed at doing just that—answering this question.

As you work with stakeholders to develop your research question, you should articulate a question that is specific and that addresses a need within the organization. The question should be one that has more than one possible answer. As you construct the question, you will have to consider other topics in this section, but you should consider the feasibility of answering the question and then think about operationalizing the concepts identified.

Feasibility

In most cases, you will want to consider the ideal circumstances for conducting your evaluation, but you will eventually have to consider the realistic conditions in which you will be working.

When thinking about feasibility, you need to give thought to pragmatic considerations. For example, what research expertise do you have access to? How much time and money can be devoted to this project? In what time frame does the evaluation need to be completed? What study participants do you have access to, or will you be using existing agency data? In any case, how can you best protect clients and/or their data?

Operationalizing Concepts

Another issue you need to consider is what each concept described in your research question means for your program/stakeholders, and then determine how best to measure these.

Earlier in this chapter, we talked about an outcome evaluation at the homeless shelter that might use the research question, "How successful are clients at moving into permanent housing?" Using information you gathered from creating your logic model and continuing to work with stakeholders, you will need to define what "success" means for your program and what "permanent housing" means. Perhaps success means leaving the shelter system within six months and not returning within six months after that. Perhaps the organization defines it differently, but in any event, this should spur a discussion, as you will ultimately want your research to yield valuable information that will be useful in improving the program. "Permanent housing" may mean that clients obtain leases in their own name; alternatively, it may mean obtaining any type of housing, even if clients do not hold a lease. As you discuss these concepts, you will be thinking back to program goals and objectives and may toss around additional ideas such as "partial success."

Once you clarify these terms, you will need to think about how best to measure these concepts. Where can you get this information? Who can best provide it for you? Do you have access to your ideal information source, or do you need to look elsewhere? These issues will be discussed later in this chapter and in the resources provided in Appendix A.

As you read through the case studies in this book, notice that research questions are explicitly stated. Writing these down in question form is particularly helpful, as ultimately you will want to provide answers to them.

CHOOSING A RESEARCH DESIGN

Selecting a research design for a program evaluation is not unlike the process you would use with other types of research. Traditionally, some research designs

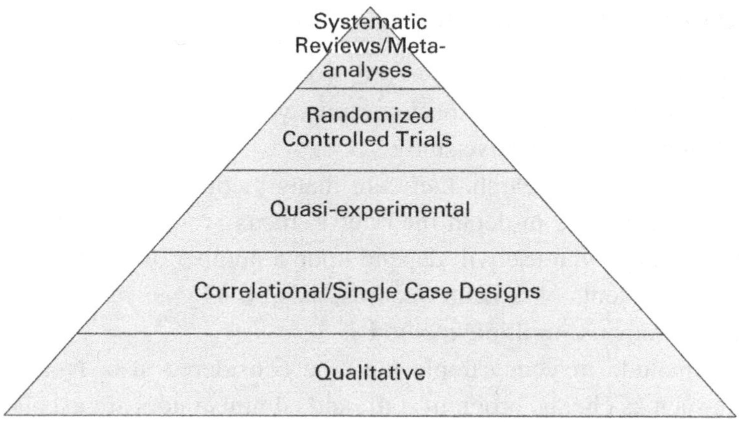

FIGURE 2.2 Hierarchy of scientific rigor of research designs.

have been thought of as more rigorous and more likely to explain causal relationships, with systematic reviews and meta-analyses considered superior to other designs, as displayed in Figure 2.2 (Becker, Bryman, & Ferguson, 2012; Rubin & Bellamy, 2012).

It is not always practical to use the most rigorous designs, and there have been well-documented effective evaluation studies that have used single case designs, correlational studies, and quasi-experimental designs (e.g., Auerbach & Mason, 2010; Auerbach, Mason, Zeitlin, Spivak, & Sokol, 2013; Epstein, 2010; Schudrich, 2012; Spivak, Sokol, Auerbach, & Gershkovich, 2009).

Decisions regarding research design will be based, in part, upon your research question, but will also be driven by other factors. For example, if a comparison group is available, how feasible and ethical would it be to randomly assign clients to an experimental condition? You can imagine that randomized controlled trials are rarely conducted in real-world practice settings and may not be the ideal method for answering questions related to outcome evaluations.

Another issue you will want to consider in designing your study is your preference for a prospective or retrospective study. Retrospective studies can use existing organizational data, if they are available, while prospective studies may allow for selecting new tools that could be used to specifically measure a construct identified in your research question.

In addition, you will want to determine whether your research question can best be answered with a longitudinal study or a cross-sectional one. Again, the methods you ultimately select will be based upon a number of factors, but this is one that needs to be considered.

Quasi-experimental designs are often the most realistic methods to use in practice settings. These may include cohort studies. Correlational designs, with pre-test/post-test designs and single-subject designs, are also frequently employed effectively.

DATA COLLECTION AND SAMPLING

When planning an evaluation of any type, you will need to determine your data sources. If you are planning a prospective study, you may have more flexibility than if you are planning a retrospective study.

As with any type of research, there are many methods available for collecting data. These could include in-depth interviews, focus groups, records reviews, and surveys. The methods you use will depend upon a number of factors, including the availability and contents of existing records, as well as your research question. In some cases, you may use multiple methods.

Who you include in your sample must be considered also. Not surprisingly, stakeholders such as clients, program staff, and administrators are excellent sources of information, but other sources should be considered as well. These could include community leaders, existing documents, and similar programs (Grinnell et al., 2012).

A WORD ABOUT VARIABLES

Before we move into a more detailed discussion about measurement, it is a good idea to discuss variables in general. A variable is anything that can differ from observation to observation. In evaluating the Family Services Program at the homeless shelter, variables could include things such as gender of the head of household, age of the head of household, number of children, and family income.

There are some factors that are important to consider in your evaluation that do not vary from observation to observation, and these are called constants. Some of the constants in the Family Services Program are that all the clients are living in the shelter, and all have one or more children. Since constants do not vary between observations, they cannot be used as comparison groups.

Levels of Measurement

Variables can be thought of in several ways. First, you can consider the level of measurement of variables. Why should you worry about this? The level of measurement matters because it determines how much precision you get in a variable, and it dictates what sorts of statistical tests you can conduct.

In general, variables can be thought of as categorical or numeric. Categorical variables are simply categories, or named groups, while numeric variables are measured as quantities. Categorical variables have less precision than numeric ones.

There are two levels of measurement within the grouping of categorical variables: nominal and ordinal. Nominal-level variables are categorical variables made up of unranked categories. That is, each indicator cannot be ranked compared to the others. A good example of a nominal-level variable is *gender*, operationalized as *male* or *female*. Notice that *male* and *female* are discrete categories, and one category does not denote more or less *gender* than the other. Variables dichotomized as yes/no conditions are also nominal. An example of this would be a variable measuring whether someone had a college education. A variable called *college* could be operationalized as *yes* or *no*.

Ordinal-level variables are categorical variables made up of ranked categories. Each indicator can be ranked as greater than or less than in some way as compared to others. An example of an ordinal-level variable could be *level of education*, operationalized as *less than high school, high school/GED, some college, BA/BS, some graduate education, graduate degree*. Notice that someone who indicated he had some college would have less education than someone with a BA/BS. In fact, if these indicators were listed on a survey, it would only be common sense to list them in the order described above. It would be illogical and confusing to list these indicators like this: *high school/GED, graduate degree, some college, less than high school, BA/BS, some graduate education*.

When summarizing categorical variables, you will typically report proportions or percentages. When you visualize these, you can present these as pie charts or bar graphs.

Notice that both types of categorical variables are made up only of words, or categories. None of these was defined by numbers. Some variables, however, are best described numerically, and there are two levels of measurement within the construct of numeric variables. Notice that, in general, numeric variables are more precise measures than categorical variables.

One type of numeric variable is the interval-level variable. Interval-level measures denote greater than or less than conditions based on the indicator; however, there is no true zero, which means that it is difficult to describe the true magnitude of difference between indicators. An example of this would be a client's *level of intelligence* as noted by an IQ score. If one person has an IQ of 100, which is considered average, and another has an IQ of 130, we could state, meaningfully, that the second person's IQ is 30 points higher than the first person's, but you would not conclude that the second person was 30% smarter than the first. It should be noted, however, that no one has an IQ of zero.

Ratio-level measures are also numeric, but in these cases, zero is meaningful and denotes the absence of something. For instance, if we were going to measure some aspect of homelessness, we could count the number of nights that clients were homeless over the course of a month. If, for one client (observation), we measured 10 nights and for another we measured 5, the observation with 10 was homeless for twice as many nights as the observation with 5. This means that with ratio-level measures, we can understand a magnitude of difference that was not the case with interval-level measures.

It should be noted that many concepts could be operationalized to be measured in several ways. Looking at the example of homelessness as a variable, we could consider obtaining this information by simply asking clients if they had been homeless in the past 30 days, which could be answered as a yes/no question. We could also measure this using an ordinal-level measure by determining if they were

TABLE 2.1 Measuring *Homelessness* as a Variable With Different Levels of Measurement

Level of Measurement	Description	Example of Measuring Homelessness	
Nominal	Unranked categories	Homeless/Not homeless	Less precision
Ordinal	Ranked categories	No nights, some nights, many nights	
Interval	Numeric values with no true zero		
Ratio	Numeric values with a true zero	Actual number of nights spent in shelter in the last 30 days	More precision

homeless no nights, some nights, or many nights. We could also simply ask clients how many nights they had been homeless in the past 30 days and a number could be obtained, which would be a ratio-level measure. If we obtained this information as a nominal-level measure, there would be no way to determine how many nights clients who answered "yes" were actually homeless. Similarly, if we asked this as an ordinal-level measure, we could collapse answers into the nominal-level measure, but we could still not determine actual numbers of nights that clients were homeless. If, however, we were to ask this as a ratio-level measure, we could determine which categories clients fell into in the ordinal-level measure, and we could determine if, in fact, clients had been homeless in the previous 30 days (i.e., if the number of homeless nights was greater than zero). This example is illustrated in Table 2.1. Notice that we did not measure homelessness as an interval because we simply were not able to determine an adequate way to measure the concept in this way.

This does not mean that all variables should be measured as ratios, as some concepts, such as gender or level of education, are best measured differently. You should, however, be aware of the level of precision achieved at various levels of measurement.

When describing numeric variables, this is typically done with some measure of central tendency and dispersion. This could be reporting a mean and standard deviation or a median and quantiles. You can visually depict numeric data in a variety of ways, including histograms, boxplots, and stem-and-leaf plots.

Relationships of Variables to One Another

For the most part, you will be interested in examining the relationship between one variable and others. In outcome evaluations, the desired result is your dependent variable, which is sometimes also referred to, not surprisingly, as an outcome variable. Variables that you think will be predictive of the dependent variable are known as independent, or predictor, variables. In general, research questions look at one dependent variable at a time, with at least one independent variable.

While we make hypotheses about the relationships between independent and dependent variables, we caution that, for the most part, causal relationships cannot be drawn. That is, we can state that there is a relationship between one or more independent variables and a dependent variable, but it is difficult to determine if the independent variable(s) cause the dependent variable. In order to draw causal inferences, three criteria must be met:

1. The cause must come before the effect in time (that is, whatever the cause is, it must precede the effect).
2. There must be a relationship between the cause and the effect. Does manipulating the causal variable result in some change in the effect variable?
3. The relationship between the cause and effect cannot be related to some other factor that is impacting each.

While the first two criteria are fairly simply to determine, it is quite difficult to conclude the third with certitude. After all, most of what is studied with regard to aspects of human behavior is quite complex. As evaluators, we have access to limited information that can help us draw inferences. Additionally, we are limited by our knowledge and creativity to identifying third (or fourth or fifth) factors that could be impacting an identified cause and effect.

Despite this, determining whether relationships exist between predictors and outcomes is important, particularly when the relationships are relatively strong. Therefore, evaluators should not be dissuaded from conducting research if causal relationships cannot be determined.

MEASUREMENT INSTRUMENTS

Once you determine your research design and identify all the concepts you need to quantify, you will have to establish how best to actually measure them. If you are conducting a retrospective study, you may want to consider using existing organizational data. An excellent resource to use if you are considering doing an evaluation with existing data is Epstein's text, *Clinical Data-Mining: Integrating Practice and Research* (2010).

If you are planning to collect data prospectively, you will have the opportunity to select existing instruments or construct your own. In many cases, it is advantageous to use previously constructed instruments, as psychometric properties of these may be known. Validated instruments, if available, can be helpful even if you are not seeking to generalize your findings to a larger population. You will have the assurance that you are measuring what you intend, particularly if the sample or population you are studying is substantially similar to those used in psychometric studies.

In other cases, you will need to create your own instruments. When you do, you will need to consider several key factors:

1. *Language proficiency*: instruments should be presented in your participants' preferred language. In some cases, instruments need to be developed in multiple languages. Translated instruments should also be back-translated to ensure that translation did not alter the original meaning of individual items.
2. *Reading level*: in many cases, instruments will require participants to read individual items. Be sure to consider your participants' reading levels. Simply translating an instrument into another language may not be sufficient if people are not literate in their preferred language.
3. *Sensitivity of the topic*: difficult topics may need to be operationalized carefully. Questions should be asked tactfully and should be physically placed within a survey in an advantageous spot. For example, it would be inappropriate to start a survey by asking people the numbers and types of crimes they may have committed.
4. *Quantitative and/or qualitative items*: some topics may be best addressed quantitatively, while others may be best addressed qualitatively. In many cases, a mixed method is most useful. It is always helpful to conclude a quantitative instrument with the open-ended question, "Is there anything else you would like to share with us?" If this is presented in a written format, be sure to provide adequate space for individuals' responses. You may be surprised at the responses you receive!
5. *Method of data collection*: how people are asked to respond to your instrument may impact how items are constructed. If, for example, you are conducting a telephone survey, you may not want to ask long or complicated questions, as it may be difficult for respondents to remember all aspects of the question without being able to visually review it or have it repeated.
6. *Comprehensiveness*: while you do not want to develop an excessively long instrument, you need to be sure to gather all the information you need, particularly if you are using a cross-sectional design. If you forget to gather data on a particular concept, it is unlikely that you will have the opportunity to do so later.

As you construct your instrument, you should do your best to ask questions in a manner that can be easily answered. Here are some tips for writing good survey items:

1. Be sure that all terms used in each item are commonly understood and are used in a way that respondents can easily interpret.
2. Ask questions that respondents can easily answer accurately. For instance, many people do not know their exact total household income, but could easily answer accurately if the answers were presented categorically. In a case like this, it may not be advisable to gather this information as a ratio-level variable, but as an ordinal variable.
3. Categorical indicators, cumulatively, should be both exhaustive and mutually exclusive. That is, response categories should not overlap and should contain

all possible responses. In some cases, it may be helpful to have an "Other" category and to allow respondents to enter their own responses if the ones that are presented do not apply.

Once you have developed your instrument, it is useful to have others review it. Reviewers could be colleagues, but should also include other individuals, such as clients or stakeholders, who could be study participants. Good feedback in the construction of an instrument is the first step in developing a valid measure.

Finally, we suggest that the instruments you develop be piloted with a relatively small sample. It is helpful to do a simple analysis in order to identify how well the instrument is working. For instance, if there is very little variability between respondents on particular items, it may be that you have too many or too few response categories. Alternatively, the concept being measured may not be worded well, or the concept that you thought may be variable may, instead, be constant.

PRESENTING YOUR FINDINGS

In almost all cases, findings from your evaluation will need to be presented in some sort of written report. Additionally, you may be asked to present your findings in other formats as well. Who you are asked to share your findings with will, in large part, dictate what you share and how you share it.

Here we offer a few tips that we have found helpful in disseminating findings with others; many of the resources in Appendix A provide additional information and guidance (e.g., Administration for Children and Families, 2010; Bond, Boyd, & Rapp, 1997; Centers for Disease Control and Prevention, 2011; Morris, Fitz-Gibbon, & Freeman, 1987; Substance Abuse and Mental health Services Administration National Registry of Evidence-Based Programs and Practices, 2012; W. K. Kellogg Foundation, 2004):

1. *Consider your audience*: many people interested in your findings may be neither researchers nor statisticians. Therefore, in order to provide accurate and relevant information, you may need to "translate" what you have done into laymen's terms. If you provide statistical information, be sure to explain what it means. For instance, if you conduct a logistic regression, which is explained later in the book, you will want to describe what that procedure ultimately does (i.e., it explains the odds that an event will occur greater than chance).
2. *Consider your content*: for the most part, you will be told to report certain things (e.g., how you conducted your evaluation, whom you studied, etc.). Be sure to provide everything that is requested. This may sound simple, but you will save yourself and your colleagues aggravation and time if you keep your reporting requirements in mind as you conduct your research.

3. *Consider your actual presentation*: as we stated earlier, almost all evaluations include some sort of written report, but sometimes you will be asked to present your findings in other ways as well. These could include webinars, conference presentations, or articles. You can scale these presentations up or down according to your audience to make best use of your comprehensive report.
4. *Consider using graphics*: regardless of the composition of your audience, the content that you need to share, or the format of your presentation, the phrase "a picture is worth a thousand words" rings true for most people. We recommend making use of graphs, diagrams, and tables to support your text or your spoken words. In this book, we have an entire chapter devoted to creating graphs in *R*, and subsequent chapters show you how we apply graphics to various analytical situations.

All in all, when you present your findings, this is your opportunity to share what you have learned during your research endeavors. Clearly communicating this is as important as any other step in the evaluation process.

CONCLUSIONS AND A RECOMMENDATION

This chapter has provided you with an overview of factors that you will need to consider when planning for an outcome evaluation. You should realize, however, that research of any type is best played as a team sport. You will need to gain involvement from key stakeholders within your organization, but you may also want to include others, such as community members, who have an interest in your evaluation. It is helpful to collaborate with others throughout the planning and evaluation process. Thinking through the details of the evaluation and careful planning with others at early stages can avert unpleasant surprises later.

This chapter has provided an overview of factors you will need to consider when planning a comprehensive evaluation. While we present you with these topics and suggest issues for you to consider, it will be important to gain a more thorough understanding of these, as decisions made during the planning stages of research will impact every subsequent aspect. To gain more information on each of these, we again refer you to the resources recommended in Appendix A.

/// 3 /// GETTING STARTED WITH *R*

In order to work through the examples in this chapter, you will need to *install* and *load* the following packages:

- *psych*
- *Hmisc*
- *gmodels*

For more information on how to do this, refer to the Packages section later in this chapter.

WHAT IS *R?*

R is an open source, freely available statistical programming language and is compatible with Windows, OS X, Linux, and other UNIX variants. *R* is similar to *S*, a program developed at Bell Laboratories by John Chambers (Auerbach & Schudrich, 2013; The R Project for Statistical Computing, n.d.). Although *R* has been around since 1993, it has grown rapidly in popularity since 2010. It is a programming language for statistical analysis and graphics. The software offers the following features:

- an effective data handling and storage facility,
- a suite of operators for calculations on arrays, in particular matrices,
- a large, coherent, integrated collection of intermediate tools for data analysis,
- graphical facilities for data analysis and display, either on-screen or on hard copy, and
- a well-developed, simple, and effective programming language, which includes conditionals, loops, user-defined recursive functions, and input and output facilities (The R Project for Statistical Computing, n.d., paragraph 5).

In other words, *R* provides an environment where statistical techniques can be implemented (The R Project for Statistical Computing, n.d.). *R*'s capabilities have been extended through the development of functions and packages. Fox and Weisberg state, "one of the great strengths of R is that it allows users and experts in particular areas of statistics to add new capabilities to the software" (2010, p. xiii).

For all of these reasons, we have begun working extensively in *R*, and we recommend that you do, too!

In order to make working with *R* a bit easier, a number of freely available graphical user interfaces, or GUIs, have been developed. Among these are *RStudio, R Commander*, and *RKWard*. We use *RStudio*, as we have found it to be flexible and useful. The screen shots depicted throughout this book are based upon our use of *RStudio*.

INSTALLING *R* AND *RSTUDIO*

In this section you will learn how to install *R*, open *R* files, and enter *R* commands using the *RStudio* GUI.

Begin by downloading *R* and *RStudio* free of charge from links on the homepage of the Single-System Design Analysis website (www.ssdanalysis.com). On this site you will also find videos on how to install the software. When you click the links for installing *R* and *RStudio*, you will be taken to external sites. Both *R* and *RStudio* are completely free and are considered safe and stable downloads.

Once these are installed, open *RStudio*. When you open it, your screen should look like Figure 3.1.

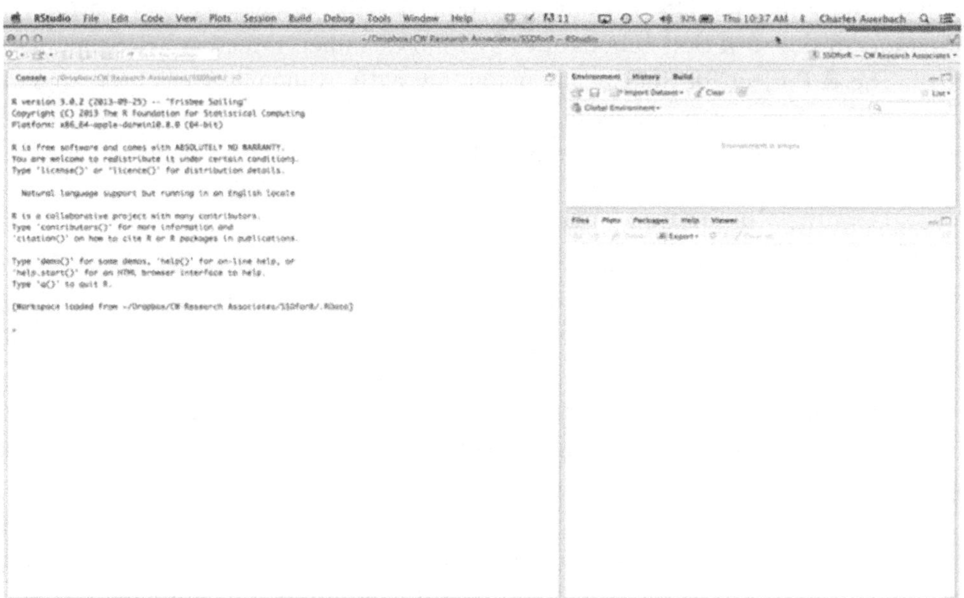

FIGURE 3.1 A first look at *RStudio*.

NAVIGATING *RSTUDIO*

The Console located in the left pane of Figure 3.1 is the area in which *R* commands are typed. After entering a command, pressing the <RETURN> key executes it. Pressing the up and down arrows scrolls through commands in your history directly into the Console.

The top right pane contains three tabs: "Environment," "History," and "Build." The "Environment" tab is where any files, known in *R* as data frames, that you open or create during a session are listed, along with vectors and variables. The "History" tab keeps a list of all *R* commands you enter. Clicking any command stored in the history will copy it into the Console. Pressing <RETURN> will execute the copied command. Your history is continuous from session to session and will not be cleared unless you clear it manually by clicking on the broom icon. The "Build" tab is used for programing *R* and will not be covered in this text.

The pane at the bottom right contains five tabs: "Files," "Plots," "Packages," "Help," and "Viewer." The "Files" tab lists all files that are located in your default directory. The "Plots" tab opens a window that contains the most recent plot created during the session. Using the arrows in this tab helps you scroll through plots created during that session only. In this window there is an Export button that enables you to copy plots to the clipboard or save them in various formats, such as a PDF, TIFF, or JPEG. The "Help" tab gives you access to *R* help files.

SETTING YOUR WORKING DIRECTORY

It is good practice to begin your session by setting your default directory. To accomplish this, in the menu bar click on **Session / Set Working Directory / Choose**

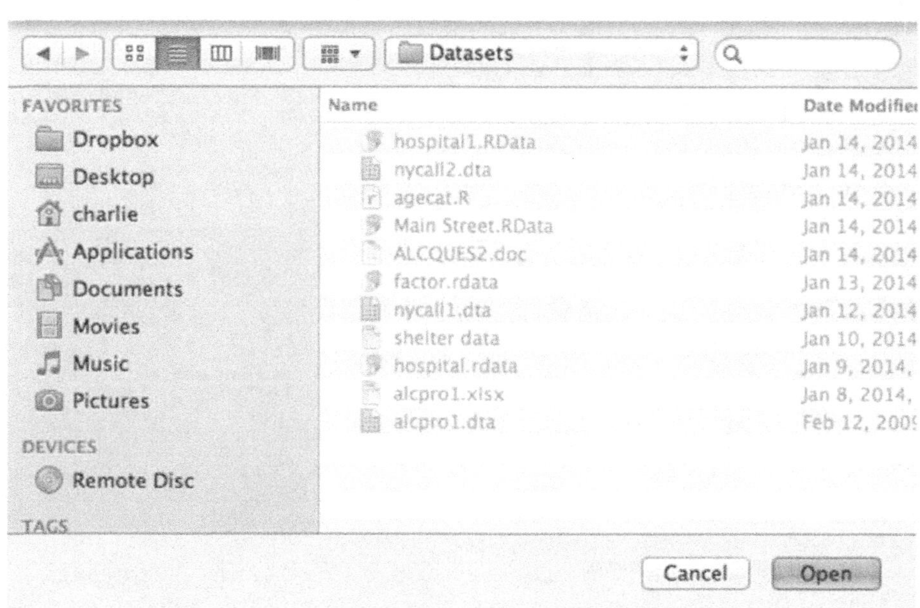

FIGURE 3.2 Setting your working directory.

Directory. After you press <RETURN>, you will see the dialogue box presented in Figure 3.2. Use this dialogue to navigate to the directory that contains the example files for this book, and select Open.

OPENING A FILE

There are a number of methods for opening files in *RStudio*. The most common method is to employ the **File / Open File** menu choice located at the top of the menu bar of *RStudio*. As shown in Figure 3.3, a dialogue box is presented, similar to the one opened when the working directory was set. With this dialogue box, you can navigate to the directory containing files. Double click the file *hospital.rdata* to open it in *RStudio*. Notice, as displayed in Figure 3.4, *RStudio* queries you to click *Yes* to load the file into the global environment, which will complete the process.

The *hospital* data set is now listed in the top right *RStudio* pane. Alongside the *hospital* file are the number of observations, 161, and the number of variables, 20. Clicking on the spreadsheet icon to the right of the file in the "Environment" tab will display your data in a spreadsheet format it in the upper left pane, as displayed in Figure 3.5. When you do this, the Console will automatically drop into the lower left pane.

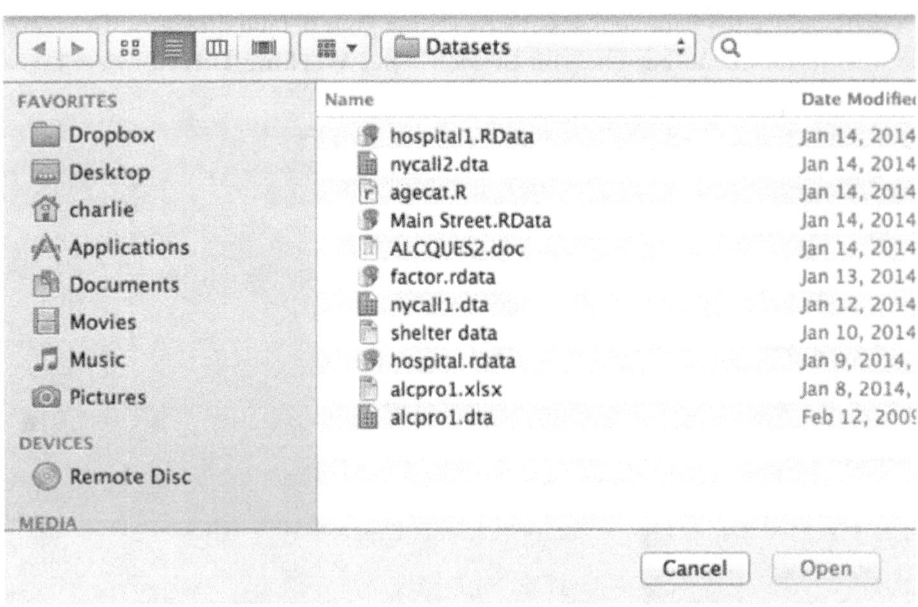

FIGURE 3.3 Opening a file in *RStudio*.

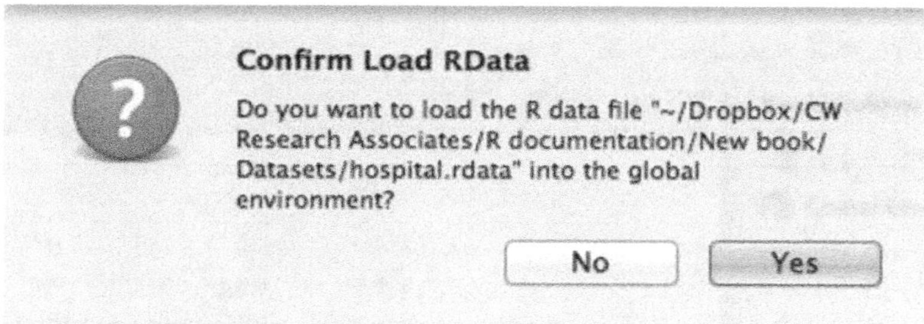

FIGURE 3.4 Accepting your choice.

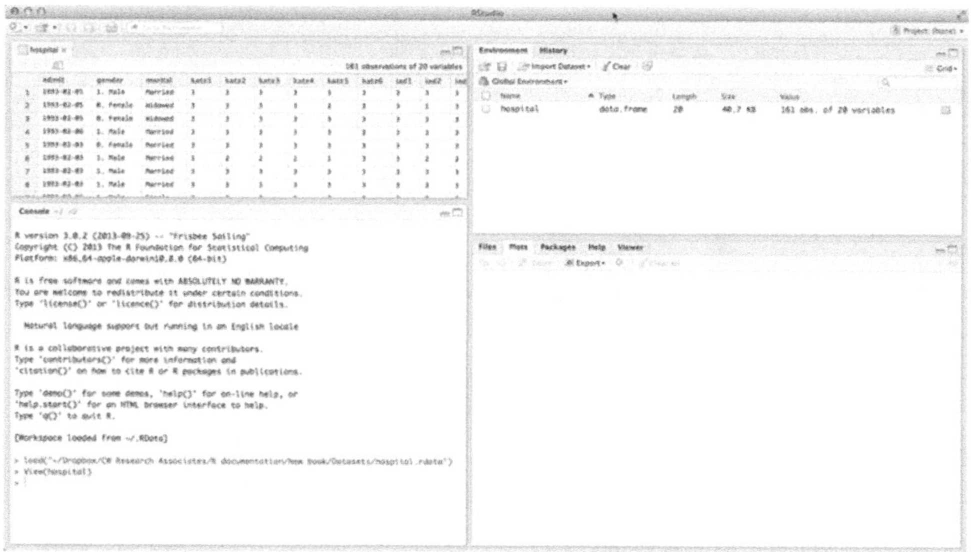

FIGURE 3.5 Viewing your data in *RStudio.*

You cannot edit your data in this pane, but you can easily view it by scrolling left, right, up, or down. Additionally, simply grabbing the handles between the panes and stretching them or compressing them, as desired, can modify the size of each of these.

As displayed in Figure 3.6, you can also view the list of files in your working directory by clicking on the "File" tab in the bottom right pane. You can double click on an *R* file (a file with the extension *.RData* or *.rdata*) to open it in *RStudio.* Try this by double clicking *factor.RData*. The data set *factor* appears in the Environment window in the top right *RStudio* pane. As displayed in the pane, the file contains one variable and 161 observations.

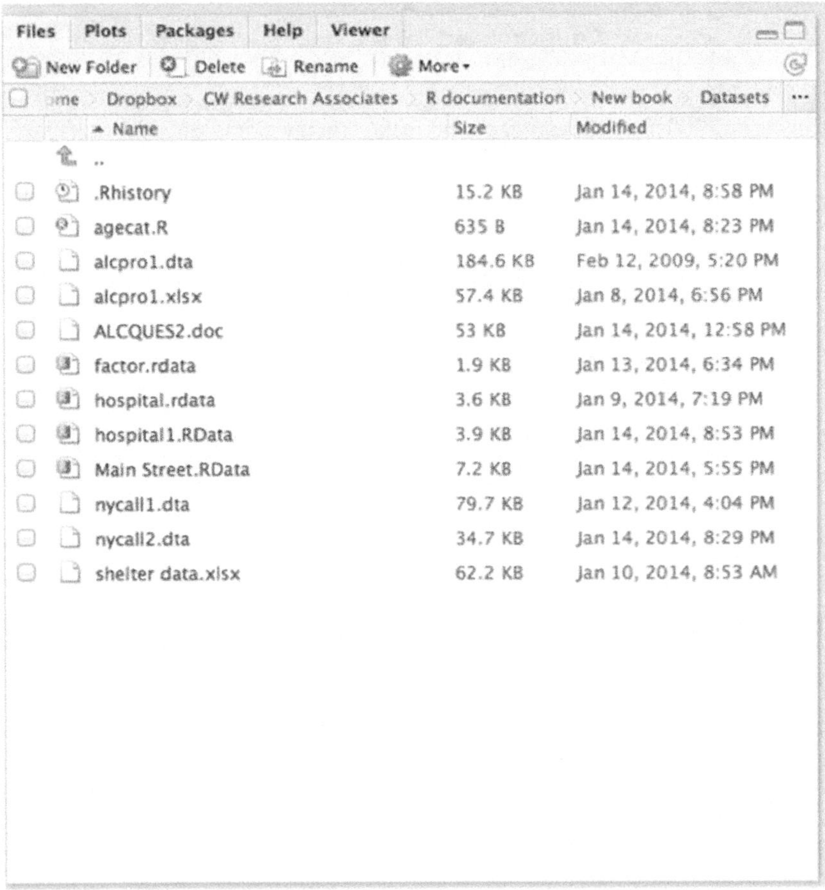

FIGURE 3.6 Files listed in the Files tab.

ENTERING YOUR FIRST *R* COMMAND

Enter the following command into the Console in the bottom left pane of *RStudio:*

`>names(hospital)` and press <RETURN>.

You will obtain the results displayed in Figure 3.7.

The **`names()`** function simply reports the names of variables contained in an *R* file. Do the same for the *factor* file and the following will be displayed:

```
>names(factor)

[1] "marital"
```

Notice that both the *hospital* data set and the *factor* data set contain a variable called *marital*. More on that in a moment.

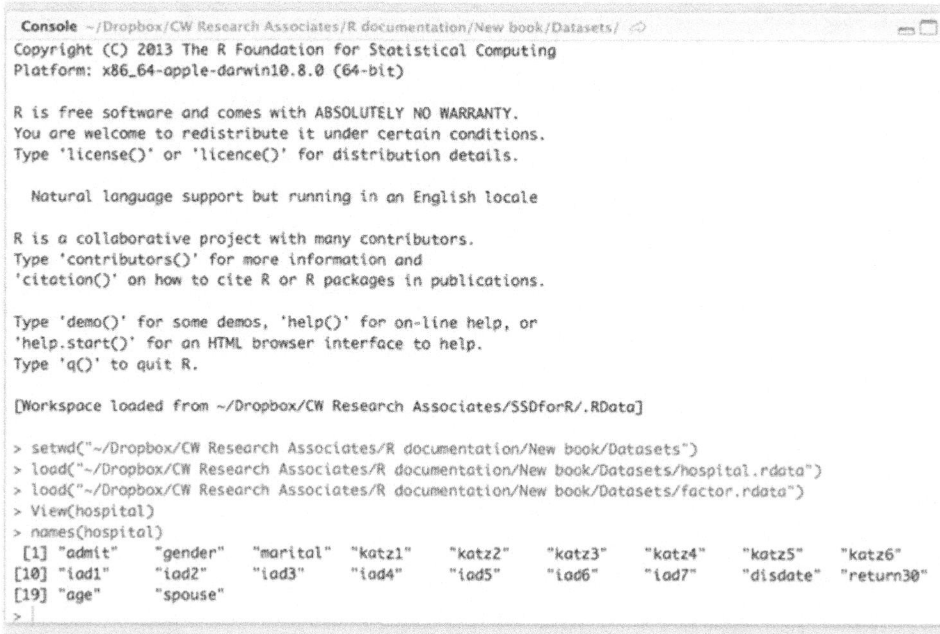

```
Console ~/Dropbox/CW Research Associates/R documentation/New book/Datasets/
Copyright (C) 2013 The R Foundation for Statistical Computing
Platform: x86_64-apple-darwin10.8.0 (64-bit)

R is free software and comes with ABSOLUTELY NO WARRANTY.
You are welcome to redistribute it under certain conditions.
Type 'license()' or 'licence()' for distribution details.

  Natural language support but running in an English locale

R is a collaborative project with many contributors.
Type 'contributors()' for more information and
'citation()' on how to cite R or R packages in publications.

Type 'demo()' for some demos, 'help()' for on-line help, or
'help.start()' for an HTML browser interface to help.
Type 'q()' to quit R.

[Workspace loaded from ~/Dropbox/CW Research Associates/SSDforR/.RData]

> setwd("~/Dropbox/CW Research Associates/R documentation/New book/Datasets")
> load("~/Dropbox/CW Research Associates/R documentation/New book/Datasets/hospital.rdata")
> load("~/Dropbox/CW Research Associates/R documentation/New book/Datasets/factor.rdata")
> View(hospital)
> names(hospital)
 [1] "admit"    "gender"   "marital"  "katz1"    "katz2"    "katz3"    "katz4"    "katz5"    "katz6"
[10] "iad1"     "iad2"     "iad3"     "iad4"     "iad5"     "iad6"     "iad7"     "disdate"  "return30"
[19] "age"      "spouse"
>
```

FIGURE 3.7 Entering your first command: `names(hospital)`.

TO ATTACH OR NOT TO ATTACH? THAT IS THE QUESTION

R can have multiple files entered into the environment at one time; however, you need a method to identify the file you want to analyze. The **`attach()`** function is one way that enables *R* to recognize the file in its search path so that you can manipulate it. However, before opening a new file, you must remember to use the **`detach()`** function to remove it; otherwise, opening a different file with variables containing the same names as the current one will cause a conflict and an error message, as displayed in Figure 3.8.

Because both the *hospital* and *factor* files contain a variable called *marital, R* reported a conflict when the second file was attached. It is very common to overlook detaching a file from the *R* environment. As a result, we generally recommend not using the **`attach()`** function. Instead, you can access variables in a file by using the *filename$* convention. Figure 3.9 shows an example using this convention. Type the following:

`>table(hospital$marital)` and <RETURN>

Now enter the following:

`>table(factor$marital)`

```
Console ~/Dropbox/CW Research Associates/R documentation/New book/Datasets/
> attach(hospital)
> attach(factor)
The following object is masked from hospital:

    marital

> |
```

FIGURE 3.8 Example of variable conflict between files.

```
> table(hospital$marital)

  Single  Married  Widowed Divorced
      16       95       44        4
> table(factor$marital)

 1  2  3  4
16 95 44  4
```

FIGURE 3.9 Using the "filename$" convention.

The **`table()`** command provides the frequencies for the categorical variables *spouse* from the *hospital* file and *marital* from the *factor* file.

Using the name of the file followed by a "$" prevented any potential conflicts, such as the error we observed in Figure 3.8.

ENDING YOUR SESSION

When you are ready to leave *RStudio*, end your session by simply clicking on **File / Quit RStudio** in the menu bar. *RStudio* will then query you with the following, as displayed in Figure 3.10.

Since we do not care to save anything, click "Don't Save" and *RStudio* will close.

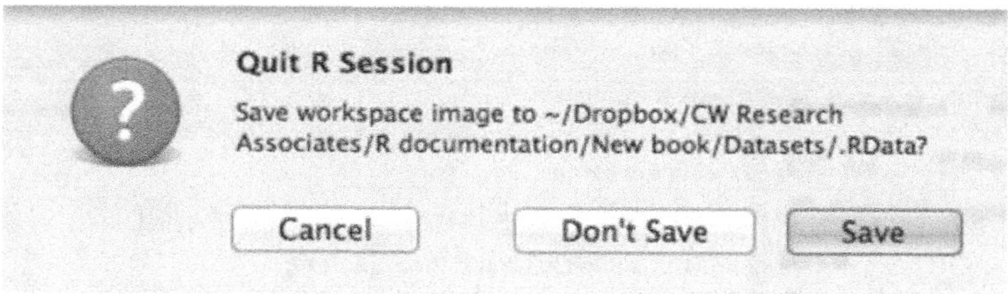

FIGURE 3.10 Ending your *RStudio* session.

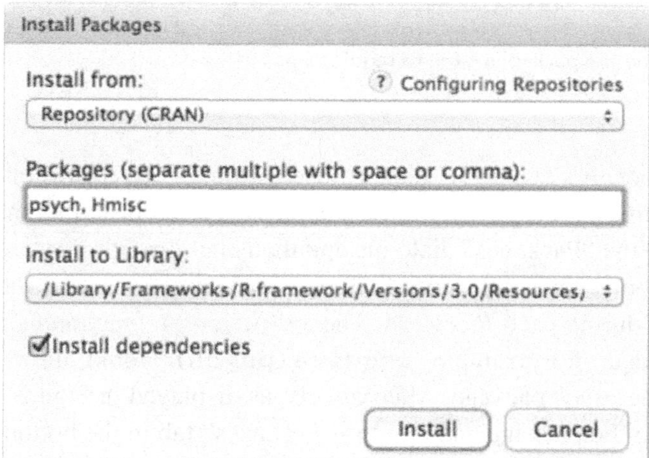

FIGURE 3.11 Installing packages.

PACKAGES

One of the appeals of *R* is the easily accessible collection of user-contributed packages. Currently, there are close to 5,000 packages on the Comprehensive R Archive Network (CRAN) written by over 2,000 user-developers (The R Project for Statistical Computing, n.d.). A package is simply a collection of pre-written *R* code to accomplish a particular task. For example, the *foreign* package allows users to import and transform files from other popular statistical packages, such as SPSS and Stata, to the *R* format. Another example is a package written by the authors, *SSDforR*, to analyze single-subject data.

It is likely that if a statistical method exists, there are one or more packages for it on CRAN. Once you open *RStudio*, you are connected to the world of CRAN and you can install any of the available packages.

Installing Packages

To install an *R* package, click on the "Packages" tab in the bottom right *RStudio* pane. Click on "Install" and the dialogue shown in Figure 3.11 will be displayed. Make

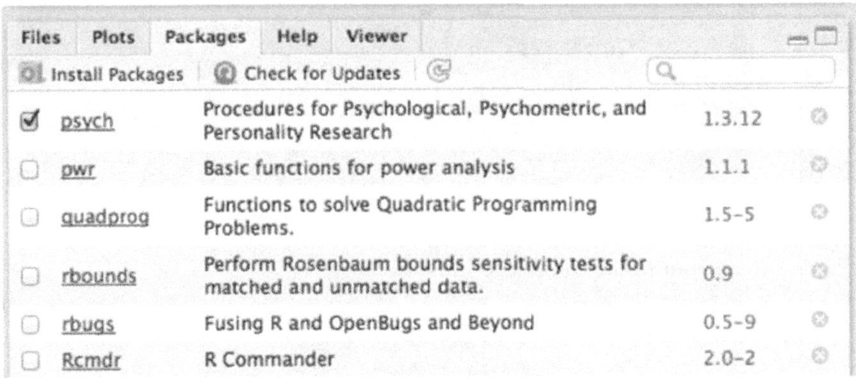

FIGURE 3.12 Using the packages pane to require a package.

sure that "Repository (CRAN)" under "Install from" is selected. Later in the book you will be utilizing the *psych* and *Hmisc* packages. To install them now, type the following into the "Packages" dialogue and then click Install: `psych, Hmisc.`

Packages only need to be installed once; however, to access them, they must be "required" during each *R* session. The **`require()`** function can be utilized to invoke a package. For example, **`require(psych)`** would allow you to access functions in the *psych* package. Alternatively, as displayed in Figure 3.12, checking the box next to the package name in the "Packages" tab in the bottom right pane of *RStudio* would also make the package available for use.

SOME BASICS OF *R*

R Can Do Math

Because *R* is a statistical programming language, it can be used to perform basic mathematical functions. Entering 2 + 3 into the console and pressing <RETURN> produces the following:

```
> 2 + 3
[1] 5
```

Now try your hand at multiplication by typing 3*4 into the Console and pressing <RETURN>. The results are as follows:

```
> 3*4
[1] 12
```

More complex computations can be accomplished, but you will need to be mindful of the standard order of operations. They are as follows:

Parentheses
Exponents
Multiplication/Division
Addition/Subtraction

Operations inside parentheses take priority and are performed prior to any other process. For example, type **(20-10) / 2** into the Console and press <RETURN>. This produces the following results:

```
> (20-10) / 2
[1] 5
```

In this case, the subtraction is performed first, followed by division.

Exponents are entered into *R* with the ^ symbol. For example, try the following:

```
> 10^2
[1] 100
```

VARIABLES

There are different methods for assigning values to variables. The most common methods are using the <- (less than symbol followed by a dash) or the = sign. You will obtain the same result using either method; however the convention in *R* is to use <-. Type the following into the Console and press the <RETURN> key:

```
> x<-7
> x
[1] 7
```

You could repeat the same operation using the equal sign (=) to obtain the same result.

Now that *x* is stored in memory, it appears as a value in the Environment tab.

Be aware that *R* is case-sensitive, so it differentiates between lowercase and uppercase variable names. Therefore, the variable *x* is not the same as the variable *X*. Also, variable names must start with an alphanumeric character. Furthermore, there cannot be any spaces between characters; however, the underscore (_) and dot (.) can be used to connect words. Special characters like the dash (-), asterisk (*), and slash (/) are not permissible as part of a variable name.

You can remove a variable from memory using the **remove()** function. You can use the shortcut for the **remove()** command, **rm()** to remove the variable *x* from memory. Simply type **rm(x)** into the Console and press <RETURN>. As shown in the following, if **x** is typed into the Console after it is removed, the error presented below will appear. You will also notice that *x* was removed from the Environment tab.

```
> rm (x)
> x
Error: object 'x' not found
```

TYPES OF VARIABLES

A variable in *R* can contain numbers, characters, or dates.

Numeric Variables

Numeric variables can be integers, both positive and negative, or decimals. We will recreate the *x* variable used in the previous section:

```
> x<-7
> x
[1] 7
```

A very useful function in *R* is **is.numeric()** that can be utilized to test if a variable is stored in *R* as a number. Try it out on the *x* variable by typing the following into the Console:

```
> is.numeric(x)

[1] TRUE
```

For integers, *R* expects an "L" to be attached to the number. For example, type the following:

```
> y<-6L
> is.integer(y)

[1] TRUE
```

It is also true that the *y* is a numeric value so using the **is.numeric()** function would also produce a result of "TRUE." Try the **class()** function:

```
>class(y)

[1]"integer"
```

Character Variables

Although character string variables are non-mathematical, they are commonly used in data analysis. As displayed here, you can assign a character string to a variable.

```
x<-"hello"
>x

[1] "hello"
```

As mentioned, *R* differentiates between upper- and lowercase characters; therefore, *R* would evaluate the same word in the following examples differently: *hello, Hello*, and *HELLO*.

Dates

R contains a number of functions that provide for the manipulation of dates. A date can be directly entered employing the **as.Date()** function, for example:

```
> admitted<-as.Date("2013-05-03")
> discharged<-as.Date("2013-05-23")
```

These dates represent when a patient was admitted to and discharged from a hospital. Notice that the dates were entered as a four-digit year, followed by a two-digit month, and a two-digit day, all entered within quotation marks. This is the preferred method.

To calculate the total length of stay for the patient in days, the **as.numeric()** function can be utilized to convert a date into the number of days since January 1, 1970. With this function, the patient's length of stay in days can easily be calculated:

```
> discharged<-as.Date("2013-05-23")
> los<-as.numeric(discharged)-as.numeric(admitted)
> los

[1] 20
```

VECTORS

A vector is a collection of elements that can be stored as a variable. Vectors can be numbers, characters, dates, or any combination of these. The **c()**, or combine, command is a frequently used method to enter elements into a vector. For example, x<-c(1, 2, 3, 4, 5) is a numeric vector named *x* containing five elements: the numbers 1, 2, 3, 4, and 5. *R* is a vectorized programming language; any operation applied to a vector affects all the elements within it simultaneously. We can multiply our vector *x* by a factor of 10. This example and its results are shown below. Notice that a comma separates each element. Remember to put the "c" in front of the opening parenthesis.

```
> x<-c(1, 2, 3, 4, 5)
> x

[1] 1 2 3 4 5

> x<-x10
> x
[1] 10 20 30 40 50
```

A vector can also contain characters like the following: c("Tom", "Dick", "Harry"). Each character element must be placed between quotation marks. The vector can be assigned to a variable as follows:

```
> y<-c("Tom", "Dick", "Harry")
> y

[1] "Tom"   "Dick"   "Harry"
```

A more complex example of the power of vectors is displayed below. Four patients admitted on different days are discharged from a hospital on the same day. Notice the **as.Date()** and **as.numeric()** functions are applied once to the vector *admitted* in the first and third steps, respectively.

```
> admitted<-as.Date(c("2013-12-20", "2013-12-9",
"2013-12-11", "2013-12-27"))
> discharged<-as.Date("2013-12-31")
> los<-as.numeric(discharged)-as.numeric(admitted)
> los

[1] 11 22 20 4
```

FACTOR VARIABLES

A factor variable is a type of categorical variable that can be represented as a string or a number. Converting categorical variables to factors has a number of advantages, especially when tables and graphics are used in data analysis. Factor variables are also useful in advanced statistical models such as linear regression or logistic regression. These topics will be discussed in detail in Chapters 8 and 9.

To illustrate, open the example data set named *factor.rdata*. To do this in *RStudio* select **File** and then **Open File** and navigate to where the file is located. You will be prompted to load the file into *R*; select *Yes*. This data frame contains a single variable, *marital*. To look at the values of *marital*, use the **`table()`** command.

```
> table(factor$marital)

 1  2  3  4
16 95 44  4
```

Notice the *factor$* in the command before the variable name *marital*. As previously mentioned, a common variable such as *age* or *gender* can be present in multiple files you may be analyzing. Using the "filename$" convention in front of the variable name allows *R* to differentiate from which data set you are selecting your variable and prevents any potential conflicts.

In your output, the first row represents the various categories of marital status, and the second row represents the number of clients in each category. For example, we see that category 2 has 95 clients. The categories represent the following: 1 = single, 2 = married, 3 = widowed, and 4 = divorced, which you would need to know in order to interpret this table.

Any client who was single was entered as a 1, a married client was entered as a 2, and so on. If *marital* were converted to a factor variable, the table would be more easily interpreted. The **`factor()`** function can be utilized to accomplish this. This is depicted as follows:

```
>f.marital<-factor(factor$marital,levels=c(1,2,3,4),
labels=c("single","married","widowed","divorced"))
```

In the *R* command above, the levels are defined using the **`c()`** function described previously. The **`labels()`** option is then used to assign labels to the categories in the order in which they are presented. Finally, a new vector/variable *f.marital* was created containing this factor information. The following are the results of the **`table()`** command on the new factor variable. Note how this produces a more readable table.

```
> table(f.marital)

single  married  widowed divorced
    16       95       44        4
```

In the section on data frames you will learn how to save a newly created variable to an existing file.

MISSING VALUES

Missing responses are very common in social science research, particularly survey research. Respondents often decide not to answer a particular question on a survey and skip it. *R* handles this by using "NA" to represent a missing response. The following is an example that extends the previous example on hospital admission and discharge dates. Note that the third *admitted* date is missing and was entered into the *admitted* vector as "NA."

```
> admitted<-as.Date(c("2013-12-20","2013-12-9",NA,
"2013-12-27"))
> discharged<-as.Date("2013-12-31")
> los<-as.numeric(discharged)-as.numeric(admitted)
> admitted

[1] "2013-12-20" "2013-12-09" NA "2013-12-27"

> los

[1] 11 22 NA  4
```

In the fourth step, when *admitted* was entered into the Console, the displayed result contained the "NA" for the third patient. Finally, the number of days for *los* could not be calculated for this third patient, and an "NA" was assigned for this occurrence.

The **is.na()** function can be utilized to test for missing values. The use of this command is presented below. As indicated by the "TRUE," the third value is missing.

```
> is.na(los)

[1] FALSE FALSE  TRUE FALSE
```

DATA TRANSFORMATION

When analyzing data, there is often a need to modify or transform data into groups or to combine individual items in some way to form, for example, a scale.

TABLE 3.1 *hospital.RData* Variable Descriptions

Variable	Description	Values	Variable Type
admit	Date admitted to the hospital	Actual date	Date
gender	Gender of patient	Female/male	Factor
marital	Marital status	Single, Married, Widowed, Divorced	Factor
katz1	Bathing	3 = Receives no assistance (gets in and out of tub) 2 = Receives assistance in bathing only one part of body 1 = Receives assistance in bathing more than one part of the body	Numeric
katz2	Dressing	3 = Gets clothes and gets completely dressed without assistance 2 = Gets clothes and gets dressed without assistance except in tying shoes 1 = Receives assistance in getting clothes or in getting dressed	Numeric
katz3	Toileting	3 = Goes to "toilet room," cleans self, and arranges clothes without assistance 2 = Receives assistance in going to the "toilet room," or in cleaning self or in arranging clothes 1 = Doesn't go to the room termed "toilet" for elimination process	Numeric
katz4	Transfer	3 = Moves in and out of bed as well as in and out of chair without assistance (may use object for support) 2 = Moves in and out of bed or chair with assistance 1 = Doesn't get out of bed	Numeric
katz5	Continence	3 = Controls urination and bowel movement completely by self 2 = has occasional "accidents" 1 = Supervision helps keep urine or bowel control; catheter is used, or is incontinent	Numeric
katz6	Feeding	3 = Feeds self without assistance 2 = Feeds self except for getting assistance in cutting meat or buttering bread 1 = Receives assistance in feeding or is fed partly or completely by using tubes or intravenous fluids	Numeric

(continued)

TABLE 3.1 Continued

Variable	Description	Values	Variable Type
iad1	Telephone	3 = Able to look up numbers; can dial, receive, and make calls without help 2 = Able to look up numbers, dial, receive and make calls with help 1 = Unable to use the telephone	Numeric
iad2	Traveling	3 = Able to drive own car or travel alone on bus or taxi 2 = Able to travel, but not alone 1 = Unable to travel	Numeric
iad3	Shopping	3 = Able to take care of all shopping with transportation provided 2 = Able to shop but not alone 1 = Unable to travel	Numeric
iad4	Preparing meals	3 = Able to plan and cook full meals 2 = Able to prepare light foods, but unable to cook full meals alone 1 = Unable to prepare any meals	Numeric
iad5	Housework	3 = Able to do heavy housework (e.g. scrub floors) 2 = Able to do light housework, but needs help with heavy tasks 1 = Unable to do any housework	Numeric
iad6	Medication	3 = Able to take medication in the right dose at the right time 2 = Able to take medication, but needs reminding or someone to prepare it 1 = Unable to take medication	Numeric
iad7	Money	3 = Able to manage buying needs, write checks, pay bills 2 = Able to manage daily buying needs, but needs help managing checkbook, paying bills 1 = Unable to manage money	Numeric
disdate	Discharge date	Date of discharge	Date
return30	Returned within 30 days	No; yes	
age	Age in years	Actual age	Numeric
spouse	Living spouse	Yes; no	Factor

The *hospital.rdata* file will be used to illustrate some examples. If you do not already have this data set open, in *RStudio* select **File** and then **Open File** from the menu bar and navigate to where you have saved your files. Double click the file *hospital.rdata*. When queried whether you want to load the file into the Global Environment, select *Yes*. You can now use the **names()** function to list the variable names in the file. This is displayed below.

```
>names(hospital)

[1] "admit"      "gender"     "marital"    "katz1"
"katz2"      "katz3"      "katz4"      "katz5"
[9] "katz6"      "iad1"       "iad2"       "iad3"
"iad4"       "iad5"       "iad6"       "iad7"
[17] "disdate"   "return30"  "age"         "spouse"
```

Table 3.1 provides a description for each of these variables.

Recoding Data

Recoding is used to combine, collapse, or correct data. For example, the variable *age* is a numeric variable. In the *hospital* data set, patients range in age from 65 to 100 years. For the purposes of analysis it may be helpful to collapse the data into the following categories: *65 to 69, 70 to 74, 75 to 79,* and *80 or older*, making it a categorical, or factor, variable. In order to do this recode, you will need to use a number of *R's* logical operators, presented in Table 3.2.

In order to recode the variable *age*, enter the following into the Console:

```
> agecat<-NA
> agecat[hospital$age >= 65 & hospital$age < 70]<-1
> agecat[hospital$age >= 70 & hospital$age < 75]<-2
> agecat[hospital$age >= 75 & hospital$age < 80]<-3
> agecat[hospital$age >= 80 ]<-4
```

The first statement creates a new variable called *agecat* and assigns missing values ("NA") to it initially as a default. The second statement assigns the value "1" to any observation whose age is greater than or equal to (>=) 65 and (&) less than (<) 70. This means that a "1" is assigned to *agecat* for any case that has an *age* value between 65 and 69.9 years. Similarly, the third statement assigns a value of "2" to *agecat* for any observation that has an *age* value between 70 and 74.9. The same applies for the last two statements.

Once you enter these commands, use the **table()** function to see the number of observations in each category. The results are displayed below.

```
> table(agecat)

agecat
 1  2  3  4
41 32 35 46
```

As mentioned earlier, it is more efficient to store a categorical variable as a factor variable. The syntax for doing this is displayed below.

```
> agecat<-factor(agecat,levels=c(1,2,3,4),
labels=c("65-69","70-74","75-79","80 or older"))
> table(agecat)

agecat
          65-69          70-74          75-79 80 or older
             41             32             35          46
```

In this situation, *R* assigns numeric values sequentially to the factor variable so *65–69* = 1, *70–74* = 2, *75–79* = 3, and *80 or older* = 4.

The **ifelse(*test,yes,no*)** function can also be used to recode data. This function would be perfect if we wanted to create a dichotomous variable for observations that are 80 years of age or older compared to all other ages.

TABLE 3.2 Logical Operators

Operator	Description
<	Less than
<=	Less than or equal to
>	Greater than
>=	Greater than or equal
==	Exactly equal to
!=	Not equal to
!X	Not X
X | Y	X or Y
X & Y	X and Y
isTRUE(x)	Test if x is true

```
> age80<-ifelse(agecat=="80 or older",1,0)
> table(age80)
```

```
age80
  0   1
108  46
```

In this example, if an observation was exactly equal to *80 or older, age80* is assigned a value of "1." Otherwise, *age80* is assigned a value of "0." Because *agecat* is a factor variable, the category name was used in the test portion of the **ifelse()** and, therefore, needs to appear between quotation marks. As displayed below, this could be avoided by using the **as.numeric()** function.

```
>age80<-ifelse(as.numeric(agecat)==4,1,0)
```

Combining Variables

In Table 3.1, there are six items from the Katz Activities of Daily Living (ADL) scale, labeled *katz1* through *katz6*. This scale is a measure of how independently a person can care for himself or herself. A value of 3 for each item is the most independent, 2 is partially dependent, and 1 is the most dependent. It would be helpful to create a total combined score for each observation. As shown below, this can be accomplished by adding the six items in the Katz ADL scale together.

```
>tkatzsum<- hospital$katz1+hospital$katz2+hospital$katz3+
hospital$katz4+hospital$katz5+hospital$katz6
> summary(tkatzsum)
```

```
Min. 1st Qu. Median    Mean 3rd Qu.  Max. NA's
6.00   13.75   18.00   15.62   18.00 18.00    1
```

The scale, *tkatzsum,* has a low value of 6 and a high value of 18. The higher the value, the more independent the patient is. Using a sum may not be the best method, though, when there are missing values, since the more items answered, the higher the score. For example, if one patient answered all six items, each with a value of three, the sum would be 18. If another answered five of six items, each with a value of three, the sum score would be 15, but it may appear as if the second patient were less independent than the first. In this case, it may be more appropriate to get the average of individual items. The **rowMeans()** function is another method to combine items from a scale that takes into account missing data. This command is illustrated below.

```
>tkatzmean<-rowMeans(cbind(hospital$katz1,
hospital$katz2, hospital$katz3, hospital$katz4,
hospital$katz5, hospital$katz6), na.rm=T)
>summary(tkatzmean)
```

```
   Min. 1st Qu.  Median    Mean 3rd Qu.    Max.
  1.000   2.167   3.000   2.598   3.000   3.000
```

The **cbind()** function combines *R* objects, in this case the variables *katz1* through *katz6*. Because **na.rm** option is set to (**T**)rue, cases with missing values are omitted from analysis.

Saving Your Transformations

Before the data set can be saved, the new variables need to be added to the *hospital* file. As shown below the **data.frame()** function can be utilized to accomplish this.

```
>hospital1<-data.frame(hospital,agecat,age80,tkatzsum,
tkatzmean)
```

This command is appending the newly created variables to the *hospital* vector into a new vector called *hospital1*, which we are defining as a data frame. To save this vector you will first need to set your directory to the folder in which you have your data sets stored. To do this in *RStudio*, select the desired working directory, as previously described. Now enter the command below:

```
>save(hospital1,file="hospital1.RData")
```

Alternatively, you can check the box next to the newly created data frame in the Environment tab and then click on the disk icon. You will then be presented with a dialogue box. From there, you can navigate to where you would like the new file saved.

SOME BASIC *R* COMMANDS

Categorical Data

In the previous section, the **table()** command was used to describe categorical data. This function can also be used to display percentages and totals. If the *hospital1* data set you created is not open, access it in *RStudio* by selecting **File / Open File** from the menu bar and navigate to where the file is located. Double click the file to open it.

To begin, create the vector below.

```
> t.agecat<-table(hospital1$agecat)
> t.agecat

    65-69        70-74        75-79 80 or older
       41           32           35          46
```

You can use the **prop.table()** function to display proportions. Notice that you need to have created a table vector first in order to do this.

```
> prop.table(t.agecat)


    65-69        70-74        75-79 80 or older
0.2662338    0.2077922    0.2272727   0.2987013
```

You can convert the proportions to percentages by multiplying by 100, as displayed below.

```
> prop.table(t.agecat)100

    65-69        70-74        75-79 80 or older
 26.62338     20.77922     22.72727    29.87013
```

As displayed below, the **addmargins()** function can be utilized to obtain totals.

```
> addmargins(t.agecat)

    65-69    70-74    75-79 80 or older        Sum
     41         32          35          46     154
```

Numeric Data

Table 3.3 displays a number of functions to describe numeric data.

Below is an example for calculating the mean of *age*.

TABLE 3.3 Functions for Numeric Variables

Function	Description
mean(x)	Calculates the mean of x
median(x)	Calculates the median of x
sd(x)	Calculates the standard deviation of x
var(x)	Calculates the variance of x
range(x)	Calculates the range of x
sum(x)	Calculates the sum of x
min(x)	Displays the minimum value of x
max(x)	Displays the maximum value of x

```
> mean(hospital1$age,na.rm=T)

[1] 76.13433

> mean(hospital1$age)

[1] NA
```

Because *age* has some missing values, the **na.rm=T** argument is included in the statement. *R* returned a mean of "76.13433." Notice that in the second statement the **na.rm=T** was excluded, and *R* returned "NA." Because missing values are often present in data, it is preferable to include the missing value option.

Below is an example of how to obtain a standard deviation.

```
> sd(hospital1$age,na.rm=T)

[1] 7.300806
```

Here is an example of how to obtain a median.

```
>median(hospital1$age,na.rm=T)

[1] 75.50411
```

Typing each function to describe a variable can be tedious. The **summary()** command, displayed below, combines a number of calculated values. Notice that we do not need to include the missing values argument in this statement. Also notice that the standard deviation is not included in the **summary()** output. Later in the book you will be introduced to a package, *psych*, which includes a function that has a wider range of descriptive statistics in a single command.

```
>summary(hospital1$age)

 Min.   1st Qu.   Median   Mean   3rd Qu.     Max.   NA's
64.46    69.79     75.50  76.13     80.49   100.00      6
```

/// 4 /// GETTING YOUR DATA INTO *R*

In order to work through the examples in this chapter, you will need to *install* and *load* the following packages:

- *foreign*
- *memisc*

For more information on how to do this, refer to the Packages section in Chapter 3.

INTRODUCTION

In this chapter you will learn how to get data into *R*. One of the easiest ways to do this is to use Excel or another spreadsheet package. You will then be able to import this data into *R* and analyze it. The first part of this chapter will show you how to use Excel or another spreadsheet program to quickly and effectively record your data. In the second part of this chapter you will learn how to enter the data directly in *R*. Finally, you will learn how to import data from other popular statistical packages and web-based applications directly into *R*.

In this chapter, we also introduce you to *The Clinical Record*, a free downloadable database package that we created to help you easily collect data related to the helping professions. Chapter 10 provides details on how to download and use *The Clinical Record.*

This chapter concludes with a section on data management. This includes instruction on how to add more observations to an existing *R* data set, how to add variables to an existing *R* data set, how to sort a data set, how to delete variables from a data set, and how to create a sub-set of a data set.

GETTING STARTED

Variables

If you think about it, gathering data for analysis is the process of entering the operationalized representation of a variable. A variable can be expressed as a coherent

ID__________

1. What is your gender? ☐ Female ☐ Male

2. What is your age in years at you last birthday?

3. What is your Job Type?

☐ Administration /Management (CEO, Program Director, IT, Dept Head, etc.)

☐ Direct Service (child care worker, residential care worker, youth counselor, etc.)

☐ Clinical (social worker, psychologist, guidance counselor, etc.)

☐ During the past year have you thought of leaving child welfare? ☐Yes ☐ No

☐ If you turn back the clock and revisit your decision to take your current job, would you make the same decision? ☐Yes ☐ No

Perceptions of Child Welfare

The purpose of this survey is to gain your perception of the general public's view of child welfare workers.

Below is a list of statements about how various individuals and groups perceive child welfare. For each statement, please indicate if you: Strongly Disagree (SD); Disagree (D); Agree (A) Strongly Agree (SA)

	SD	D	A	SA
1. Most people respect you for your choice to work in child welfare.	☐	☐	☐	☐
2. People feel that child welfare work is important.	☐	☐	☐	☐
3. People make me feel proud about the work I do.	☐	☐	☐	☐
4. People just don't understand what you have to go through to work in child welfare.	☐	☐	☐	☐
5. When people find out I am a child welfare worker, they seem to look down on me.	☐	☐	☐	☐
6. The government should take more responsibility for improving child welfare services.	☐	☐	☐	☐
7. The work I do is valued by others.	☐	☐	☐	☐
8. Government officials only pay attention to our work when there is a serious incident.	☐	☐	☐	☐
9. Most people blame the child welfare worker when something goes wrong with a case.	☐	☐	☐	☐
10. Most people think that child welfare workers do too little to help the children and the families who are their clients.	☐	☐	☐	☐

FIGURE 4.1 Example survey

	SD	D	A	SA
11. Most people wonder how I can do this kind of work.	☐	☐	☐	☐
12. I feel uncomfortable admitting to others that I am a child welfare worker.	☐	☐	☐	☐
13. People look down on my work because of the types of clients I serve and the needs they have.	☐	☐	☐	☐
14. Most of my friends and family act like they don't want to know anything about my work.	☐	☐	☐	☐

FIGURE 4.1 Example survey (continued)

combination of attributes that can vary from person to person in a research project. For example, Figure 4.1 contains an example of a survey distributed to child welfare workers to learn about a workforce issue: how they believe those outside the child welfare system view them. In this survey, the first question asks the respondent his or her gender. The variable *gender* consists of two attributes: *female* and *male*. The attributes of gender can vary from one subject to the next. For data entry into a spreadsheet we could easily assign an operational value to *male* and *female*, for example, 1 = *female* and 2 = *male*. Once all the data are entered for this variable, you can then calculate the number and percentage of males and females in your study sample.

For the variable *age*, the attribute, or the operational value, is the respondent's actual age in years. If a respondent enters 29 for *age* on a survey, that is the value you would record for him or her in a spreadsheet holding your data. Once all the ages of the respondents are entered, various descriptive statistics can be calculated, such as the mean, median, and standard deviation.

ENTERING DATA INTO MICROSOFT EXCEL

In this section, we will walk you through the steps necessary to accurately enter data into Excel for import into *R*.

One of the simplest ways to bring your data into *R* for analysis is by entering it into Excel, Numbers, or any other program that can create *.csv* files. Since Excel is the most commonly used spreadsheet program, this chapter will show you how to enter data into Excel. Other programs used for entering data will use a method similar to, although not exactly like, Excel.

In some situations, you may not be able to use Excel or another program to enter your data, and in these cases you may want to enter your data directly into *R*. This is explained in detail later in this chapter in the section titled Entering Data Directly in R.

To look at a relevant example, we will return to the example in Figure 4.1. An agency executive of a large child welfare program is interested in studying how child welfare workers' attrition is affected by how they think they are perceived by others, and the Perceptions of Child Welfare scale is included in the survey (Auerbach et al., 2014). Figure 4.1 is an example of a blank survey used in this evaluation.

Creating an Excel file that can be imported into *R* must be done in a particular manner. To do this, complete the following steps:

1. Create a folder that will be used to store your data. We suggest that you create this on your hard drive and name this folder *Rdata*.
2. Open Excel.
3. As displayed in the "Variable name" in Table 4.1, on the first row (labeled "1"), enter the names of your variables across the columns beginning with column

TABLE 4.1 Question Items and Coding for Data Entry

Survey Item	Excel Column	Variable Name	Values
ID	A	ID	sequential number
What is your gender?	B	gender	1 = female; 2 = male
What is your age in years at your last birthday?	C	age	enter age in years
What is your job type?	D	job	1 = Administration / Management 2 = Direct service 3 = Clinical
During the past year, have you thought of leaving child welfare?	E	leave	1 = yes; 2 = no
If you could turn back the clock and revisit your decision to take your current job, would you make the same decision?	F	clock	1 = yes; 2 = no
Most people respect you for your choice to work in child welfare (+)	G	pcw1	SD = 1; D = 2; A = 3; SA = 4
People feel that child welfare work is important. (+)	H	pcw2	SD = 1; D = 2; A = 3; SA = 4
People make me feel proud about the work I do. (+)	I	pcw3	SD = 1; D = 2; A = 3; SA = 4
People just don't understand what you have to go through to work in child welfare. (–)	J	pcw4	SD = 1; D = 2; A = 3; SA = 4
When people find out I am a child welfare worker, they seem to look down on me. (–)	K	pcw5	SD = 1; D = 2; A = 3; SA = 4

(continued)

TABLE 4.1 Continued

Survey Item	Excel Column	Variable Name	Values
The government should take more responsibility for improving child welfare services. (+)	L	pcw6	SD = 1; D = 2; A = 3; SA = 4
The work I do is valued by others. (+)	M	pcw7	SD = 1; D = 2; A = 3; SA = 4
Government officials only pay attention to our work when there is a serious incident. (–)	N	pcw8	SD = 1; D = 2; A = 3; SA = 4
Most people blame the child welfare worker when something goes wrong with a case. (–)	O	pcw9	SD = 1; D = 2; A = 3; SA = 4
Most people think that child welfare workers do too little to help the children and the families who are their clients. (–)	P	pcw10	SD = 1; D = 2; A = 3; SA = 4
Most people wonder how I can do this kind of work. (–)	Q	pcw11	SD = 1; D = 2; A = 3; SA = 4
I feel uncomfortable admitting to others that I am a child welfare worker. (–)	R	pcw12	SD = 1; D = 2; A = 3; SA = 4
People look down on my work because of the types of clients I serve and the needs they have. (–)	S	pcw13	SD = 1; D = 2; A = 3; SA = 4
Most of my friends and family act like they don't want to know anything about my work. (–)	T	pcw14	SD = 1; D = 2; A = 3; SA = 4

A and ending with column T. Always use simple but descriptive aliases with no spaces or special characters as variable names. This will assure that the names you use in your Excel spreadsheet will be acceptable in *R*.

4. Starting in row 2, you can begin entering your data for each worker, as displayed in Figure 4.2.

The numeric values displayed in the column "Values" in Table 4.1 were used to transfer the responses from the surveys into Excel. For example, the first respondent (ID = 1) entered in row 1 was a female whose age was 29 years. The worker also indicated that she thought of leaving child welfare (*leave* = 1), and would not have made the same decision to take her current job if she could decide all over again (*clock* = 2). Often respondents do not answer every item on a survey. The simplest method for dealing with this is to leave the entry blank for the item. For example, notice that for the last worker (ID = 15, row = 16), the cell for *pcw5* is blank (Figure 4.2). When the data are imported into *R*, cell "j16" will be interpreted as missing.

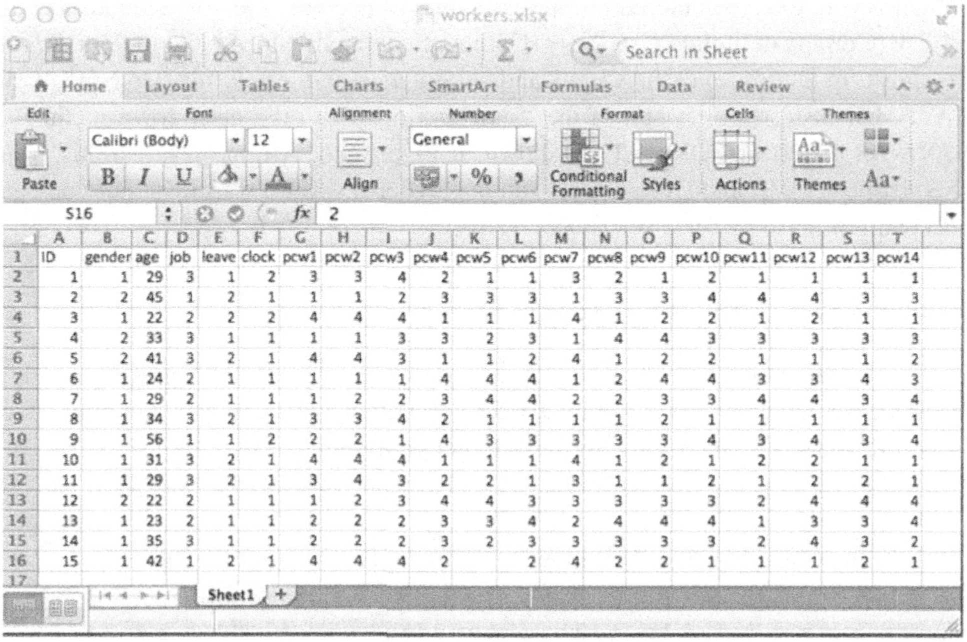

FIGURE 4.2 Data entry example in Excel.

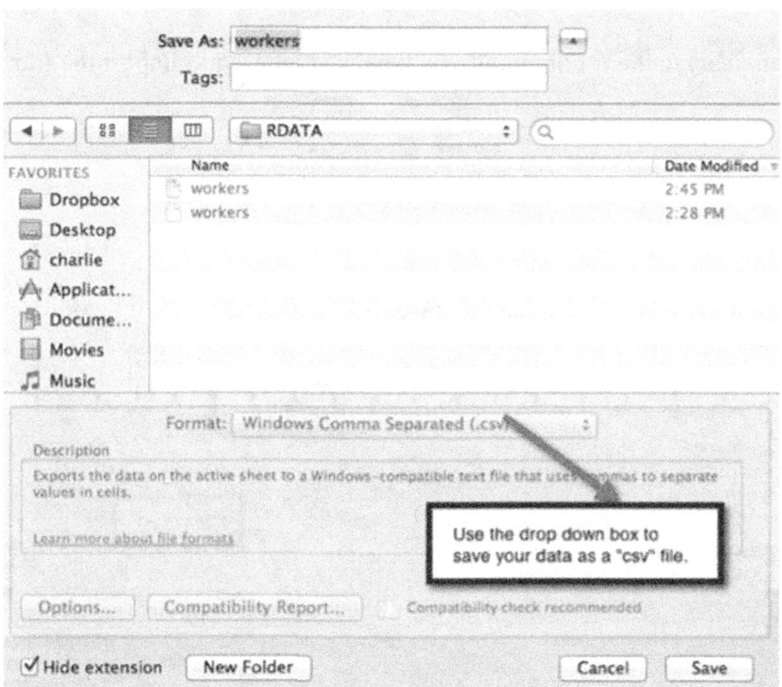

FIGURE 4.3 Saving a Microsoft Excel file in ".csv" format.

Once your data are entered into Excel, you will need to save your spreadsheet as a ".csv (Comma delimited)" or ".csv (Comma Separated Values)" file in your *Rdata* directory. To do this, click SAVE AS and choose a name for your file. Do NOT click SAVE, but instead select one of the ".csv" options from the drop down menu for SAVE AS TYPE or FORMAT, as shown in Figure 4.3. After you finish this, you should click SAVE and close Excel. You may receive several warnings, but you can accept all of these by selecting CONTINUE.

IMPORTING AN *EXCEL* SPREADSHEET INTO *R*

Once you enter your data into Excel, you can import it into *R* and begin your analysis. Because the data were saved in *.csv* format, you can use a simple *R* command to import the data. Use the following steps to get your data into *R*.

1. Open *RStudio*
2. In the Console, enter the following command and press ENTER:

```
>worker<-read.table(file.choose(),header=TRUE,sep=',')
```

You will be prompted with the dialogue box shown in Figure 4.4, which you use to navigate to the *workers.csv* file:

3. Select the file *workers.csv* and click "Open."

We can analyze the *R* command you have just entered to import the file:

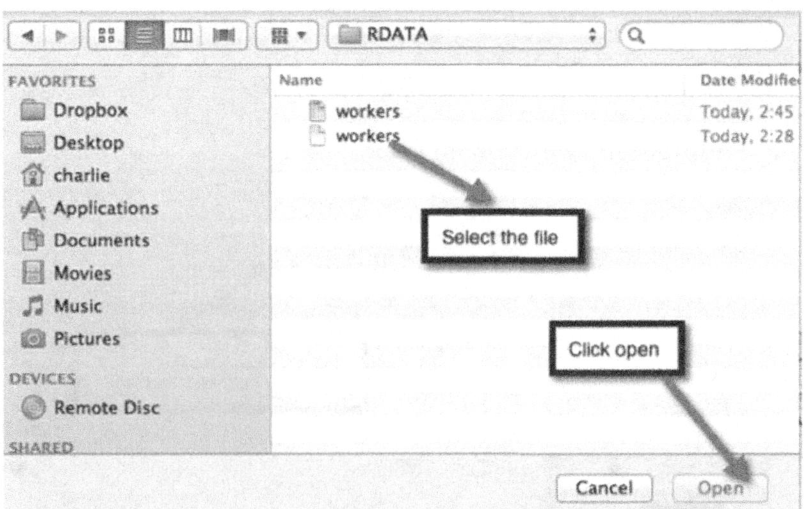

FIGURE 4.4 Opening a *.csv* file in *R*.

```
>worker<-read.table(file.choose(),header=TRUE,sep=',')
```

The **worker** portion of the command is the name of the vector into which the spreadsheet will be copied. The **read.table()** command is used for importing text data. The **header** option informs *R* that the variables' names are included in the first row and **sep=','** informs *R* that the variables in the *.csv* file are separated by commas.

The **file.choose()** command provides navigation to the file. This command can be used over again to import data from other *.csv* files by simply changing the vector name. For example, if you saved data on who attends a self-help group in a different *.csv* file, just replace the vector name with "shelp" or any name of your choosing and import the file.

As displayed here, typing **names(worker)** will provide a list of the variables in the *worker* vector:

```
[1] "ID"      "gender" "age"     "job"     "leave"
"clock"  "pcw1"    "pcw2"    "pcw3"    "pcw4"    "pcw5"
[12] "pcw6"    "pcw7"    "pcw8"    "pcw9"    "pcw10"
"pcw11"  "pcw12"   "pcw13"   "pcw14"
```

Now that your data have been brought into *R*, you can run various commands to analyze your data. For example, you can see how many of the workers thought of leaving within the past year. Type the following command into the Console:

```
>prop.table(table(worker$leave))*100
```

The following will be displayed:

```
1        2
53.33333 46.66667
```

The output shows us that a little more than half of the workers thought of leaving within the past year.

As discussed in Chapter 3, you can also create factor variables. A factor variable is a special type of categorical variable that can be represented as a string or a number. Converting categorical variables to factors has a number of advantages, especially when tables and graphics are used in data analysis. This will be discussed further in Chapter 5.

SOME MORE ABOUT THE `read.table()` FUNCTION

The **read.table()** function is quite flexible. For example, you can read in a tab delimited file by changing the **sep** option to **sep = "\t"**. It should be noted that character variables will be treated as factor variables by default. This function can be turned off by adding the option **Factors=FALSE**. There are also situations in which column names are not included with the file (i.e., there is no header). For example, open the file *worker.txt* included with the example files using a text editing or word processing software (e.g., MS-Wordpad or MAC-Textedit). You will notice that there are no variable names. To read this file in *R*, you first need to create a vector containing the column/variable names.

In the Console, type the following command:

```
>names<-
c("ID","gender","age","job","leave","clock","pcw1",
"pcw2","pcw3","pcw4","pcw5","pcw6","pcw7","pcw8",
"pcw9","pcw10","pcw11","pcw12","pcw13","pcw14")
```

Now you are ready to import the file. In the Console, type the following command:

```
>workertxt<-
read.table(file.choose(),header=F,sep="\t",
col.names=names)
```

Observe that the **header=F** was included because header information was not included in the file. Also notice the **sep="\t"** was used because tabs separate the columns. If the file were tab delimited but included variable names (i.e., there was a header), the following command would be used instead:

```
>workertxt<-read.table(file.choose(),header=T,sep="\t")
```

Once the file is read into *R*, you can modify, analyze, and save it. For example, we can use a command you learned in the section on entering data in Excel. Enter the following in the Console:

```
>prop.table(table(workertxt$leave))*100
```

The following will be displayed in the Console:

```
1        2
53.33333 46.66667
```

This is the same result you acquired in the section on entering data in Excel.

SAVING YOUR DATA AS AN *R* FILE

Once you have imported your data, they can be saved in *R* format. To accomplish this, in the menu bar, click on **Session / Set Working Directory / Choose Directory**. After you press <RETURN>, you will see a dialogue box. Use this dialogue to navigate to the directory that contains the *worker.csv* file, and select **Open**. Use the following command to save the file:

```
>save(worker,file="worker.RData")
```

The first **`worker`** after the opening parenthesis is the vector name, and it was saved in a file called *worker.RData.*

Alternatively, you can check the box in *RStudio* next to the data frame you wish to save and click the disk icon in the Environment pane. You will then be prompted to select a directory in which to save your file. The file will automatically be saved in the *R* data format, *.RData.*

OPENING AN *R* FILE

Once your data have been saved in *R* format, they can be easily retrieved in *RStudio.* To accomplish this, in the menu bar click on **File** and navigate to the directory that contains your data. Click on the file *worker.RData* and click **Open File**. You can now analyze your data. For example, type **`summary(worker$age)`** in the Console, and you will see the following output:

```
Min.  1st Qu.   Median    Mean  3rd Qu.    Max.
22.0     26.5     31.0    33.0     38.0    56.0
```

ENTERING DATA DIRECTLY INTO *R*

Data can be directly entered into *R* by creating a data frame. The function to accomplish this is illustrated in the following example. Notice the following:

- A plus sign (+) starts on the second line and is shown on each subsequent line of the function. DO NOT enter the plus sign; it will be added automatically by *R* to denote a command continuation.
- Each item in the data frame denotes the name of a variable in the order in which you would like it to appear in the data frame. Each is separated from the others by a comma (,).
- The entire data frame is enclosed in parentheses. Note, then, that the last variable entered will have two closed parentheses after it.

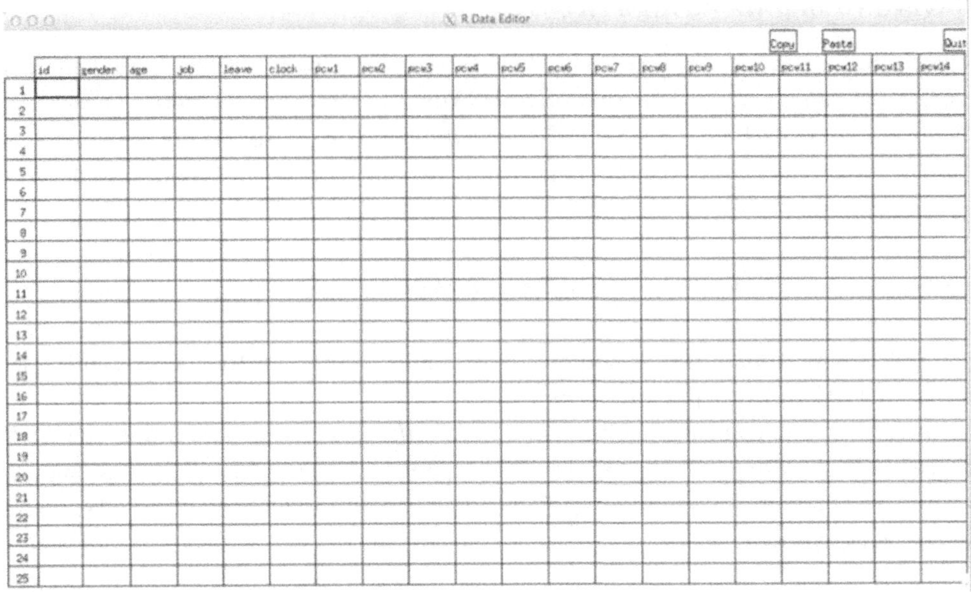

FIGURE 4.5 Example of empty *R* spreadsheet.

```
> worker1 <- data.frame(id=numeric(0), gender=numeric
(0),age=numeric(0),
+ job=numeric(0),leave=numeric(0),clock=numeric(0),
+ pcw1=numeric(0),pcw2=numeric(0),pcw3=numeric(0),
+ pcw4=numeric(0),pcw5=numeric(0),pcw6=numeric(0),
+ pcw7=numeric(0),pcw8=numeric(0),pcw9=numeric(0),
+ pcw10=numeric(0),pcw11=numeric(0),pcw12=numeric(0),
+ pcw13=numeric(0),pcw14=numeric(0))
```

The **data.frame()** function is used to define each of the variables and their type. In this case, all the variables are numeric. Since we are creating a blank spreadsheet, the definition of each variable as numeric is followed by "(0)." If you would want to enter a character variable called *lname* to denote the respondent's last name, you would use the following function: **lname=character(0)**.

After you have defined the variables, entering the function **fix(worker1)** in the Console will display the spreadsheet shown in Figure 4.5. You can now begin entering the data from Figure 4.2 into the spreadsheet. When you are finished entering data, you can save the spreadsheet using one of the two methods described above. Once your data have been saved in *R* format, they can be easily retrieved in *RStudio*, as described earlier in this chapter.

IMPORTING DATA FROM OTHER PROGRAMS

Data from other statistical packages like STATA, SPSS, and SAS can be imported directly into *R*. The *foreign* package is included with the initial installation of *R* and can read files written in different formats. One advantage to using *foreign* is that variables with value labels will automatically be read into *R* as factor variables.

Importing STATA Files

There is an important caveat to importing STATA files into *R* using *foreign*. ***Foreign*** **will not translate files above STATA Version 12.** If you are using STATA 13 or above, in the menu bar in STATA click on **File / Save as**, and a save data dialogue will appear. Under **Format** be sure to select STATA 12 and save your file in the desired folder.

As an example, we can import a STATA file into a vector called *workerstata*. Enter these steps for using *foreign* to read and translate a STATA file:

1. Type `require(foreign)` in the Console and press RETURN or check the box next to *foreign* in the Packages pane. You now have access to all the functions in this package.
2. Type `workerstata<-read.dta(file.choose())` in the Console and press RETURN.
   The `file.choose()` function provides the ability to navigate to the file of your choice. Navigate to where you have the example data sets installed, select the file `worker.dta`, and click Open.
   The file is now stored in a vector called *workerstata*. Type `names(workerstata)` in the Console, and the variables in the vector will be listed.
3. The imported data can be saved as an *R* file using one of the two methods described earlier. One way to do this is to click on **Session / Set Working Directory / Choose Directory** in the menu bar. After you press <RETURN>, you will see a dialogue box. Use this dialogue to navigate to the directory that contains the *worker.csv* file, and select Open. Use the following function in the Console to save the file:

```
>save(workerstata,file="workerstata.RData")
```

Alternatively, you can check the box in *RStudio* next to the data frame you wish to save and click the disk icon in the Environment tab. You will then be prompted to select a directory in which to save your file. Once you navigate to the desired directory, enter *workerstata* in the *Save As* box.

Importing SPSS System Files

Our preference is to not import SPSS files directly into *R* as was demonstrated with STATA files. Rather, we believe it is better to first save the SPSS file as a STATA file and then read it into *R* using *foreign*, as described above. This is because the *read.spss* function in *foreign* does not import the data as a data frame. As an example of importing an SPSS file as we recommend, do the following:

1. Open the *worker.sav* file in SPSS.
2. While in SPSS, select **File / Save as** from the menu bar and you will see the dialogue in Figure 4.6.
3. Navigate to the directory in which you wish to save the file.
4. Click the arrow next to the *Save as type* shown in Figure 4.6.
5. Scroll down to **Stata Version 8 SE (.data)**
6. Select **Save.**

Except for changing the vector name file (e.g., *workerspss*), you can simply repeat the steps from the section on importing data from STATA.

If you do not have access to SPSS, but would like to import an SPSS file into *R*, the *memisc* package can be used as an alternative for importing SPSS systems files (*.sav*). This package needs to be installed first from CRAN and required before using any of

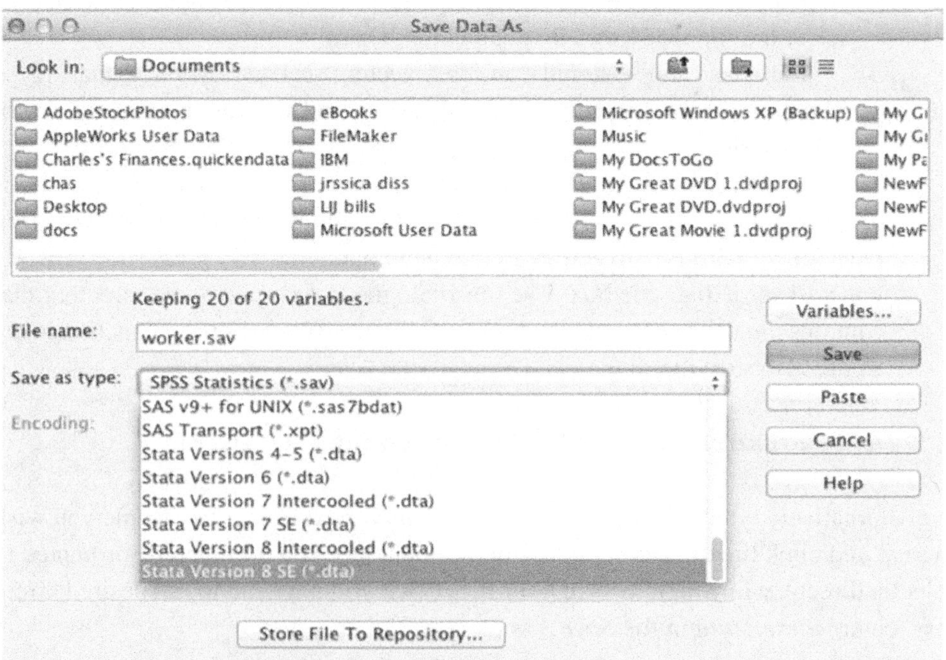

FIGURE 4.6 Saving an SPSS file as a STATA file.

its functions. You can review the steps for installing *R* packages described in Chapter 3. Once the package has been successfully installed, follow these steps to import your data.

1. Type **require(memisc)** and press <RETURN>.
2. Enter the following into the Console:

```
>workerspss <-
as.data.set(spss.system.file(file.choose()))
```

(Notice that the function **file.choose()** is included for navigation to the file. Be mindful of the matching parentheses.)

3. Navigate to where you have stored your example files and open the file called *worker.sav*.
4. Enter the following function into the Console to save this data as a data frame:

```
>workerspss <-as.data.frame(workerspss)
```

5. The data frame can be saved as an *R* file using the directions described in the section on importing and saving STATA files. Because the variable *gender* includes value labels (i.e., *female* and *male*), gender was imported as a factor variable. As displayed in Figure 4.7, if you click on the *Environment* tab in the top right pane, a listing for the data frame will appear. When you double click on *workerspss* or click on the spreadsheet icon, a spreadsheet view will be available in the upper left pane. Notice that the variable *gender* contains *female* and *male* attributes for various observations.

An SPSS portable file (*.por*) can also be imported into *R*. Repeat the steps for importing an SPSS system file by replacing the function in step 2, above, with

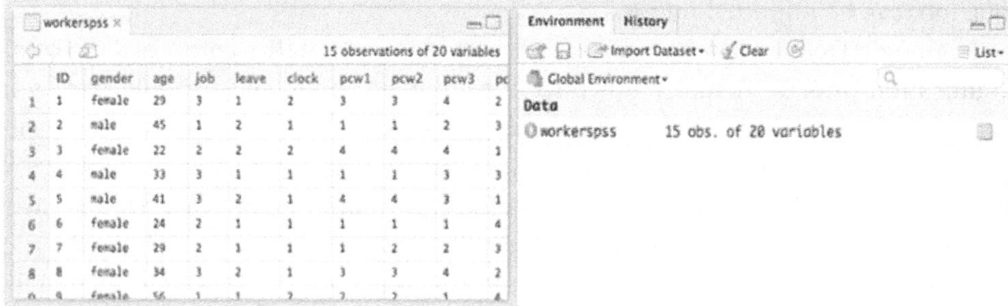

FIGURE 4.7 Translated SPSS system file.

```
>workerpor<-
as.data.set(spss.portable.file(file.choose()))
```

Also replace the function in step 4, above, with

```
>workerpor<-as.data.frame(workerpor).
```

Importing SAS Files

SAS files can be imported using the *foreign* package described earlier in this chapter. As an example, enter the following in the Console:

1. If *foreign* has not already been required for the session, do so: `require(foreign)`
2. Type `workersas<- read.xport(file.choose())` and navigate to the folder that contains the example data and double click on *worker.xpt*.
3. Your data can be saved in *R* format using the steps outlined in the section on importing and saving STATA files.

Another Alternative

There is a commercial program called StatTransfer (http://www.stattransfer.com) that allows for the transfer of files between numerous file formats, including *R*. When transferring from SPSS and STATA, StatTransfer does not retain value labels; however, it does have the advantage of being able to transfer newer version of STATA into *R*. StatTransfer 11 has the ability to transfer between 37 different file formats, including the ones discussed earlier in this chapter. Examples of other supported data formats include 1-2-3, FoxPro, and Statistica.

IMPORTING DATA FROM WEB APPLICATIONS

There are several web applications such as Google Docs and Survey Monkey, in which you can create web-based survey instruments that are completed online. These data, too, can be imported into *R*.

In Google Docs, when you work with your data, you will want to make a small modification prior to actually downloading the data. First, the variable names in Google Docs are actually the questions that you defined in your form. You will want to, in the spreadsheet, change the variable names to ones that are acceptable to *R*. Then, in Google Docs, select **File / Download as / comma-separate values (.csv, current sheet)**. You will then be presented a dialogue box and you can **Save** the file.

Now, you can use the command for importing other .csv files, as described in the section titled Importing an Excel spreadsheet Into *R*, earlier in this chapter.

Survey Monkey is another popular program, and you will import data into *R* in a similar fashion as instructed for Google Docs. To download your data in the proper format, in Survey Monkey, navigate to the **Analyze Results** tab. On the left side of your screen, select **Download Responses**. You will then be prompted to select a type of download. Choose **All Responses Collected and Advanced Spreadsheet Format**. Then click on the **REQUEST DOWNLOAD** button.

You will then be prompted to either save or open your file. You will need to save this .ZIP file and then unzip it to access the files.

Open the CSV file folder and then open the file entitled *sheet_1.csv* in your spreadsheet software. As with Google Docs, you will need to change your variable names to ones that are acceptable to *R*, as the existing names will be too long and cumbersome to manage. Then, save your file in a convenient place. You can now use the command for importing other .csv files, as described in the section titled Importing an Excel Spreadsheet Into *R*, earlier in this chapter.

THE CLINICAL RECORD

The Clinical Record is an application we created to help those in the helping professions collect and store data in a user-friendly manner. You can learn how to download *The Clinical Record* for free in Chapter 10. Complete instructions for use are also included in that chapter.

The format for collecting data using *The Clinical Record* is different from that of any of the statistical packages or web applications described above. Instead, it was designed to be used in practice settings to collect data while working with clients. Data collected in *The Clinical Record* can be downloaded to *R* for analysis. Complete instructions and a comprehensive example are also presented in Chapter 10.

MANAGING YOUR DATA

There are times when you may need to modify a data set. In this section we will cover a number of data management functions that include adding more observations to an existing *R* data set, adding variables to an existing *R* data set, sorting a data set, deleting variables from a data set, and sub-setting data.

Combining Files: Adding Observations

The `rbind()` function can be utilized to add observations to an existing file. Open the *workera.rdata* data set, which is located in the folder that contains the example files for this book. In the Environment tab, you will see the information depicted in Figure 4.8.

Note that this file contains 15 observations and 20 variables. To view this data, you can double click the spreadsheet icon to the right of the listing of the data file. Alternatively, you can type `head(workera)` in the Console and,

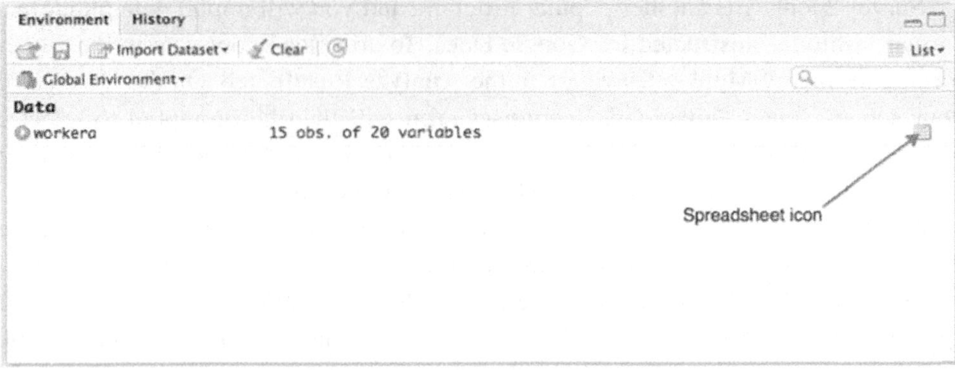

FIGURE 4.8 Example of Environment tab.

```
  ID gender age job leave clock pcw1 pcw2 pcw3 pcw4 pcw5 pcw6 pcw7 pcw8
1  1      1  29   3     1     2    3    3    4    2    1    1    3    2
2  2      2  45   1     2     1    1    1    2    3    3    3    1    3
3  3      1  22   2     2     2    4    4    4    1    1    1    4    1
4  4      2  33   3     1     1    1    1    3    3    2    3    1    4
5  5      2  41   3     2     1    4    4    3    1    1    2    4    1
6  6      1  24   2     1     1    1    1    1    4    4    4    1    2
  pcw9 pcw10 pcw11 pcw12 pcw13 pcw14
1    1     2     1     1     1     1
2    3     4     4     4     3     3
3    2     2     1     2     1     1
4    4     3     3     3     3     3
5    2     2     1     1     1     2
6    4     4     3     3     4     3
```

FIGURE 4.9 Using `head()` function to display *workera* file.

```
  ID gender age job leave clock pcw1 pcw2 pcw3 pcw4 pcw5 pcw6 pcw7 pcw8
1 16      1  29   3     1     2    3    3    4    2    1    1    3    2
2 17      2  45   1     2     1    1    1    2    3    3    3    1    3
3 18      1  22   2     2     2    4    4    4    1    1    1    4    1
4 19      2  33   3     1     1    1    1    3    3    2    3    1    4
5 20      2  41   3     2     1    4    4    3    1    1    2    4    1
  pcw9 pcw10 pcw11 pcw12 pcw13 pcw14
1    1     2     1     1     1     1
2    3     4     4     4     3     3
3    2     2     1     2     1     1
4    4     3     3     3     3     3
5    2     2     1     1     1     2
```

FIGURE 4.10 Using `head()` function to display *worker1* file

as shown in Figure 4.9, the first six observations in the data frame will be displayed.

Now open the file called *worker1.rdata*. This file contains information for IDs 16 through 20. To see a partial listing (displayed in Figure 4.10) of what is in this file, enter **head(worker1)** in the Console.

Note that both files contain the same number of variables, and the variable names are identical. Because of this, the files can be merged using the following function.

```
>rworker<-rbind(workera,worker1)
```

In this command, the files are combined and copied into a new vector called *rworker*. Look in the Environment tab and notice that *rworker* contains 20 observations and 20 variables. The file can now be saved using the **save()** function described in Chapter 3.

You can view the results of the **rbind()** command in the same way you viewed the data files described above. If you double click on the spreadsheet icon, you will notice that *R* created a variable called *row.names*. This variable is not visible if you view the results using the **head()** function or the **names()** function.

HELPFUL HINT: We suggest that you always retain your original data files in case you make a mistake or need to refer back to your original unaltered data at some later point. As a very wise professor once told us, "Deleting data and variables is dangerous!"

Combining Files: Adding Variables

Often there are times when you will need to combine two data sets that contain the same observations but have different variables. For example, the files *workera.rdata* and *worker2.rdata* contain information about the same employees, but each contains different variables. If *workera.rdata* is not open, open it. Once it is open, type **names(workera)** and the following will be displayed:

```
[1] "ID"      "gender" "age"     "job"     "leave"
"clock"   "pcw1"
[8] "pcw2"    "pcw3"    "pcw4"    "pcw5"    "pcw6"
"pcw7"    "pcw8"
[15] "pcw9"    "pcw10"   "pcw11"   "pcw12"   "pcw13"
"pcw14"
```

Now, open *worker2.rdata* and type **names(worker2)** in the Console. The following will be displayed:

```
[1] "ID"      "jobsat" "exper"
```

Notice that both files contain a common "ID," which represents the same worker in each file. This ID can be used as a unique identifier for the employee. Their common ID (unique identifier) can be used to merge the data from each data set while attributing the data to the correct observation by linking it with the unique identifier. The unique identifier informs *R* of how to match each of the cases.

The **merge()** function is used to merge files with common observations but different variables. Type the following command in the Console:

```
>newworker<-merge(workera,worker2,by="ID")
```

The two data sets are merged linking the two on the variable *ID* into a new vector called *newworker*. Notice that *newworker* now contains 22 variables: 20 from *workera* plus 2 from *worker2*. Once the vector is created, it can be viewed and saved. Also notice that the variables from *worker2* are appended to those from *workera*; that is, in the newly created vector, the order in which the original files are listed determines the order in which the variables appear.

There are times when you need to combine files that cannot be identified by a single unique identifier. Take, for example, the files *merg1.rdata* and *merg2.rdata*. Each contains different variables but has an *id* and a *siteid* common to both files. The *id* is not unique across sites but it is within sites. As a result, we

69 observations of 8 variabl

	row.names	id	siteid	pay	promotion	supervison	benefits	contingent	operating
1	58	8	2	9	10	7	11	7	8
2	5	11	2	11	9	15	10	13	13
3	23	17	2	10	9	11	9	11	11
4	24	19	2	10	11	16	14	15	9
5	27	22	2	10	8	13	8	11	8
6	31	32	2	10	13	10	NA	NA	NA
7	51	72	2	6	10	16	9	10	11
8	53	73	2	10	4	11	12	10	12
9	40	57	3	11	12	16	15	15	12
10	42	63	3	10	NA	12	12	11	12
11	3	101	3	12	12	16	12	15	14
12	6	110	3	7	11	16	12	11	10
13	26	2	5	9	8	7	11	5	9
14	32	4	5	9	10	13	12	13	10
15	41	6	5	11	13	15	14	12	12
16	48	7	5	7	7	14	11	11	12
17	59	8	5	7	7	14	14	4	13
18	64	9	5	NA	NA	NA	NA	NA	11
19	1	10	5	10	11	NA	NA	8	11
20	14	13	5	9	8	11	11	7	9
21	22	15	5	8	11	9	12	10	7
22	25	19	5	10	11	14	8	8	9

FIGURE 4.11 Display of vector *cwsort*.

have to merge the files using both *id* and *siteid*, the variable representing the various sites.

Open both of theses files. When you enter the following syntax in the Console, you will merge the files.

```
>totalcw<-merge(merg1,merg2,by=c("id","siteid"))
```

The two files are merged into a new vector, *totalcw*. This vector can be sorted first by *siteid*, followed by *id*, into a new vector *cwsort* using the following syntax:

```
>cwsort<-totalcw[order(totalcw$siteid,totalcw$id),]
```

Click on the spreadsheet icon next to the vector name in the Environment tab and the information depicted in Figure 4.11 will be displayed in the top left pane.

Notice that the vector is now in order by *id* within *siteid*. Also notice that observations 4 and 22 have the same id, 19, but different values for *siteid*.

Combining Files With Different Numbers of Observations

So far, we have only looked at instances where we merged files that had the same number of observations in each file. There are times when you may need to merge files that have unequal numbers of observations.

We will create an example in Table 4.2. We will begin by creating two vectors (*id* and *x*) that we will then use to build a data frame, *file1*. Then, we will create two other vectors (*id* and *y*) that will then be used to build a second data frame, *file2*. You will notice that both of these data frames have different numbers of observations, but we will be able to merge them.

TABLE 4.2 Creating and Merging Data Files With Different Numbers of Observations

Command	Explanation
`>id<-c(1,2,3,4,5,6,7,8,9,10)`	Create *id* vector with 10 elements
`>x<-c(10,20,30,40,50,60,70,80,90,100)`	Create *x* vector with 10 elements
`>file1<-data.frame(id,x)`	Create a data frame combining *id* and *x* into *file1*
`>id<-c(1,2,3,4,6,8,9,10)`	Create new *id* with 8 elements
`>y<-c(1,2,3,4,5,6,7,8)`	Create *y* variable with 8 elements
`>file2<-data.frame(id,y)`	Create data frame combing *id* and *y* into *file2*
`>file3<-merge(file1,file2,by="id", all=TRUE)`	Merge *file1* and *file2* into *file3*

file1

	id	x
1	1	10
2	2	20
3	3	30
4	4	40
5	5	50
6	6	60
7	7	70
8	8	80
9	9	90
10	10	100

file2

	id	y
1	1	1
2	2	2
3	3	3
4	4	4
5	6	5
6	8	6
7	9	7
8	10	8

file3

	id	x	y
1	1	10	1
2	2	20	2
3	3	30	3
4	4	40	4
5	5	50	NA
6	6	60	5
7	7	70	NA
8	8	80	6
9	9	90	7
10	10	100	8

FIGURE 4.12 Creation of three data files.

As Figure 4.12 illustrates, three files have been created. *file1* has ten rows with ids 1 through 10. *file2* has eight rows, as it is missing *ids* 5 and 7. *file3* is the result of the merge command used in Table 4.2. By including the **all=TRUE** option in the command, *R* included all the *ids* from *file1* while adding *NA* for the each of the missing *y* values for *ids* 5 and 7.

Deleting a Variable

There will be situations in which you will need to delete variables. One way to do this is to use the column/variable numbers.

As an example, consider the *totalcw* data frame constructed earlier. Begin by listing the variable names in the Console:

```
> names(totalcw)
[1] "id"          "siteid"      "pay"         "promotion"
"supervison" "benefits"
[7] "contingent" "operating"
```

Perhaps you want to delete the variables *pay* (column 3), *promotion* (column 4), and *operating* (column 8). To accomplish this, you could use the following syntax:

5 observations of 20 variables

	row.names	ID	gender	age	job	leave	clock	pcw1	pcw2	pcw3	pcw4	pcw5	pcw6
1	1	1	1	29	3	1	2	3	3	4	2	1	1
2	4	4	2	33	3	1	1	1	1	3	3	2	3
3	7	7	1	29	2	1	1	1	2	2	3	4	4
4	9	9	1	56	1	1	2	2	2	1	4	3	3
5	14	14	1	35	3	1	1	2	2	2	3	2	3

FIGURE 4.13 Display of *leave* vector.

```
>totalcw1<-totalcw[c(-3,-4,-8)]
```

Notice that a new vector called *totalcw1* is created. As stated earlier, deleting variables can be dangerous, so we recommend creating a new data frame and keeping the original intact.

Instead of using column numbers, you can use the actual names of the variables you want to delete. This is a two-step process: first you should make a copy of the original vector, as shown in Step 1; next, as shown in Step 2, the variables you want deleted are set to NULL and are removed from the vector. After the variables have been removed, the vector can be saved as a file.

```
Step 1- >totalcw2<-totalcw
Step 2-  >totalcw2$pay <- totalcw2$promotion <-
totalcw2$operating <- NULL
```

Creating Subsets of Your Data

Often, you will want to be able to create subsets of your data. For example, if you wanted to create a data frame from the *workera.rdata* file that contains workers who say they are thinking of leaving (1 = yes) and are older than 25, you can use the following syntax that uses the **subset()** function.

```
>leave<-subset(workera, leave==1 & age >25)
```

If you double click the spreadsheet icon in the Environment tab, the information depicted in Figure 4.13 will be displayed in the top left pane.
Note that all the observations have a value of 1 for *leave* and are older than 25.

If you wanted to create a data frame from the *merg1* data with only respondents from site 5, you would use the following syntax:

```
>Site5<-subset(merg1,siteid==5)
```

The **subset()** function includes an option, **select**, which can be used to create subsets of variables. From the *merg1* data frame, if you wanted a subset of sites less than 5 and only containing variables *id, siteid*, and *promotion*, you would use the following syntax:

```
>site2<-
subset(merg1,siteid<5,select=c(id,siteid,promotion))
```

You have now created a much smaller data frame with fewer variables and less observations. A new vector, *site2*, has been created, containing data for *id, siteid*, and *promotion* only for sites 2 and 3.

/// 5 /// BASIC GRAPHICS WITH *R*

In order to work through the examples in this chapter, you will need to *install* and *load* the following packages:

- *ggplot2*
- *car*

For more information on how to do this, refer to the Packages section in Chapter 3.

INTRODUCTION

This chapter explains how to create basic graphs using *R*. The chapter will cover the creation of pie charts, bar graphs, histograms, boxplots, and scatterplots. Very sophisticated graphics can be generated using the *R* base graphics package as well as user-developed ones. Before you begin working through this chapter, you will need to install the *ggplot2* and *car* packages. As described in Chapter 3, you can use the "Install Packages" tab in the lower right pane in *RStudio* to accomplish this. Alternatively, you can type the following in the Console:

```
>install.packages(c("ggplot2", "car"))
```

Regardless of the method used to install the packages, the following output will appear in the Console:

```
trying URL
'http://lib.stat.cmu.edu/R/CRAN/bin/macosx/
contrib/3.0/ggplot2_0.9.3.1.tgz'
Content type 'application/x-gzip' length 2650041
bytes (2.5 Mb)
opened URL
==================================================
downloaded 2.5 Mb
```

```
trying URL
'http://lib.stat.cmu.edu/R/CRAN/bin/macosx/con-
trib/3.0/car_2.0-19.tgz'
Content type 'application/x-gzip' length 1326452
bytes (1.3 Mb)
opened URL
==================================================
downloaded 1.3 Mb
```

SOME BASIC GRAPHING IDEAS

Keen (2010) points out that statistical analysis usually involves a great deal of "data reduction." This process often involves calculating and presenting various descriptive statistics such as the mean and standard deviation. Compressing data can lead to possible loss of information, but can be offset through the use of graphics (Keen, 2010). Graphics can display features in the data not revealed by descriptive statistics alone. In fact, combining the two leads to an even more accurate illustration of data.

Characteristics of the data must be considered when deciding what type of graph to use. For example, a pie chart would not be appropriate for the display of numeric data (e.g., the number of days a student was truant from school), but would be for categorical variables like *gender*. Likewise, a histogram would not be an appropriate graph type for categorical variables such as *marital status*. Burn (1993) and Keen (2010) provide an in-depth discussion of the principles of statistical graphics, and we refer you to their texts for more in-depth discussions (Burn, 1993; Keen, 2010).

PIE CHARTS

Pie charts are appropriate for displaying univariate counts and percentages of categorical data. As an example, we will work with the *hospital1* data set you created in

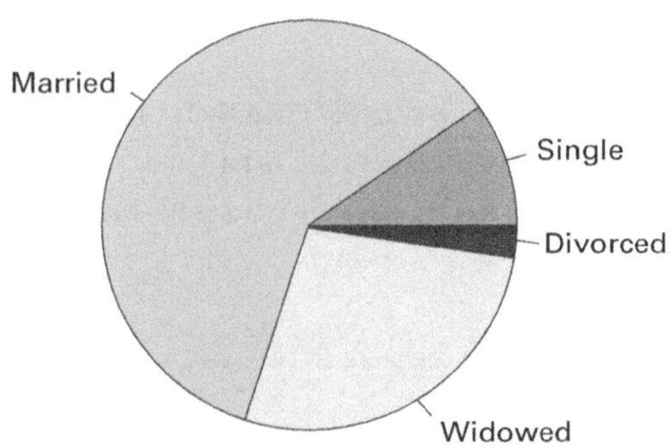

FIGURE 5.1 Pie chart example with counts.

Chapter 3. You can also download the file from the www.ssdanalysis.com website. In *RStudio,* click **File / Open** in the menu bar to navigate to the folder containing the data set, and open it.

Use the **head(hospital1)** function to display the variable names and first six cases. Figure 5.1 displays a pie chart of the count of the categories of marital status.

The first step in the creation of this pie chart is to create a vector that contains the counts for *marital status*. The following displays how this is accomplished:

```
>maritalp<-table(hospital1$marital)
>maritalp

Single  Married  Widowed Divorced
   16        95       44        4
```

From the table output, four categories are observed: Single, Married, Widowed, and Divorced. By creating a vector, colors can be assigned to each category in the same order as the table output. Here is what you need to enter:

```
>colors<-c("gray","darkgray","lightgray","black")
```

Typing **colors()** in the Console and <RETURN> will produce a list of the names of over 600 colors from which you can choose.

To draw the graph with this gray scale scheme, enter the following in the Console and press <RETURN>:

```
>pie(maritalp,col=colors)
```

Because *marital* is a factor variable, the slices of the pie are automatically labeled with the corresponding value labels. If, however, this were not a factor variable, you could add labels. To do this, you would create a vector containing a list of label names in the same order as displayed in the table output. In this case, you would add the **labels** option to the **pie()** function in much the same way as you added the **col** option.

Table 5.1 provides a review of the commands in the creation of this pie chart.

The steps contained in Table 5.2 can be used to create a pie chart displaying percentages, as illustrated in Figure 5.2.

The output in the Console after the first two functions displays the following:

```
Single     Married    Widowed     Divorced
0.10062893 0.59748428 0.27672956  0.02515723
```

TABLE 5.1 Commands to Create Pie Chart of Counts

Command	Purpose
`>maritalp<-table(hospital1$marital)`	Create table vector of counts of marital status
`>maritalp`	Display counts
`>colors<-c("gray","darkgray","lightgray","black")`	Assign colors
`>pie(maritalp,col=colors)`	Draw pie with counts

TABLE 5.2 Commands to Add Percentage to Pie Chart

Command	Purpose
`>pct<-prop.table(maritalp)`	Create table vector of proportions of marital status
`>pct`	Display proportions
`>pct<-round(pct*100,1)`	Create rounded percentages
`>pct`	Display percentages
`>lbls<-c("Single", "Married", "Widowed", "Divorced")`	Create labels based upon the table categories
`>lbls<-paste(lbls,pct,"%")`	Attach actual percentages and "%" to labels
`>pie(pct,labels=lbls,col=colors,main="Marital Status")`	Draw pie chart with percentages

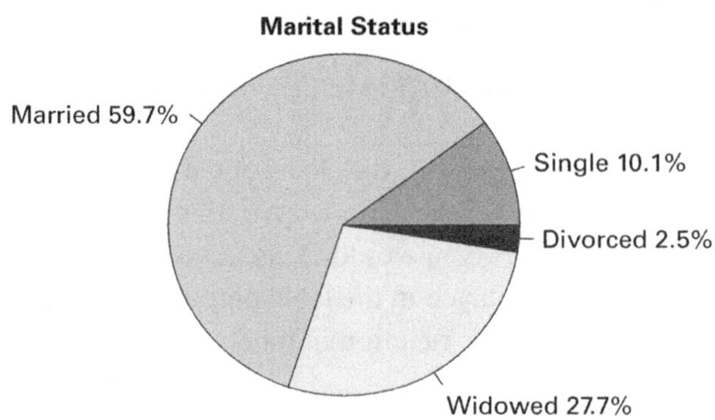

FIGURE 5.2 Pie chart example with percentages.

Using the third command in Table 5.2, the **`round()`** function, multiplies the proportions in the **`pct`** vector by 100 and rounds them to one decimal place. Entering **`pct`** and <RETURN> in the Console yields the following display:

```
Single  Married  Widowed Divorced
 10.1     59.7     27.7       2.5
```

The **paste()** function in the sixth command concatenates the labels created in the previous function with the calculated percentages and then adds the "%" sign. Therefore, when the pie chart is ultimately created, the marital status followed by the percentage attributed to each is accurately displayed.

BAR GRAPHS

Comparing Two Categorical Variables

Bar graphs can also be utilized to compare frequencies and proportions between two categorical variables. Using the *hospital1* data, we may be interested in developing a profile of which patients are more likely to be readmitted within 30 days of discharge. If you were an administrator, you might wish to identify some of the risk factors that are associated with readmission so that services to address these could be provided early in a patient's stay. From your experience, you think that patients with a spouse may be less likely to return within a 30-day window. You could use a bar graph to display this relationship.

As in the previous example, we have to start with a table vector; however, this time it will be a two-dimensional table. You can accomplish this by entering the following in the Console:

```
>g1<-table(hospital1$return30,hospital1$spouse)
>g1
```

The following output is displayed in the Console:

```
      yes  no
no    81   52
yes   5    23
```

Notice that the dependent variable, *return30*, was entered first, followed by the independent variable, *spouse*. Doing so puts the dependent variable in the rows and the independent variable in the columns. The table shows that 23 of the 28 patients who returned within 30 days had no spouse (column = *no* and row = *yes*), indicating that patients without a spouse are more likely to return within 30 days of discharge.

The stacked frequency bar plot in Figure 5.3 was created by entering **barplot(g1)** in the Console and pressing <RETURN>.

The figure in its current form is difficult to interpret. We do not readily know what *yes* and *no* mean on the *x*-axis, we do not readily know what the values represent on the *y*-axis, we do not know what the colored blocks represent, and, without a title, it is hard to discern what this bar graph is illustrating.

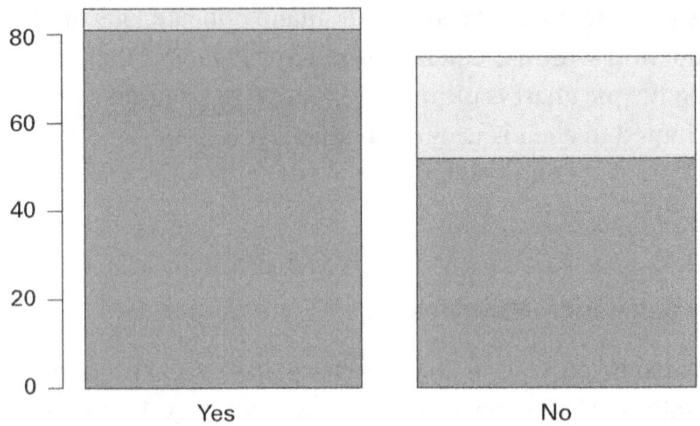

FIGURE 5.3 Stacked frequency bar graph.

Using column percentages (i.e., percentages within the *spouse* variable) will make interpretation easier, as will labels for the *x*-axis, the *y*-axis, and the main bar graph.

Typing the following command in the Console will produce a table vector containing the necessary percentages.

```
>g2<-prop.table(g1,2)*100
>g2
              yes         no
  no    94.186047  69.333333
  yes    5.813953  30.666667
```

The **prop.table()** function creates proportions of a table vector, in this case *g1*. The "2" after **g1** instructs *R* that column proportions are to be calculated. If row percentages were desired, the "2" would be replaced with a "1." Finally, to obtain percentages, the expression is multiplied by 100.

By looking at the output in the Console, we see that a much larger percentage (30.7%) of patients without a spouse returned within 30 days of being discharged, as compared to those with a spouse (5.8%). Now you are ready to draw the more comprehensible bar graph displayed in Figure 5.4.

Observe that Figure 5.4 combines two graphs into a single figure. To accomplish this, begin by entering the following in the Console to set the graphics environment:

```
>par(mfrow=c(1,2))
```

(Note: It is a good idea before changing the graphics environment to clear it. To do this, type **graphics.off()** in the Console and press <RETURN>).

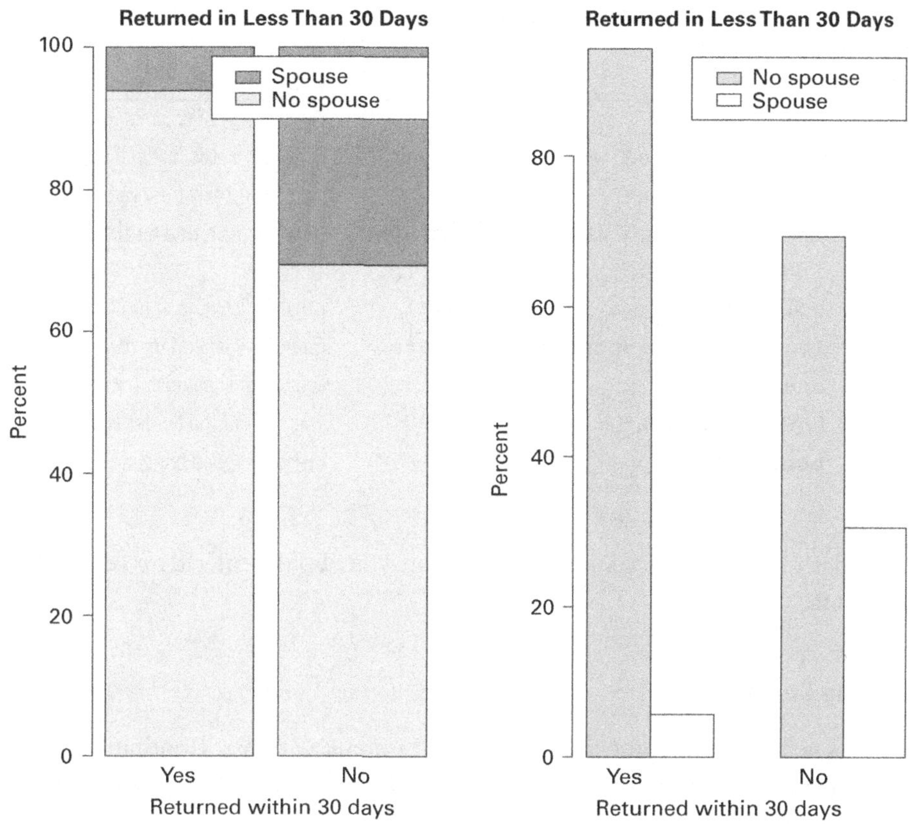

FIGURE 5.4 Stacked and grouped bar chart with percentages.

The function above modifies the graphical parameters in the environment to accept two graphs. The numbers between the parentheses [(1,2)] represent the desired number of rows and columns. In this case, we are stating that we want the graphs in one row, but in two columns. After modifying the environment, two graph commands were issued to create a stacked and a group bar chart:

```
>barplot(g2,xlab="returned within 30 days",ylab="Percent
",main="Returned in Less Than 30 Days",col=c("lightgray"
,"darkgray"), legend=c("no spouse","spouse") )

>barplot(g2,xlab="returned within 30 days",ylab="Percent
",main="Returned in Less Than 30 Days",density=30,border
="black",legend=c("no spouse","spouse") ,beside=T)
```

There are a number of options in the above commands that need some explanations, and these are described in Table 5.3.

TABLE 5.3 Steps in Creating a Stacked and Group Bar Chart

Graph	Function	Explanation
1 & 2	`g2`	Table vector of column percentages
1 & 2	`xlab="returned within 30 days"`	Label the *x*-axis (column variable)
1 & 2	`ylab="Percent"`	Label the *y*-axis (row variable)
1 & 2	`main="Returned in Less Than 30 Days"`	Define a main title for the graph
1 & 2	`col=c("lightgray","darkgray")`	Define the colors of the bars
1 & 2	`legend=c("no spouse","spouse")`	Define the legend for row variable
2	`density=30`	Degree of shading in bars
2	`border="black"`	The color of the border between bars
2	`beside=T`	Create grouped bar chart

In order to reset the graphics environment, you should enter **`dev.off()`** into the Console.

Comparing Group Data

Often it is necessary to compare groups on a numeric variable. Continuing with the question posed above, you might be interested in knowing if patients who return within 30 days of discharge have lower overall levels of activities of daily living (ADL), which we defined as the variable *tkatzmean*. Because *tkatzmean* is a numeric variable, means can be compared between those patients who did and did not return within 30 days of discharge.

To do this, the first step is to create a vector with a table containing the necessary information. Enter the following command into the Console:

```
>returnkatz<-
aggregate(hospital1$tkatzmean,by=list
(hospital1$return30),FUN=mean,na.rm=T)
```

Type **`returnkatz`** in the Console, and press <RETURN> to obtain the following output.

```
Group.1        x
1      no 2.804511
2     yes 1.750000
```

The first variable in the **`aggregate()`** function is the numeric variable *tkatzmean* and the variable in the "list" is the grouping variable, *return30*. **`FUN`** is the

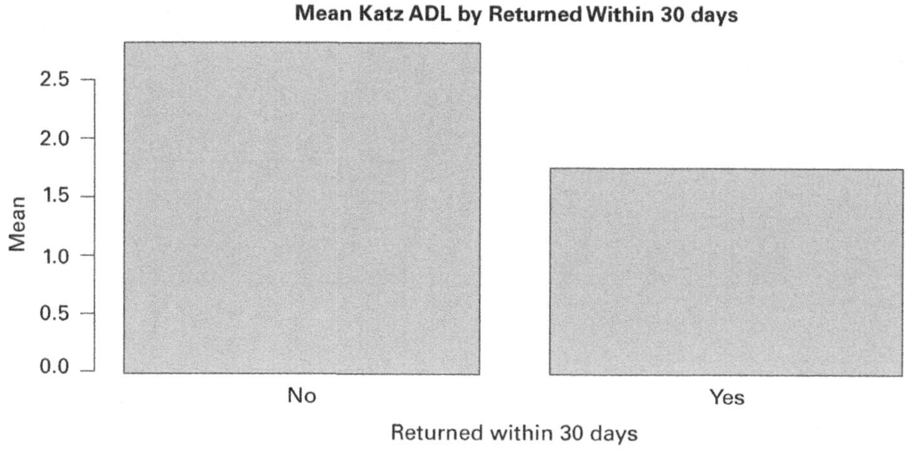

FIGURE 5.5 Mean graph by a grouping variable.

function we are requesting—in this case, the mean. Finally, **na.rm** is set to true to remove missing values.

The output displays that the *yes* (returned within 30 days) group's ADL mean is over a point lower than the *no* group's mean. To graph the table, enter the following two commands. The results are shown in Figure 5.5.

```
>barplot(returnkatz$x,names.arg=returnkatz$Group.1,
col="gray",xlab="return within 30 days",ylab="mean")
>title("Mean Katz ADL by Returned within 30 days")
```

The term **returnkatz$x** is the variable in the vector containing the mean values—see the values listed under *x* in the output from entering **returnkatz** in the Console. The **names.arg** is set equal to *returnkatz$Group.1*, which contains labels for the groups—again, refer to the output for *returnkatz*.

Using ggplot2 to Create Enhanced Bar Graphs

The *ggplot2* package, developed by Hadley Wickham, produces a number of aesthetically pleasing graphs. It also improves upon *R*'s graphic language (Wickham, 2009). The first step in using *ggplot2* is to require it. If you installed it as directed in the first section, go to the Packages tab in the lower right pane and check the box next to *ggplot2*. Alternatively, you can also type **require(ggplot2)** in the Console to require the package. The first step in creating an enhanced bar graph is the same as in the previous example:

```
>returnkatz<-aggregate(hospital1$tkatzmean, by=list
(hospital1$return30),FUN=mean,na.rm=T)
```

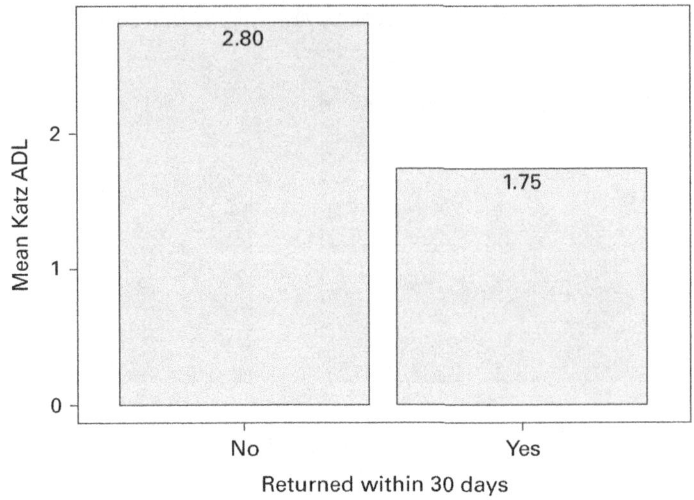

FIGURE 5.6 *ggplot* graph with labeled bars.

To obtain the graph in Figure 5.6, type the following *ggplot* command:

```
>ggplot(returnkatz,aes(x=Group.1,y=x)) +
geom_bar(stat="identity",fill="gray") +
geom_text(aes(label=paste(format(x,digits=3))),vjust=
1.5,colour="black",size=6) +
labs(x="return within 30 days",y="mean Katz ADL") +
theme_bw()
```

You can type one line at a time; be sure to include the plus sign (+) to let *R* know that you will be continuing the command.

The command begins by naming the vector *returnkatz* . The *x* (Group.1) and *y* (x) variables for the graph are defined within the **aes()** clause. The **geom_bar** defines the graph type. The **stat=** function is set to use the means of x by the keyword **identity**. The **geom_text** is used to place the group means on the bars. Finally, **theme_bw()** provides a scheme with a white background. You can try rerunning the graph removing the **+ theme_bw()** to see the default background.

Although a number of other *ggplot2* graphs will be presented in this section, for a more in-depth discussion, we recommended Winston Chang's book on *R* graphics (Chang, 2012).

BOXPLOTS

Boxplots are excellent for describing differences between groups on a numeric variable in that they provide what Keen (2010) has termed "data reduction" and "data expression" (Keen, 2010). Boxplots reduce data while, at the same time, providing a

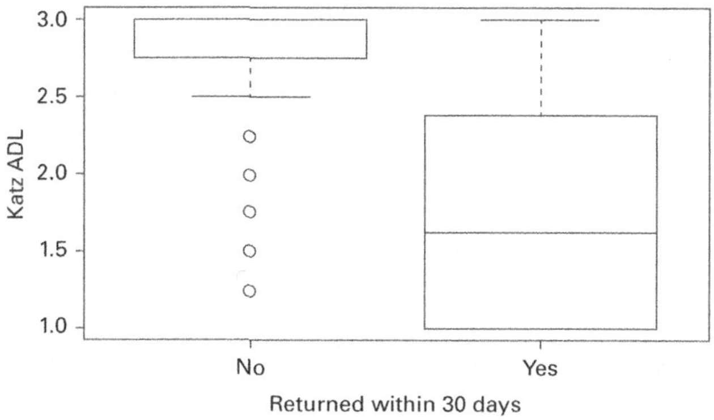

FIGURE 5.7 Comparison of ADLs by hospital readmission.

lot of information about the distributions of the groups. For example, Figure 5.6 displayed the difference in means between groups, but provided no information about their distributions. Figure 5.7, on the other hand, displays an example of a boxplot, which compares difference in ADL levels for patients who returned within 30 days of discharge to those who did not.

The following statement was used to produce the figure:

```
>boxplot(hospital1$tkatzmean~hospital1$return30,ylab=
"Katz ADL",xlab="return withn 30 days")
```

Notice in the command that the numeric variable is listed first, followed by a tilde (~) and then the grouping variable.

As a review of boxplots in general, the dark black line in each box represents the median, the circles are outliers (i.e., data points beyond 1.5 times the interquartile range), and the gray thin lines at the top and bottom are the upper and lower bounds. The bottom of the box itself represents the 25th percentile, while the top of the box represents the 75th percentile.

Boxplots provide more information than a bar plot about the distribution of data while still demonstrating that, as a group, patients returning within 30 days have lower ADLs than those who did not return.

Using ggplot2 to Create Enhanced Boxplots

The following statement creates the same graph using *ggplot2*, which is illustrated in Figure 5.8:

```
>ggplot(hospital1,aes(x=return30,y=tkatzmean,fill=
return30)) + ylab("Katz ADL") + xlab("return within
30 days") + geom_boxplot(fill="grey") + theme_bw()
```

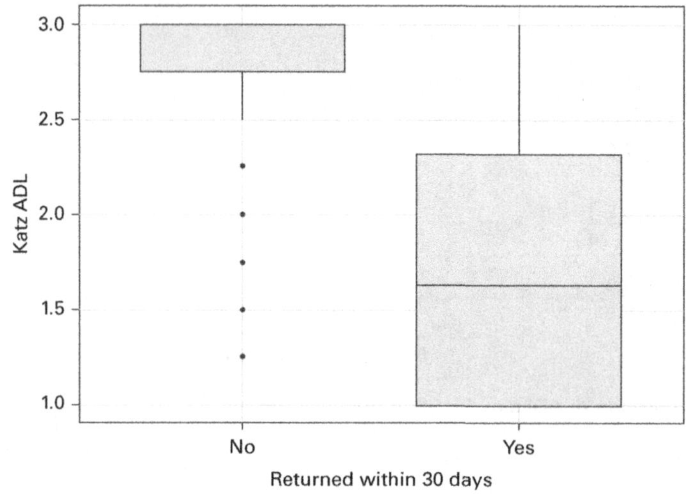

FIGURE 5.8 Boxplot created by *ggplot* package.

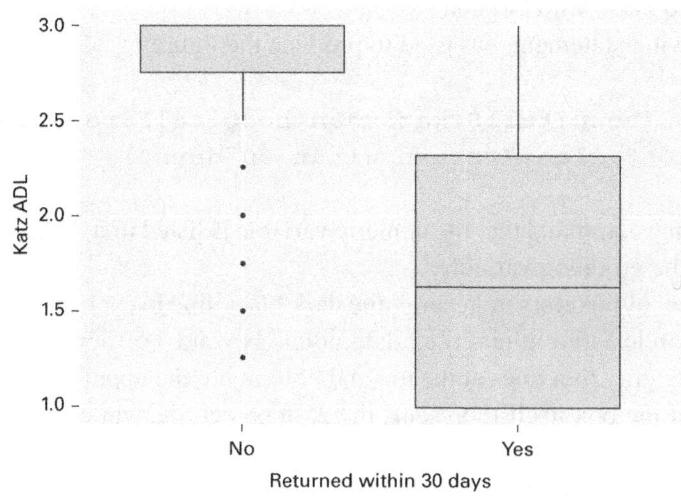

FIGURE 5.9 Boxplot created by *ggplot* with gray background.

Alternatively, you could use the following command to create the boxplot shown in Figure 5.9:

```
>ggplot(hospital1,aes(x=return30,y=tkatzmean,fill=
return30)) + ylab("Katz ADL") + xlab("return within
30 days") + geom_boxplot(fill="grey")
```

The `+ theme_bw()` function was removed to include a gray background.

SCATTERPLOTS

Scatterplots are one of the most widely used types of statistical graphs. They are used to display the relationship between two numeric variables, such as patient length of hospital stay in days (LOS) and patient levels of ADL. One variable, usually the dependent variable, occupies the *y*-axis, and the other, the *x*-axis.

Scatterplots should always be employed when conducting correlational or regression analyses. They provide an easy method for visually determining linearity, a necessary condition for understanding these types of analyses. Using the *hospital1* data, the following command will create a scatterplot with a regression line, presented in Figure 5.10:

```
>plot(los~tkatzmean,data=hospital1,xlab="Katz
ADL",ylab="length of stay (days)")
>abline(lm(los~tkatzmean,data=hospital1),col="gray",
lwd=3,lty=1)
```

In the command above, the **plot()** function draws the scatterplot. The *y*-axis variable is entered first, and the *x*-axis variable follows the tilde (~). Also notice, because of the inclusion of **data=hospital1**, it was not necessary to put **hospital1$** in front of the *x* and *y* variables. The **abline()** command is used to draw the regression line. The command uses the data from the simple regression function, **lm()**, which has similar syntax to the **plot()** command. The **col** parameter sets the color of the line; the **lwd=** parameter sets the thickness of the line; finally, the **lty** parameter sets the type of line (in this case a solid line). Figure 5.11 displays the line type that each **lty** number represents.

The *car* package provides a convenient function for creating scatterplots and a regression line in a single step. To do this, make certain the *hospital1* data set is open. If you have not installed the package, you need to do so by typing **install.packages("car"** in the Console, or download it from CRAN as described in

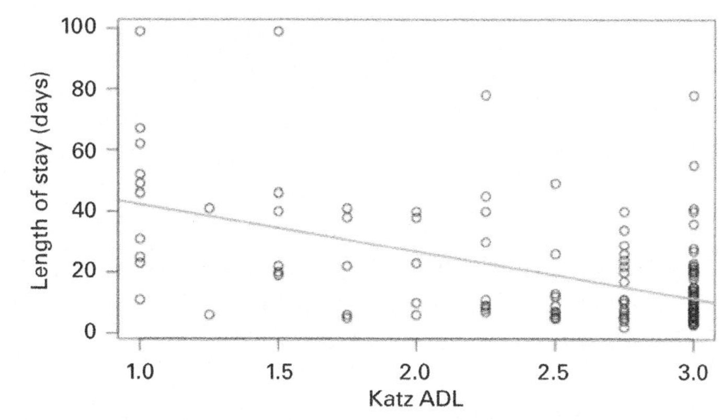

FIGURE 5.10 Scatterplot with regression line.

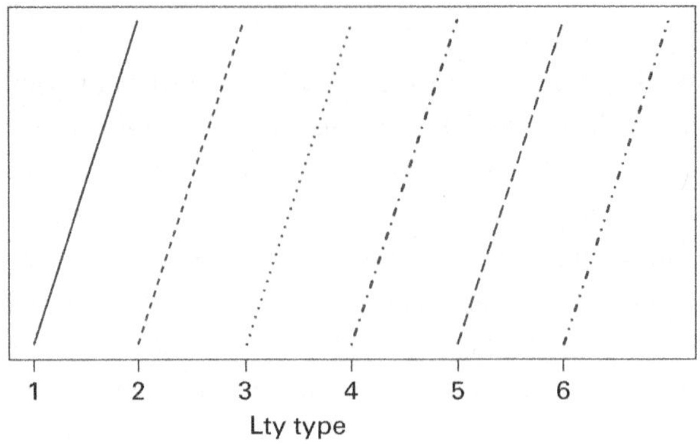

FIGURE 5.11 Line types produced by *lty*.

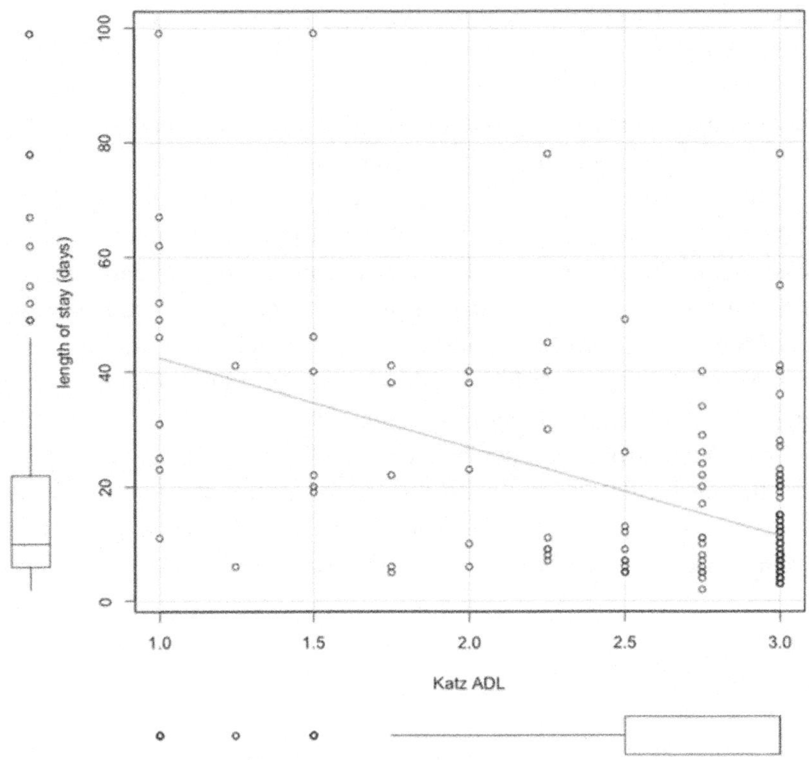

FIGURE 5.12 Example of scatterplot from *car* package.

Chapter 3. Next, load the *car* package by typing **require(car)** in the Console or by clicking the box next to the package in the Packages tab. To create the scatterplot in Figure 5.12, type the following command in the Console:

```
>scatterplot(los~tkatzmean,data=hospital1, xlab="Katz
ADL",ylab="length of stay (days)",smooth=F)
```

Notice that the plot also includes a boxplot for each of the variables, which highlights the influence of outliers and displays a different image of the distribution of the data. The boxplots can be removed by including the following option: **`boxplot=F`**. You can also remove the grid by including the following option: **`grid=F`**. Options need to be separated from main functions by commas.

The output in both Figures 5.10 and 5.12 provide a good deal of information. The *y* variable is plotted on the vertical axis, while the *x* variable is plotted on the horizontal axis. Each dot represents a patient's ADL score relative to his or her length of stay. We can see that the relationship is somewhat linear in that as ADL increases, length of stay in the hospital decreases. Since the relationship between these variables move in opposite directions (i.e., as one increases, the other decreases), this is referred to as an inverse, or negative, relationship. The scatterplot also displays a number of "outliers," which are scores that are distant (low or high) from other scores. In Figure 5.12, we can view the outliers as the data points corresponding to the dots in the boxplots.

Using ggplot2 to Create Enhanced Scatterplots

Visually pleasing scatterplots can be created with the *ggplot2* package. The following statement produced the plot in Figure 5.13:

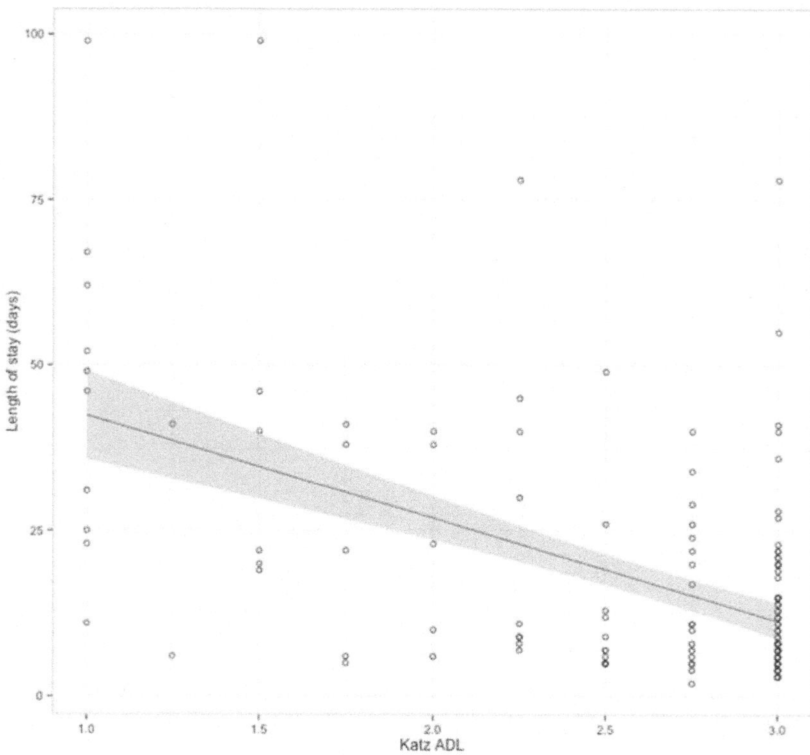

FIGURE 5.13 Scatterplot with confidence interval created by the *ggplot* package.

```
>ggplot(hospital1,aes(x=tkatzmean,y=los)) +
geom_point(shape=1) + stat_smooth(method=lm,level=.95) +
xlab("Katz ADL") + ylab("Length of stay (days)") +
theme_bw()
```

Each of the options can be added to the basic **ggplot()** command to enhance the plot. Notice that *hospital1* is entered first in the command, instructing *ggplot* to use the variables in that data set. The *x* and *y* variables are defined in the **aes()** function; the **geom_point()** defines the type of symbol used to represent observations; the **stat_smooth()** function defines the type of line fitted to the data (in this case, a linear model); the **level=** function defines the confidence interval for the shaded area (in this case, the 95th percentile).

There are many situations in which you might need to display trends between groups. For example, does the trend between the Katz ADL and length of stay differ between men and women? This can be shown visually by employing the following *ggplot* statement:

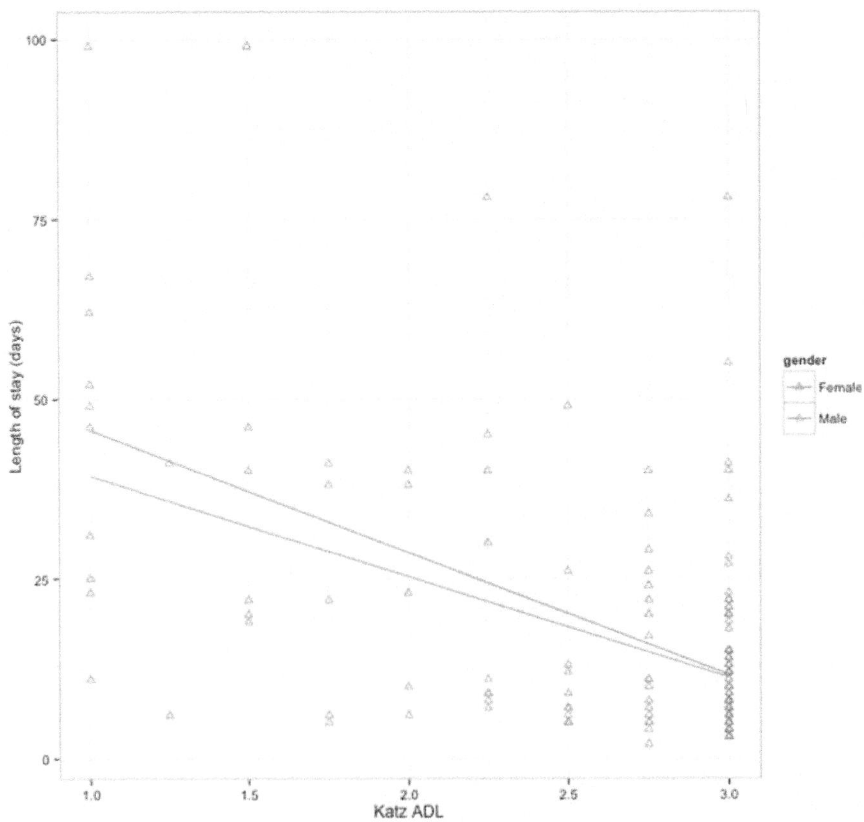

FIGURE 5.14 Scatterplot created using *ggplot* comparing groups.

```
>ggplot(hospital1,aes(x=tkatzmean,y=los,colour=
gender)) +
geom_point(shape=2)  +
xlab("Katz ADL") + ylab("Length of stay (days)") +
theme_bw() + stat_smooth(method=lm,se=F)
```

Just a number of small changes were made to the previous statement to accomplish what is illustrated in Figure 5.14. The statement **colour=gender** (notice the British spelling of "colour") was added to the **aes()** statement, which instructs *ggplot* to use the variable *gender* as a grouping variable. Finally, **se=F** was added to remove the shaded confidence interval.

The scatterplot displays *male* observations in one color and *female* in another. Separate regression lines for each gender are drawn. The plot tells a story: patients who have higher ADLs experience shorter hospital stays than those with lower ones. The plot also reveals a small gap between men and women. Regardless of ADLs, women have longer stays; however, this gender gap decreases as ADL level increases.

HISTOGRAMS

The histogram can be employed when there is a need to display the distribution of a numeric variable such as length of hospital stay in days or age in years. The following code produced Figure 5.15:

```
>par(mfrow=c(1,2))
>hist(hospital1$los, main="Histogram of
LOS",xlab="LOS")
>hist(hospital1$los,breaks="FD",col="lightgray",
xlab="LOS",main="Histogram of LOS" )
```

The **par()** command sets the graphics parameters. In this case, **mfrow=c(1,2)** instructs *R* to create a figure with two graphs placed in one row and two columns. The next command draws the first graph in Figure 5.15. The third command adds a second histogram with different qualities. The color of the bars in this histogram is set with **col="lightgray"**. The **breaks = "FD"** sets the number of bins (i.e., the number of bars displayed in the histogram). The number of bins will affect the shape of the histogram. As Fox (2011) suggests, too few bins may prevent revealing important characteristics of the data, while too may bins may lead to an inaccurate interpretation of the data (Fox & Weisberg, 2011). Fox (2011) suggests using the rule set by Freedman and Diaconis (1981) for setting the number of bins (Freedman & Diaconis, 1981; Weisberg & Fox, 2010). The formula uses a weighted range (i.e., the difference between the minimum and maximum values, divided by the interquartile range). The **breaks="FD"** option uses this formula for determining the optimal number of bins.

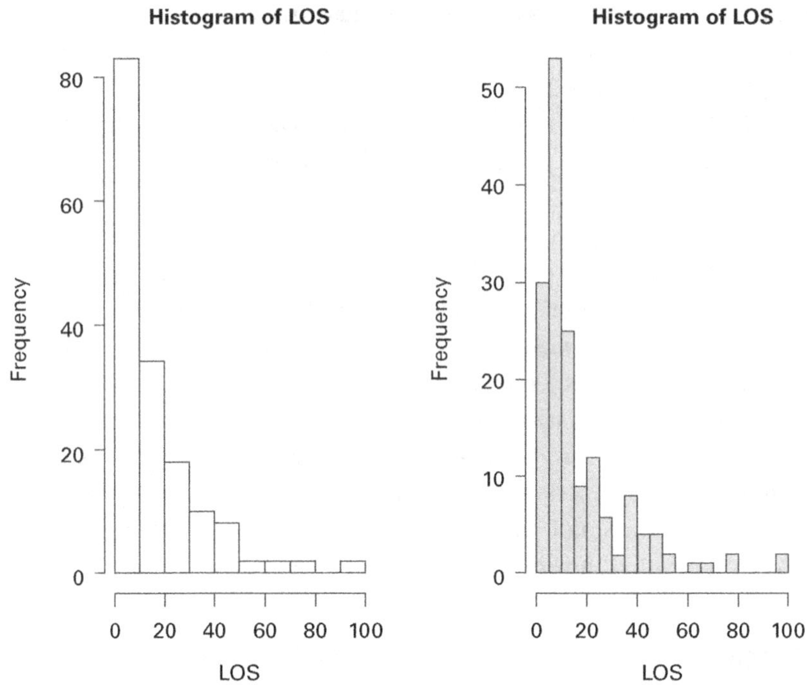

FIGURE 5.15 Histograms created using *R*.

An interpretation of Figure 5.15 indicates that LOS has a skewed right distribution, which suggests that there are a number of outliers in the sample. This is important to know because it can impact the type of analysis we conduct later and is common in count data.

The kernel density plot is a nonparametric method for the estimation of the probability of a random variable. Because of smoothing, this type of plot can provide a more accurate depiction of a variable's distribution as compared to a frequency histogram. Figure 5.16 displays a kernel density plot superimposed on a histogram for LOS. The following commands were used to create the graph:

```
>dev.off()
>hist(hospital1$los,breaks="FD",freq=F,col="lightgray",
xlab="LOS",main="Histogram of LOS")
>lines(density(hospital1$los,na.rm=T),lwd=3)
```

The **dev.off()** was issued first to set the graphic environment to expect a single graph, the default in *RStudio*. The second command draws the histogram, but notice that **freq=F** was added to the command. This instructs *R* that density will be used, instead of frequency, on the *y*-axis. As a result, the total area of the histogram will be equal to one. The third command is issued to overlay the kernel density line.

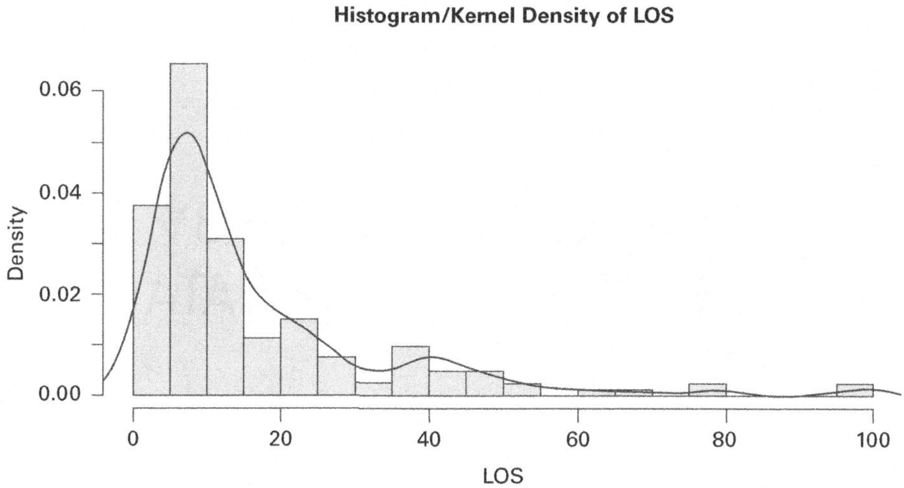

FIGURE 5.16 Kernel density histogram.

The visualization of the kernel density plot highlights the skewed nature of the distribution and the impact of the outliers on it.

SUMMARY

A number of graphs were introduced in this chapter to illustrate features of your data. *R* provides choices to create very basic and more detailed graphs through the use of options. Categorical data, such as those found in factor variables, can be illustrated through pie charts; however, bar charts are often favored over pie charts. In this chapter, you learned methods for creating both pie charts and various bar charts. We demonstrated that it is possible to create one or more graphs placed side by side in a single image. We also demonstrated how to create stacked bars, or bars placed side by side. The addition of legends and labels makes bar charts easy to understand.

Numeric variables can be displayed easily using boxplots, scatterplots, histograms, and kernel density plots. The type of graphs you use will be based upon the qualities of the data that you wish to highlight. Again, adding options to commands can easily enhance basic graphs.

In this chapter, we introduced *ggplot2*, a package for augmenting graphics. While we illustrated a number of graphs with *ggplot*, this package can create a wide range of static and dynamic graphs. We suggest that those interested in enhanced graphics beyond what was demonstrated in this chapter refer to one or more of the excellent texts on the use of the more complex facets of *ggplot2*. A listing of these can be found in Appendix A.

/// 6 ///

MAKING YOUR CASE BY DESCRIBING YOUR DATA

In order to work through the examples in this chapter, you will need to *install* and *load* the following packages:

- *psych*
- *Hmisc*

For more information on how to do this, refer to the Packages section in Chapter 3.

The simplest way to answer a research question regarding your program is by describing it in some way: how many clients you serve, the types of clients seen in the program, the characteristics of service utilization, and so on. In this chapter we will walk you through the basics of describing and reporting data in *R* accurately, succinctly, and powerfully.

CASE STUDY #1: THE MAIN STREET WOMEN'S CENTER

The Main Street Women's Center is located in the town of Redflower, which has suffered economically since the financial downturn of 2008. The Women's Center is a multi-service agency helping women who live in the town and surrounding area. Services include help with immigration, domestic violence, benefits screening, job referral, and mental health services. The overall goal of the agency is to be responsive to the social and behavioral health needs of the women in the community.

Recently, it seems as if more and more women coming to the Center are in financial distress, and the staff is concerned that these women, many of whom have children living at home, are at risk for becoming homeless. The executive director would like to start a new program, called the Housing Protection Program, to address this problem directly; however, more funds are needed to launch it and, once the program has sufficient funding, the agency would like to know what services are most urgently needed in order to prevent homelessness.

The pressing issue is that the executive director requires support from stakeholders, such as the Community Board, in order to develop and implement this new program. Support for this program, however, has been lacking. The executive director has been told time and again that support would not be forthcoming because these women are "lazy" and "trying to get a free ride."

In order to build support for the Housing Protection Program, the executive director has requested that you make the case for why this program is important. Specifically, she would like you to try to debunk, empirically, the myth that the agency's clients are undeserving of assistance by describing who the clients are, as well as their financial situations. To address these concerns, we must form a research question. Here, our overall question will be, "Are the at-risk clients in poor financial shape?"

The data you have is intake information from the previous 6 months of clients coming to the Main Street Women's Center. These are only the clients that staff are concerned are most at risk for losing their current housing.

Open the data set called *Main Street.rdata*. You will notice that you have 23 variables, which are described in Table 6.1. The name of each variable as it appears in the data set is in the column marked *Variable*; a more complete description of the variable is in the next column, and how categories are defined is listed in the last column. If the variable consists only of a numeric response, there will be no description of indicators in the third column.

CONSIDERATIONS IN DESCRIBING YOUR DATA

Notice several things about the variables listed in Table 6.1. First, if a variable would hold a numeric value, there is no value listed for the variable in the table above, as the value is simply the numeric response itself. For instance, *persons* is simply the number of people living in the client's household. The same is true for *rfaminc, fertil, hours, rearning*, and *arrears*. The remaining variables are categorical, that is, they are measured by the agency as a category. This includes whether or not the client owns a telephone (*yes* or *no*) and the primary language spoken by the client. The variable *rent* is categorical. In this case, the client is asked if her rent is less than \$200 per month, if it is between \$200 and \$300 per month, if it is between \$301 and \$400 per month, if it is between \$401 and \$500 per month, or if it is over \$500 per month. In this way, numerical values may be collapsed into categories.

You should notice two things about the categorical variables listed above. First, the categories are exhaustive; the response categories account for every possible situation. For example, the variable *hhlang* has the following possible responses: *English, Spanish, Other European, Asian language*, and *Other*. Because of the wide range of possible languages spoken, the agency assigned an additional response, *other*, to capture any languages that may not be listed but are primarily spoken by a client. The other thing to notice is that categories are mutually exclusive. Being in one category automatically precludes the responding client from also

TABLE 6.1 Variables in *Main Street.rdata* File

Variable	Description	Indicators (if appropriate)
persons	Number of people living with client	
rent	Monthly rent broken into categories	less than $200; $200–$300; $301–$400; $401–500; over $500
telephon	Whether the client has a telephone	yes; no
rgrapi	Rent as a total percentage of household income	less than 30%; 30%–39%; 40%–49%; 50%–59%; 60%–69%; 70%–79%; 80%–89%; 90–99%; 100% or more
rfaminc	Monthly household income	
rhhlang	Primary language spoken by the client	English only; Spanish; Other European; Asian language; Other
rlingiso	Is the head of household linguistically isolated	yes; no
race	Race/ethnicity of head of client	white; black; Filipino; Eskimo; Hispanic; Native American
age	Age of the client	Actual age of the client in years
marital	Marital status of client	married; widowed; divorced; separated; never married
immigr	Is client an immigrant	born in the US; immigrant
school	Is client in school	not attending; attending
yearsch	Client's highest level of education	less than HS; HS or GED; some college; associate's degree or trade certificate; bachelor's degree
english	How well the client speaks English	very well; well; not well; not at all
fertil	How many children the client has given birth to	
rlabor	Is the client in the labor force	employed; unemployed; not in the workforce
worklwk	Did the client work last week	yes; no
hours	Number of hours the client worked last week	
looking	Is the client looking for a job	Looking; Not looking
rearning	Client's monthly earnings	
hhage	Whether the head of the household is over 20 years old	Above 20; Below 20
food	Does the client's household have enough food to meet their needs	yes; no
arrears	Number of months behind in rent	

belonging to another category. For example, for the variable *immigr*, a responding client would either be born in the United States or be an immigrant; she could not belong in both categories.

As you are thinking about describing your data, it is important to consider whether the variables you are describing are categorical (i.e., to be defined as factor variables in *R*) or numeric, as each are best described differently. Categorical variables, which we will refer to as factor variables from now on, as this is the terminology used in *R*, are typically described as a proportion. For instance, we may want to know the proportion of clients who own a telephone, pay more than 50% of their monthly income in rent, or have enough food. Numeric variables, on the other hand, are best described by using some measure of central tendency, usually as a mean or median. Therefore, we may want to summarize the clients at risk for homelessness at the Main Street Women's Clinic by stating the median household size, the average number of children a woman has, or the average number of months that clients' rents are in arrears.

DESCRIBING THE CLIENTS AT THE MAIN STREET WOMEN'S CENTER

With this information in mind, we can see if we can gather some useful information to report to the executive director. Are the clients whom the staff believe are at risk for homelessness lazy? Does it appear as if they are trying to get a free ride? Are they really in severe financial distress?

There are numerous ways to describe data in *R*. We will begin with the simplest functions, those readily available in native *R*.

Describing Numeric Variables

We will begin by describing some of our numeric variables. We can use the **summary()** function in *R* to get some basic information. Type the following at the prompt and you will see the following output:

```
> summary(mainstr$persons)
Min.   1st Qu.   Median    Mean   3rd Qu.    Max.
1.000    1.000    2.000   2.439    3.000   7.000
```

Here we see that the average household size for these at-risk clients is 2.44. The smallest size household, shown as *Min.*, is only one person, while the largest household size is seven, shown as *Max.* The median household size is two people.

If we were planning to report the mean household size, we should also report the standard deviation, which quantifies how variable the data is about the mean:

```
> sd(mainstr$persons)
[1] 1.401993
```

We can also look at the number of children these clients have, as there seems to be a general conception that poor women often have an abundance of children. We will use the same functions we used to describe household size, since this variable is also numeric.

```
> summary(mainstr$fertil)
   Min. 1st Qu.  Median    Mean 3rd Qu.    Max.
  0.000   1.000   2.000   2.232   3.000   9.000

> sd(mainstr$fertil)
[1] 1.757011
```

While there are some clients who have had many children, the average number of children is 2.23, with a standard deviation of 1.76.

While this is interesting, it would also be helpful for us to visualize the data (see Figure 6.1). There are two simple yet powerful graphs that are good for displaying numeric data: histograms and boxplots. To create a basic histogram, enter the following in the Console:

```
> hist(mainstr$fertil)
```

Here we see that the data is positively skewed (i.e., pulled to the right), with the majority of the data on the lower end and a few individuals having four or more children.

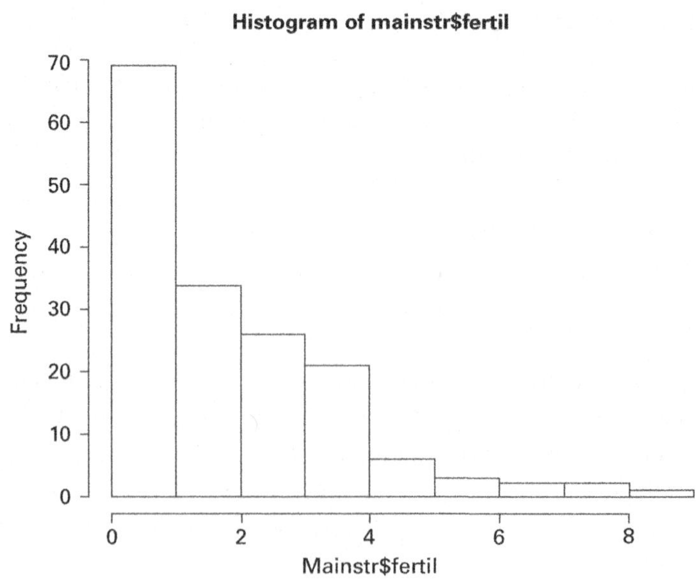

FIGURE 6.1 Basic histogram.

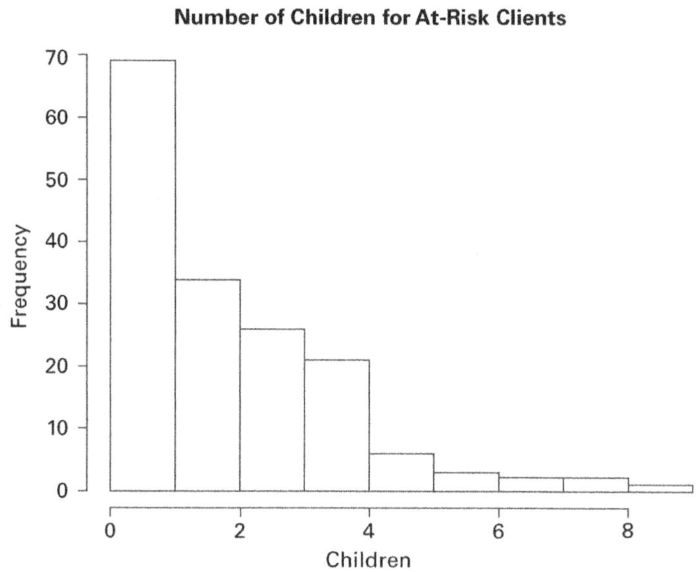

FIGURE 6.2 Histogram with titles.

While this histogram shows us some important information, the title of the graph and the label for the x-axis are not particularly useful if you would wanted to share this with a stakeholder. If we make a few minor adjustments, we can get a more useful histogram (see Figure 6.2):

```
> hist(mainstr$fertil, xlab="Children", main="Number
of Children for At-Risk Clients")
```

Another way we can visualize this data is by examining a boxplot, which provides an excellent representation of data range and variation (Figure 6.3):

```
> boxplot(mainstr$fertil, main="Children of At-Risk
Clients")
```

Now we see an illustration of the statistical output we saw in the summary function. Presenting this information together can provide a powerful message. What is particularly helpful to see here is that the majority of clients have had between one and three children, and we notice three outliers, clients who have had more children than almost everyone else. The useful range of children is between zero and six. It seems that most of these at-risk clients do not have an unusually large number of children.

FIGURE 6.3 Boxplot of *children.*

We can examine another numeric variable, *age*, in the same way that we analyzed *fertil* and *persons*:

```
> summary(mainstr$age)
   Min. 1st Qu.  Median    Mean 3rd Qu.    Max.
     19      31      41      40      50      59
```

```
> sd(mainstr$age)
[1] 11.35214
```

The output shows us that at-risk clients range in age from 19 to 59 years, with an average age of 40 and standard deviation of 11.35 years.

We can visualize this by producing a histogram (Figure 6.4) and boxplot (Figure 6.5).

```
> hist(mainstr$age, xlab="Years", main="Ages of
At-Risk Clients")
```

```
> boxplot(mainstr$age, ylab="Years", main="Ages of
At-Risk Clients")
```

The histogram and boxplot suggest that the data are not skewed, nor are there outliers. We know from the output of the **summary()** function that the bottom of the box represents 31 years, the top represents 50 years, and the middle dark line, which represents the median, is 41 years. Based on our knowledge of the

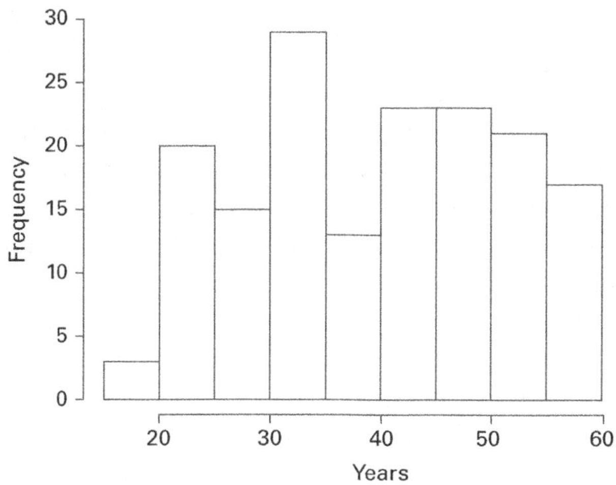

FIGURE 6.4 Histogram of age of at-risk clients.

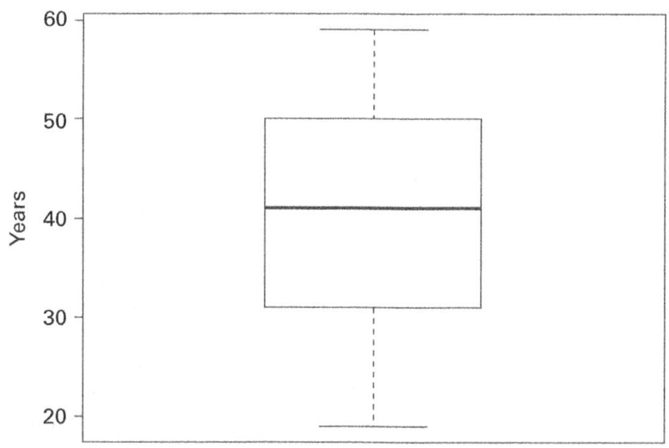

FIGURE 6.5 Boxplot of age of at-risk clients.

agency, we see that the at-risk clients are of ages typically served by the agency. One particular age group does not seem to be represented more or less than any other.

A somewhat more efficient way to describe numeric variables requires the installation of the *psych* package. Once you install and require this package, as described in Chapter 3, you can use the **`describe()`** function to better understand the characteristics of a numeric variable in a single function. We can look again at both the *fertil* and *age* variables.

```
> describe(mainstr$fertil)
```

This function provides us with additional information that could be helpful. As displayed in Figure 6.6, we now know that, in addition to the statistics we calculated before, the trimmed mean is 2.05, the median absolute deviation is 1.48, the skewness is 1.14 (a skewness of zero denotes a normal distribution), and the kurtosis, a measure of how peaked or flat a distribution is, is 1.56 (a normal distribution has a kurtosis of 3; a flatter distribution has a kurtosis of less than 3; and a peaked distribution has a kurtosis of greater than 3).

```
> describe (mainstr$age)
```

As displayed in Figure 6.7, you see an example of a distribution with very little skew, but one that is relatively flat, the depiction of which we saw in both the histogram and boxplot of *age*.

```
  vars   n mean   sd median trimmed  mad min max range skew kurtosis   se
1    1 164 2.23 1.76      2    2.05 1.48   0   9     9 1.14     1.56 0.14
```

FIGURE 6.6 Description of *fertil* variable.

```
  vars   n mean    sd median trimmed   mad min max range  skew kurtosis   se
1    1 164   40 11.35     41   40.03 14.83  19  59    40 -0.02    -1.24 0.89
```

FIGURE 6.7 Description of variable *age*.

Describing Factor Variables

You may have noticed that most of the variables that we have in this data set are factor variables. There are several variables that may be interesting to us in making our case to stakeholders. For example, there is a common assumption that recent immigrants are a drain on society compared to those native born, which serves a belief that immigrants do not deserve our support.

We can begin by looking at the variable called *immigr*. To do this in *R*, we will need to first build a table that categorizes each individual as either US born or an immigrant, and we will store our results in a vector. To do this, we can use either the **summary()** function that we used in describing numeric variables, above, or the **table()** function that we saw earlier. In either case, you will be shown the number of respondents falling into each category:

```
> immigrant<-summary(mainstr$immigr)
> immigrant
```

```
  Born US Immigrant
       84        80
OR

> i<-table(mainstr$immigr)
> i

  Born US Immigrant
       84        80
```

Looking at the output from these, we see that slightly more than half of our clients (84) are US born, while the remainder are immigrants. It would, however, be helpful if we could see those proportions exactly. The **prop.table()** function calculates the proportions for the items in a table. Multiplying the results by 100 will return the percentage of the sample that falls into each category. Again, we will store our results in a vector that we can use later.

```
> i2<-prop.table(immigrant)*100
> i2

  Born US Immigrant
 51.21951  48.78049
```

Now we can easily see that 51.2% of the clients are US born, while the remainder, 48.8%, are immigrants. So far it seems as if both native born and immigrants are vulnerable to potential homelessness.

We can now use these vectors to build bar plots to display our data. If we want to use the counts, we could use the vectors that we called *i* or *immigrant*. It might be preferable, however, to show percentages, so we will build the bar plot by using the vector that we called *i2*.

```
>barplot(i2, ylab="percentage", main="At-Risk
Clients")
```

Here again, you will see that we added labels to our graph that could be informative (see Figure 6.8).

Visually, we can now see that there are slightly more clients who are US born compared to immigrants.

Along these same lines, our stakeholders may think that those most at risk are not English speakers. We can use the same techniques we just used to describe the variable called *english*.

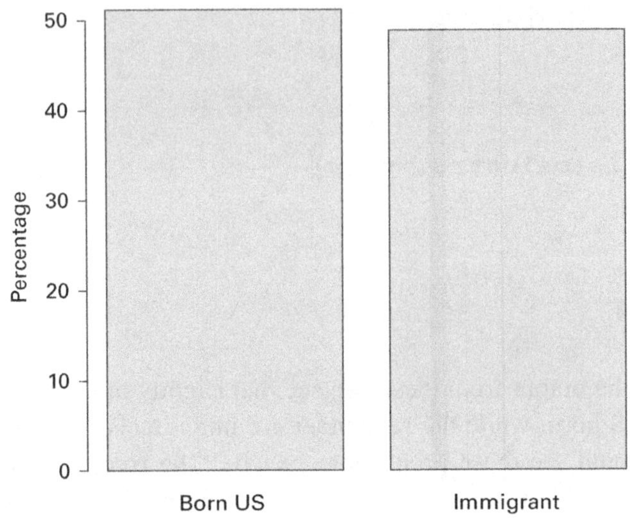

FIGURE 6.8 Bar plot of at-risk clients by immigration status.

```
> e<-table(mainstr$english)
> e

 Very well      Well    Not well Not at all
       102        26          24         12

> e2<-prop.table(e)*100
> e2

 Very well          Well    Not well Not at all
 62.195122   15.853659   14.634146   7.317073
```

Here we see that 102 clients (62.2%) speak English very well, 26 (15.9%) speak English well, 24 (14.6%) don't speak English well, and 12 (7.3%) don't speak English at all. We could also add these percentages in *R* to categorize those who speak English well or very well compared to those who do not speak English well or at don't speak it at all.

```
> 62.2+15.85
[1] 78.05
```

Here we can summarize that more than three-quarters of at-risk clients are proficient in English.

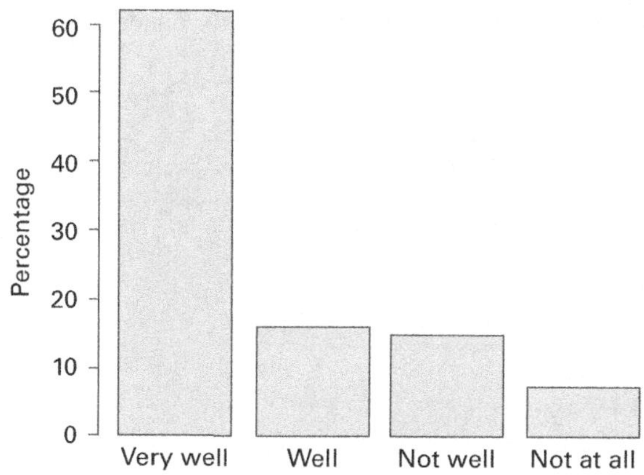

FIGURE 6.9 Bar plot of at-risk clients' English proficiency.

Again, it would be helpful to depict this graphically (Figure 6.9):

```
>barplot(e2, ylab="percentage", main="At-Risk
Clients' English Proficiency")
```

The package *Hmisc* does an outstanding job of describing factor variables without building tables first. Once you install and require this package, you can use the **describe()** function to provide useful information quickly.

NOTE: In order to avoid conflicts in the **describe()** functions in *Hmisc* and *psych*, be sure to detach the *psych* package prior to invoking the **describe()** function in *Hmisc*. You can do this by simply unchecking the *psych* box in the Packages tab.

As we have been thinking about language proficiency, we could use **describe()** to determine whether the agency's at-risk clients are linguistically isolated.

```
> describe(mainstr$rlingiso)

mainstr$rlingiso
      n missing  unique
    164       0       2

Not isolated (119, 73%), Isolated (45, 27%)
```

We see that all 164 clients answered this question and that there are two categories, *not isolated* and *isolated.* Nearly three-quarters of the clients are not linguistically isolated (119 respondents, or 73%) while the remainder are.

We can also use this function to describe clients based upon whether or not they have sufficient food in their households.

```
> describe(mainstr$food)

mainstr$food
        n missing  unique
      164       0       2

no (77, 47%), yes (87, 53%)
```

The output shows us that we have evaluated all 164 observations and there are no missing values. We have two unique factors. The factor called *no* consisted of 77 cases, which accounted for 47% of the clients, while the factor called *yes* consisted of 87 cases and accounted for 53% of the clients.

We clearly see that just under half of our at-risk clients have difficulty obtaining enough food for themselves and their household members.

We might want to think about how much these clients are paying for housing each month. Perhaps they are paying so much that they cannot afford food.

```
> describe(mainstr$rent)
mainstr$rent
        n missing  unique
      164       0       3

Less than 200 (16, 10%), 200 to 300 (46, 28%)
301 to 400 (102, 62%)
```

The agency's at-risk clients are not paying a whole lot of rent each month. Ten percent (n = 16) are spending less than $200 per month, 28% (n = 46) are spending between $200 and $300 per month, and the remaining 102 clients (62%) are spending between $301 and $400 per month.

To delve a little deeper, we could look at the percentage of monthly income that is allotted to rent by looking at the variable called *rgrapi*.

```
> describe(mainstr$rgrapi)
```

As shown in Figure 6.10, a quarter of the clients are spending between 40% and 49% of their monthly income on rent, but, alarmingly, 60 clients (37% of those at risk) are spending all or more than all of their income on rent! Despite relatively low rents, housing expenses are using up the majority of these clients' incomes.

```
mainstr$rgrapi
       n missing  unique
     164        0       7

           40-49% 50-59% 60-69% 70-79% 80-89% 90-99% 100% or more
Frequency     41     20     13     14     14      2           60
%             25     12      8      9      9      1           37
```

FIGURE 6.10 Description of variable *rgrapi*.

We may want to graph this, but in order to do so, we will need to build a table, as we did previously (see Figure 6.11).

```
> r<-table(mainstr$rgrapi)
> r1<-prop.table(r)*100
> r1
```

```
Less than 30%        30-39%        40-49%        50-59%        60-69%        70-79%        80-89%
     0.000000      0.000000     25.000000     12.195122      7.926829      8.536585      8.536585
       90-99%  100% or more
     1.219512     36.585366
```

FIGURE 6.11 Percentage of income spent on rent.

```
>barplot(r1, ylab="percentage", main="Percentage of
Monthly Income Spent on Rent")
```

In the output from entering `r1` in the Console, we see the percentages of clients falling into each category, as displayed in Figure 6.12. We can visualize that there are no individuals in the lowest categories, and the majority of clients are in the 40%–49% and 100% or more categories.

What About Work History?

One of the main challenges that the executive director has faced in her attempt to build support for the Housing Protection Program is that the clients are viewed as lazy. It may be helpful, then, to look at variables related to employment: *rlabor, worklwk, hours, looking*, and *rearning*.

You will notice that *rlabor, worklwk*, and *looking* are factor variables, while *hours*, and *rearning* are numeric. As we said earlier, we will describe factor variables differently than numeric variables, and we can use the *Hmisc* `describe()` function to get some quick information.

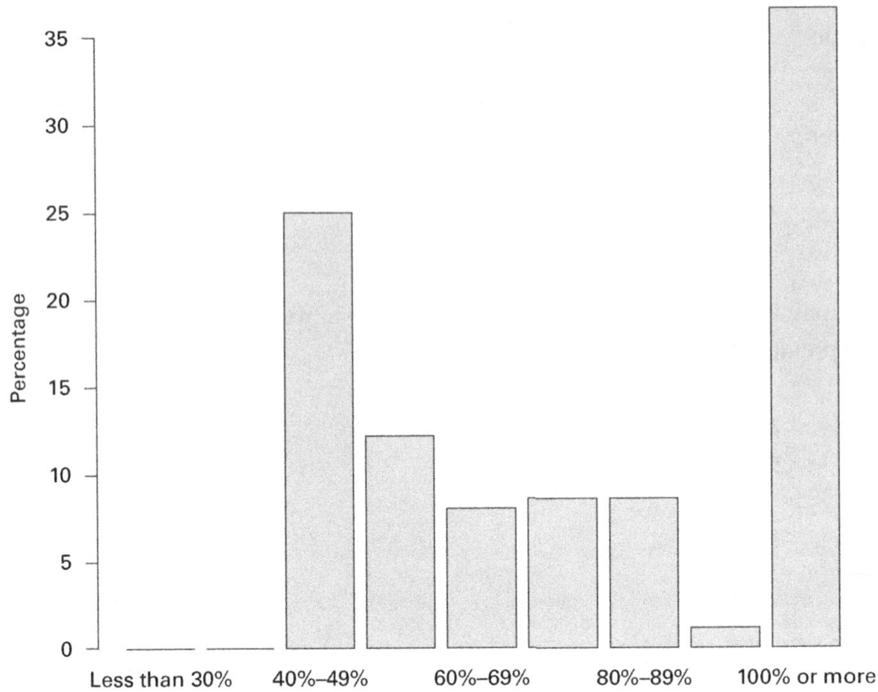

FIGURE 6.12 Bar plot of percentage of income spent on rent.

```
> describe(mainstr$rlabor)
mainstr$rlabor
       n missing  unique
     164       0       3

Employed (15, 9%), Unemployed (13, 8%), Not in lbr
force (136, 83%)
```

We see that while 9% of the at-risk clients are employed, the vast majority (136, or 83%) are not in the labor force at all. Only 8% of these clients consider themselves unemployed.

```
> describe(mainstr$worklwk)
mainstr$worklwk
       n missing  unique
     164       0       2

Worked (11, 7%), Did not work (153, 93%)
```

And only 7% of these clients worked in the last week.

```
> describe(mainstr$looking)
mainstr$looking

      n missing  unique
    164       0       2

Looking (42, 26%), Not looking (122, 74%)
```

Despite so many clients not being in the labor force, just over a quarter were looking for work; however, we do not have access to information as to why these clients are not in the labor force; that is, we do not have any variables in our data set that specifically address why clients are not working.

Now, detach *Hmisc* and attach *psych* so you can use the **describe()** function in that package to summarize our numeric variables.

```
> describe(mainstr$hours)
```

As displayed in Figure 6.13, while the mean number of hours worked weekly is very low, the standard deviation is high, and we know that the data are highly skewed and peaked. It may be helpful to look at a histogram of *hours*, displayed in Figure 6.14.

```
  vars   n mean   sd median trimmed mad min max range skew kurtosis   se
1    1 164 2.68 9.33      0       0   0   0  42    42 3.45    10.46 0.73
```

FIGURE 6.13 Description of *hours*.

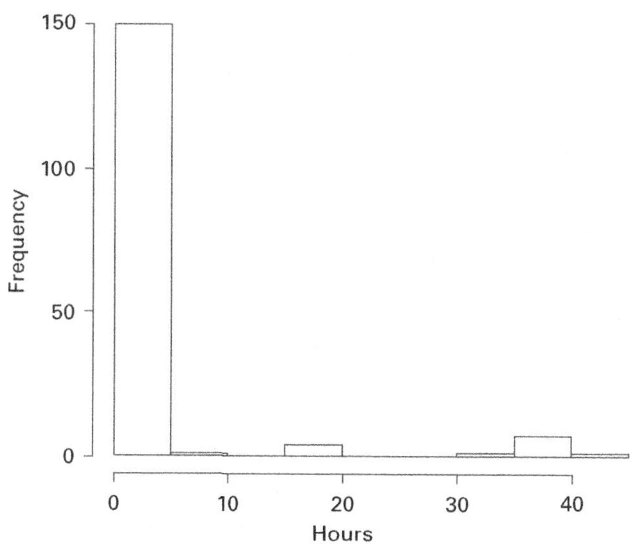

FIGURE 6.14 Histogram of hours worked weekly by at-risk clients.

```
>hist(mainstr$hours, xlab="hours", main="Hours Worked
Weekly by At-Risk Clients")
```

We can easily see that very few clients are working, despite the fact that a good number are looking for work.

```
> describe(mainstr$rearning)
```

As seen in Figure 6.15, again, we see highly skewed data with a low mean and a high standard deviation. Also, notice that the median is zero. We can visualize this as a boxplot, shown in Figure 6.16.

```
> boxplot(mainstr$rearning, main="Monthly Earnings by
At-Risk Clients")
```

This illustrates the tight clustering of data around zero and the fact that there are a number of outliers.

```
  vars   n   mean     sd median trimmed mad min  max range skew kurtosis    se
1    1 164 197.42 760.53      0    5.14   0   0 6240  6240 5.16    30.63 59.39
```

FIGURE 6.15 Description of variable *rearning*.

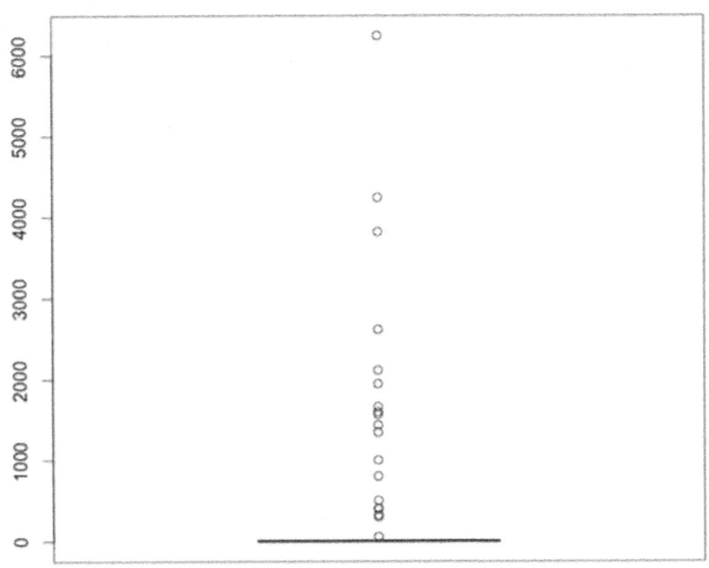

FIGURE 6.16 Boxplot of monthly earnings by at-risk clients.

One suspicion we may have could be related to clients' level of education, which is a variable in our data set. We will use the *Hmisc* **describe()** function to look at *yearsch*.

```
> describe(mainstr$yearsch)

mainstr$yearsch
      n missing  unique
    164       0       4

Less than HS (102, 62%), HS/GED (57, 35%), Some col-
lege (2, 1%)
Associate's degree or trade degree (3, 2%)
```

This gives us a clue as to why some of the agency's clients may be unemployed. Over half do not have a high school diploma, and only 3% have any type of higher education. None has a bachelor's degree or higher. This is a powerful piece of information that we would probably want to present visually, as displayed in Figure 6.17:

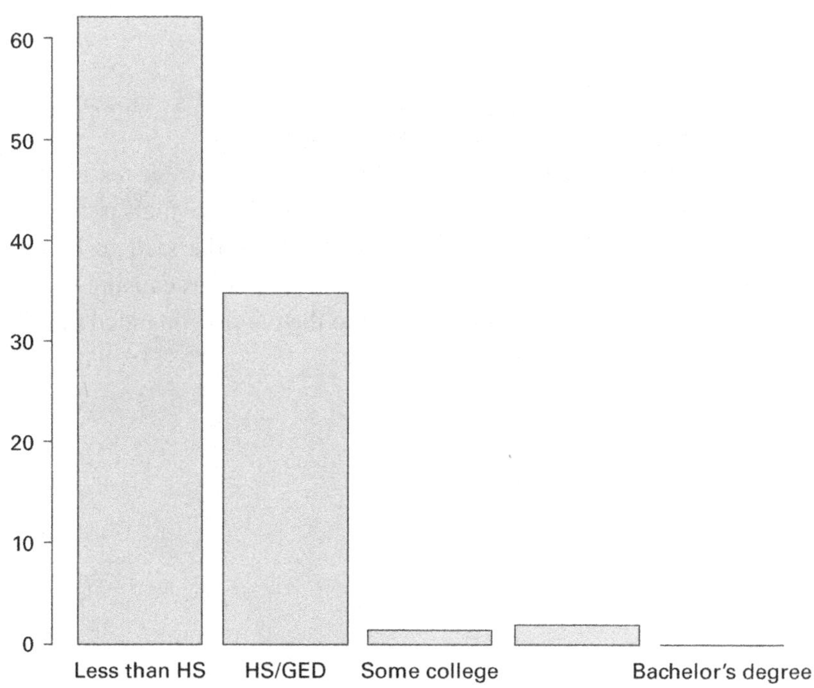

FIGURE 6.17 Bar graph of level of education for at-risk clients.

```
> educ<-table(mainstr$yearsch)
> e1<-prop.table(educ)*100
> barplot(e1, main="Highest Level of Education for
  At-Risk Clients")
```

Summarizing Our Findings

As you prepare to report back to the executive director, you will want to think about the original questions posed to you: Are the clients' most at risk for becoming homeless lazy and trying to get a free ride, and are their financial situations as dire as they seem? While we cannot get the answer to this definitively, we have some initial evidence to suggest that these clients are disadvantaged.

These clients have an extremely low monthly income, and while their housing costs are low, all of the clients pay at least 40% of their monthly income toward their housing expenses. For 37% of them, housing expenses are at or in excess of their monthly income. Additionally, nearly half of these women do not have enough food to meet their households' needs, despite having modest household sizes.

Slightly more than half of these clients were born in the United States, and 78% speak English well or very well. Nearly three-quarters of these women are not isolated linguistically.

While many of these women are unemployed, slightly more than a quarter of them are looking for work, and the vast majority of these women (87%) have only a high school education or less.

You have now begun to paint a picture of the at-risk clients that could be used to debunk the myth that these women are undeserving of help.

As an analyst, summarizing these variables individually leaves us with more questions. We see a lot of unemployment and low income, which is not surprising considering the fact that these clients are considered by the staff to be at risk for becoming homeless; however, what we do not know is what is causing this phenomenon. If we can identify factors that are related to the clients' financial problems, we may have an avenue to begin helping them.

/// 7 ///

MAKING YOUR CASE BY LOOKING AT FACTORS RELATED TO A DESIRED OUTCOME

In order to work through the examples in this chapter, you will need to *install* and *load* the following packages:

- *psych*
- *Hmisc*
- *car*
- *gmodels*
- *effsize*
- *exact2x2*

For more information on how to do this, refer to the Packages section in Chapter 3.

In the previous chapter, you learned how to describe your client data in a manner that could be helpful to stakeholders. In many cases, however, you will want to know a bit more. What client or program characteristics, for example, are related to a desired outcome?

Throughout the rest of the book, we will be looking at these issues in a number of ways. In this chapter, we will explore how to describe and depict relationships between two variables—an independent, or predictor, variable and a dependent, or outcome, variable—and decide whether the two are related.

CASE STUDY #2: THE CASE OF HEARING LOSS IN NEWBORNS

Like almost all hospitals in the United States, Memorial Hospital in Springvale screens all babies born there for hearing loss before they are sent home. Most babies that do not pass the hearing screening in the hospital do not have a hearing loss; they simply have fluid in their ears due to the birth process. However, in order to catch

TABLE 7.1 Variables in *newborn hearing* Data File

Variable	Description	Indicators	Variable Type
id	Patient id number	This is a unique identifier for each patient.	Numeric
nursery	Type of nursery the child was admitted to at birth	Well = well-baby nursery where healthy babies are admitted; NICU = neonatal intensive care where babies with significant health issues are admitted	Factor
mcd	Whether the child has Medicaid or private insurance	Yes = Medicaid; No = private insurance	Factor
rescreen	Whether the child was rescreened on time or late	On time/Late	Factor
age	The age in weeks of the baby when the rescreen occurred	Actual age of the baby in weeks	Numeric
dx	Whether the child was diagnosed on time or late	On time/Late	Factor
dxage	The age in weeks of the baby when the diagnosis occurred	Actual age of the baby in weeks	Numeric
tx	Whether the child was treated on time or late	On time/Late	Factor
txage	The age in weeks of the baby when the treatment occurred	Actual age of the baby in weeks	Numeric
fudifctr	Whether the parents followed up with the child's hearing at a different center	Yes = follow-up occurred at another center; No = follow-up occurred at Memorial Hospital	Factor
prtsref	Whether or not the parent(s) refused follow-up care	Yes = follow-up care was refused by the parents; No = follow-up care was not refused	Factor
losttofu	Whether or not the child was completely lost to follow-up (i.e., additional care was needed, but it was not pursued)	Yes = child did not receive needed care; No = child received needed care	Factor
distance	Whether or not the child lived 25 or more miles from the Hearing and Speech Center	Yes = child lives more than 25 miles from the Hearing and Speech Center; No = child lives within 25 miles of the Hearing and Speech Center	Factor
hltype	Type of hearing loss with which the child is diagnosed	Sensorineural = an inner ear hearing loss that is considered permanent; Conductive = a middle ear hearing loss that is often considered temporary, but in some cases may be permanent	Factor

(continued)

TABLE 7.1 Continued

Variable	Description	Indicators	Variable Type
hlsev	The severity of the child's hearing loss	Mild/Severe	Factor
hleffect	Whether the hearing loss is in one or both ears	Unilateral = the hearing loss is only in one ear; Bilateral = the hearing loss is in both ears	Factor

actual hearing losses early, babies that do not pass the screening done in the hospital need to be rescreened within a month of going home.

Some babies, of course, will not pass the rescreen, and those babies need to be evaluated further and, optimally, diagnosed by 3 months of age if they actually have a hearing loss. It is the hospital's aim to begin treatment for babies with actual hearing loss by the time they are 6 months old, in accordance with guidelines set by the American Speech-Language-Hearing Association (American Speech-Language-Hearing Association, 2008).

The director of the hospital's Hearing and Speech Center would like to evaluate their current program by determining factors that are related to rescreening, diagnosing, and treating these babies late or, worse yet, not at all. The goal of the evaluation is to design additional interventions to improve follow-up care. To begin, he has asked you to use existing hospital records to determine these factors.

In *RStudio*, open the data set titled *newborn hearing.RData*. Note that there are 16 variables and 192 observations. The data you have available to you are displayed in Table 7.1.

HYPOTHESIS TESTING

Throughout the remainder of this book, we will be using the case studies presented to illustrate a number of concepts, all of which will examine the relationship between one or more independent variables and a dependent variable. The first step in significance testing is to form a hypothesis of no difference, referred to as the *null hypothesis*, which is denoted as H_0. The null hypothesis states that there is no relationship between the independent variable(s) and the dependent variable. The alternate hypothesis, which is denoted as H_1 or H_A, is that there is a relationship between the variables. As you read each of the case studies, you will notice that the alternate hypothesis is explicitly stated, while the null hypothesis is implied (i.e., there is no relationship at all between the variables).

Traditionally, with group research designs, researchers are particularly interested in statistical significance, which is the assignment of a cutoff value for the chances of making a Type I error. Type I error is the probability of making an incorrect decision by rejecting the null hypothesis and accepting the alternate when, in fact, the null is correct. In the social sciences, findings are typically considered statistically significant if p, or the probability of making a Type I error, is 0.05 (5%) or less.

When $p \leq 0.05$, we reject the null hypothesis and accept the alternate; however, this does not mean that the alternate hypothesis is true and that we are correct in our hypothesis. It means that the chances of making a Type I error are low enough that we are willing to take the chance on accepting the alternate hypothesis (and, therefore, rejecting the null). We could be wrong. That is, if p is, for example, 0.02, we understand this to mean that there is a 2% chance that the null hypothesis is correct. Since this falls below our standard threshold for rejecting the null, we accept the alternate, but in two cases out of 100, we will simply be wrong. Calculated p-values are impacted by factors such as differences in mean values, variation, and sample size. Large differences in means between groups, large samples, and less variation within groups all increase the likelihood of finding statistically significant differences.

While we will be demonstrating numerous tests of Type I error, you will need to consider what your findings actually mean in the context in which you are working and with the understanding of the limitations of tests of Type I error.

More detail on hypothesis testing, in general, can be found in the texts described in Appendix A.

The type of test of Type I error that you conduct in a bivariate analysis (i.e., in looking at the relationship between two variables) is based upon the level of measurement of each variable. This is illustrated in Table 7.2.

In all cases in which the dependent variable is numeric, we have listed two tests of Type I error. The first is a parametric test and the second, listed in *italics*, is a non-parametric test. Parametric tests are based on the assumption that data are normally distributed, as in the classic "bell curve," while non-parametric tests do not make this assumption. In many cases, there is not a specific concern about normality when samples (i.e., the number of observations you have collected) are deemed "sufficiently large." What constitutes "sufficiently large" has been debated

TABLE 7.2 Bivariate Tests of Type I Error

Dependent Variable	**Independent Variable**	**Comparison**	**Tests of Type I Error**
Factor	Factor	Contingency table	*Chi-square* (X^2) or *Fisher's exact*
Numeric	Factor (with 2 factors)	Comparison of means	t-test or *Mann-Whitney Test*
Numeric	Factor (with more than 2 factors)	Comparison of means	Analysis of Variance (ANOVA) followed by post hoc analysis or *Kruskal-Wallis Test*
Numeric	Numeric	Correlation	Pearson's r or *Spearman's rho* (ρ)

by statisticians over the years, but in all cases, these sample sizes are relatively small, ranging from 15 to 40 (Allen, 1990; Casella & Berger, 1990; Cherry, 1998; Moore & McCabe, 1989). Therefore, we will be illustrating bivariate analysis in our case study using parametric tests; however, at the end of this chapter, we will illustrate the use of non-parametric tests with our data.

Also note that when both the dependent and independent variables are factors, you will need to do either a chi-square or a Fisher's exact to test for Type I error. It is appropriate to use the Fisher's exact test when the table you create is 2 × 2, that is, when both variables have two categories, and/or your expected cell sizes are small (< 5). In cases where the tables are larger, for example one variable has two categories and another has three, you would use the chi-square test.

Examples for using each of these will be illustrated throughout the rest of the chapter.

FORMULATING THE RESEARCH QUESTION

To begin, it is important to articulate the overall research question and any subordinate questions. At the Hearing and Speech Center at Memorial Hospital, there are three explicit, yet related, research questions:

1. What factors are related to different statuses on rescreen times (on-time, late, and lost to follow-up)?
2. What factors are related to different statuses on diagnosis times?
3. What factors are related to different statuses on treatment times?

As we move through the analytical process, we will consider each of these questions separately.

What Factors Are Related to Different Statuses on Rescreen Times?

Before we begin to address this problem, it would be helpful to understand how big a problem late rescreening is; that is, how many babies are actually rescreened late compared to those rescreened on time. To determine this, we will begin by sorting the babies in our sample into a table based upon their rescreen status. Enter the following in the Console:

```
> rscrn<-table(hear$rescreen)
> rscrn

On Time    Late
    129      62
```

The output shows that 129 babies were rescreened on time and 62, nearly a third of the babies, were rescreened late. To convert this to proportions, enter the following into the Console:

```
> prop.table(rscrn)

   On Time      Late
0.6753927 0.3246073
```

It is easy, now, to see that 67.5% of the sample were rescreened on time, and 32.5% were rescreened late.

As we ponder the first research question, we have to make hypotheses about what factors could be related to late rescreening. When making hypotheses, you will want to draw upon several sources: experience, a theoretical understanding of the problem, and prior research. In most cases, this will take some time, research, and consultation.

With all this in mind and by reviewing the data set, suppose we think that the following variables may be related to different rescreen statuses:

- Nursery type (corresponds to the variable called *nursery*): we might suppose that babies in the well-baby nursery have fewer health problems than those in the newborn intensive care unit (NICU); therefore, the parents of these babies might be more likely to follow-up on time since they do not need to deal with other health problems with their babies.
- Medicaid (corresponds to the variable called *mcd*): we might hypothesize that babies with Medicaid coverage may be more likely to be rescreened late or not at all. Our thinking here could be that parents may be very concerned about the ultimate cost of treatment if the child does, in fact, have a hearing loss.
- Severity of hearing loss (corresponds to the variable called *hlsev*): we might hypothesize that children who are ultimately diagnosed with a more severe hearing loss are more likely to be screened on time since it is likely that the hearing loss is more noticeable to parents and other caregivers than those children with less severe hearing losses.

As we move through the analysis process, we will need to consider the level of measurement for each of the variables. In each of our hypotheses, the outcome variable is *rescreen*, a factor variable with two factors: *on time* or *late*. The independent variables in this case, *nursery, mcd*, and *hlsev*, are all factor variables. By referring to Table 7.2, we can see that, in each case, we will want to create a contingency table and do a Fisher's exact test since all of these variables consist of only two categories.

For those variables in which we see a relationship with rescreen status, we may want to create a graph that illustrates this difference.

Nursery Type

To test this hypothesis, we will need to start by building a two-dimensional table in *R*. When you create this table, we recommend putting the outcome variable (in this case *rescreen*) in the rows, and the independent variable (in this case *nursery*) in the columns.

Enter the following in the Console:

```
> n<-table(hear$rescreen, hear$nursery)
> n

      You will see this output:

          Well NICU
  On Time   86   43
  Late      27   35
```

To see this as percentages totaled by column, enter the following in the Console to see the following results:

```
>prop.table(n, 1)
                 Well      NICU
  On Time 0.6666667 0.3333333
  Late    0.4354839 0.5645161
```

By entering the ", 1" following the vector holding the nursery data (*n*), we tell *R* that we want to total our percentages by row. Here, we see that of those babies that were rescreened on time, 67% were placed in the well-baby nursery, while 33% were in the NICU. This seems different from those babies who were screened late, with 43.5% of those babies being placed in the well-baby nursery and 56.5% being placed in the NICU.

To do a Fisher's exact test, enter the following into the Console in order to get the following output:

```
> fisher.test(n)

    Fisher's Exact Test for Count Data

data:  n
p-value = 0.002855
```

```
alternative hypothesis: true odds ratio is not
equal to 1
95 percent confidence interval:
 1.329579 5.061332
sample estimates:
odds ratio
  2.578978
```

With a calculated *p*-value of 0.002855, we consider our observed differences statistically significant since the chances of making a Type I error are far less than 5%.

Notice that our analysis so far had us write four simple commands. The *gmodels* package uses a function, **CrossTable()**, that will allow us to get all of this information in one command. To begin, you will need to download and require the *gmodels* package, as described in Chapter 3. Then, enter the following command in the Console:

```
> CrossTable(hear$rescreen, hear$nursery,prop.t=TRUE,
fisher=TRUE)
```

Notice that in order to place the dependent, or outcome, variable in the rows, we listed it first, followed by the in dependent variable. The **prop.t=TRUE** option tells *R* that we want proportions displayed for both rows and columns. The **fisher=TRUE** option tells *R* that we want to conduct a Fisher's exact test.

The output shown in Figure 7.1 is displayed in the Console. We have highlighted some of the interesting statistics in Figure 7.1 to which you will want to refer.

First, notice that the legend at the top, labeled "Cell Contents" describes the order in which output appears in each cell. The top number shows the N, or sample size, the next number shows the chi-square contribution for that cell. The next two numbers display the row and column proportions, while the last number shows the proportion attributed to that cell based upon the entire table.

Notice that the total number of observations is 191. This is the total upon which your analysis is based. The highlighted values within the tables are the counts and proportions that we retrieved from the **table()** and **prop.table()** functions previously. The highlighted values under *Row Total* are the counts and corresponding proportions to the babies screened on time and late. We see that the total number of babies screened on time was 129, which makes up 67.5% of the sample. Sixty-two babies, or 32.5% of the sample, were rescreened late. Similar information can be gleaned from the *Column Total* values; however, this information is based on nursery. We see that 113 babies (59.2% of the sample) were in the well-baby nursery, while 78 babies (40.8% of the sample) were in the NICU. Finally, *p*-values for three interpretations of the Fisher's exact are presented. The first is the one we are interested

```
   Cell Contents
|-------------------------|
|                       N |
| Chi-square contribution |
|           N / Row Total |
|           N / Col Total |
|         N / Table Total |
|-------------------------|


Total Observations in Table:  191


               | hear$nursery
hear$rescreen  |      Well |      NICU | Row Total |
---------------|-----------|-----------|-----------|
       On Time |        86 |        43 |       129 |
               |     1.228 |     1.779 |           |
               |     0.667 |     0.333 |     0.675 |
               |     0.761 |     0.551 |           |
               |     0.450 |     0.225 |           |
---------------|-----------|-----------|-----------|
          Late |        27 |        35 |        62 |
               |     2.555 |     3.701 |           |
               |     0.435 |     0.565 |     0.325 |
               |     0.239 |     0.449 |           |
               |     0.141 |     0.183 |           |
---------------|-----------|-----------|-----------|
  Column Total |       113 |        78 |       191 |
               |     0.592 |     0.408 |           |
---------------|-----------|-----------|-----------|


Fisher's Exact Test for Count Data
------------------------------------------------------------
Sample estimate odds ratio:  2.578978

Alternative hypothesis: true odds ratio is not equal to 1
p =  0.002854845
95% confidence interval:  1.329579 5.061332

Alternative hypothesis: true odds ratio is less than 1
p =  0.9992904
95% confidence interval:  0 4.571073

Alternative hypothesis: true odds ratio is greater than 1
p =  0.002008549
95% confidence interval:  1.4664 Inf
```

FIGURE 7.1 Example of `CrossTable()` output.

in, the two-tailed (non-directional) test. If we were interested in a one-tailed (directional) test, we would refer to one of the *p*-values presented below.

Because of the ease in obtaining results using the `CrossTable()` function in one command, we will be using this command in favor of the ones presented earlier. You should know, however, that this is simply a preference, and results can be obtained either way.

At this point, you may want to display this graphically. Using basic *R* functions, you can create a bar chart that breaks up the rescreen status by whether the baby was in the well-baby nursery or the NICU. To do this, enter the following code into the Console:

```
>barplot(n, col=c("lightgray", "darkgray"),
legend=rownames(n), ylab="count", xlab="Rescreen
Status", beside=TRUE)
```

The resulting graph is displayed in Figure 7.2.

What is obvious from this bar chart is that babies in the well-baby nursery were much more likely to be rescreened on time. While most babies in the NICU were screened on time, a greater number were late compared to those in the well-baby nursery.

Since our other hypotheses for this research question are made up of all factor variables, we will be using a similar method to test each of the other hypotheses to that used in the analysis of the relationship between nursery type and rescreen status.

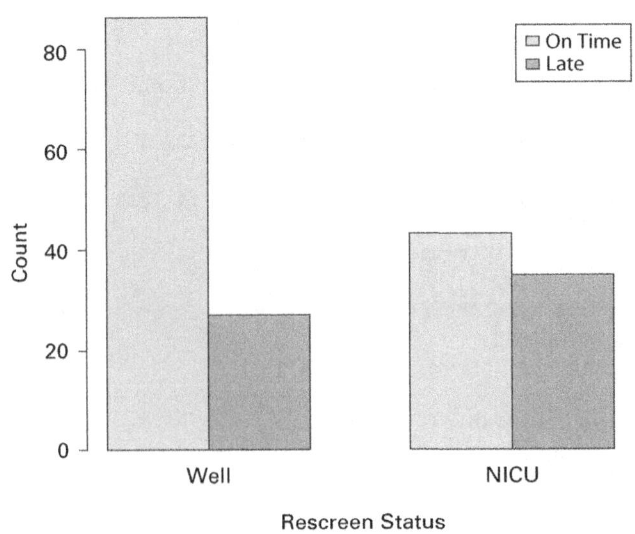

FIGURE 7.2 Rescreen status by nursery type.

Medicaid

We can use the **CrossTable()** function to determine the extent of the relationship between insurance coverage and rescreen status. Enter the following in the Console:

```
   Cell Contents
|-------------------------|
|                       N |
| Chi-square contribution |
|           N / Row Total |
|           N / Col Total |
|         N / Table Total |
|-------------------------|


Total Observations in Table:  191


               | hear$mcd
hear$rescreen  |        no |       yes | Row Total |
---------------|-----------|-----------|-----------|
       On Time |       102 |        27 |       129 |
               |     0.304 |     0.906 |           |
               |     0.791 |     0.209 |     0.675 |
               |     0.713 |     0.562 |           |
               |     0.534 |     0.141 |           |
---------------|-----------|-----------|-----------|
          Late |        41 |        21 |        62 |
               |     0.633 |     1.885 |           |
               |     0.661 |     0.339 |     0.325 |
               |     0.287 |     0.438 |           |
               |     0.215 |     0.110 |           |
---------------|-----------|-----------|-----------|
  Column Total |       143 |        48 |       191 |
               |     0.749 |     0.251 |           |
---------------|-----------|-----------|-----------|


Fisher's Exact Test for Count Data
------------------------------------------------------------
Sample estimate odds ratio:  1.927896

Alternative hypothesis: true odds ratio is not equal to 1
p =  0.07405597
95% confidence interval:  0.924885 3.99999

Alternative hypothesis: true odds ratio is less than 1
p =  0.9813637
95% confidence interval:  0 3.589421

Alternative hypothesis: true odds ratio is greater than 1
p =  0.04127776
95% confidence interval:  1.032261 Inf
```

FIGURE 7.3 Insurance coverage by rescreen status.

```
> CrossTable(hear$rescreen, hear$mcd,prop.t=TRUE,
fisher=TRUE)
```

The results, shown in Figure 7.3, are displayed in the Console.

In the output from *R*, we can see that the largest groups of babies were those covered by private insurance (n = 143, 74.9%) and were screened on time (n = 129, 67.5%). When we examine combinations of rescreening and insurance status, we see that, of those rescreened on time, nearly four out of five (79.1%) had private insurance, while 20.9% had Medicaid. Of those babies rescreened late, almost two-thirds (66.1%) had private insurance compared to 33.9% having Medicaid.

Based upon the Fisher's exact test, we cannot reject the null hypothesis that there is no difference between the groups based upon insurance status (p = 0.074). Statistically, it does not matter whether the babies have private insurance or have Medicaid when it comes to whether these children are rescreened on time or late.

Severity of Hearing Loss

To test the hypothesis that those with more severe hearing losses are rescreened differently from those with less severe hearing losses, we will again use the `CrossTable()` function:

```
> CrossTable(hear$rescreen, hear$hlsev,prop.t=TRUE,
fisher=TRUE)
```

As displayed in Figure 7.4, if we look simply at the raw numbers, it is easy to see that those screened on time were equally distributed between those with mild and severe hearing losses (65, or 50.4%, compared to 64, or 49.6%). Of the babies screened late, slightly more had severe hearing losses (i.e., 26, or 41.9%, had mild losses, compared to 36, or 58.1%, with severe losses).

Not surprisingly, the Fisher's exact two-tailed p-value is greater than 0.05, indicating that there is no significant difference between the groups.

Rescreening Summary

Despite the hypotheses developed at the beginning of this section, we were only able to identify one factor related to late rescreen status. The fact that babies in the NICU were more likely to be rescreened late is not surprising considering the serious medical conditions facing these babies at birth.

One other final bit of information that might be helpful to report with regard to rescreening is the mean age of babies screened on time compared to those screened

```
   Cell Contents
|-------------------------|
|                       N |
| Chi-square contribution |
|           N / Row Total |
|           N / Col Total |
|         N / Table Total |
|-------------------------|


Total Observations in Table:  191


               | hear$hlsev
hear$rescreen  |       Mild |     Severe | Row Total |
---------------|------------|------------|-----------|
       On Time |         65 |         64 |       129 |
               |      0.204 |      0.185 |           |
               |      0.504 |      0.496 |     0.675 |
               |      0.714 |      0.640 |           |
               |      0.340 |      0.335 |           |
---------------|------------|------------|-----------|
          Late |         26 |         36 |        62 |
               |      0.424 |      0.386 |           |
               |      0.419 |      0.581 |     0.325 |
               |      0.286 |      0.360 |           |
               |      0.136 |      0.188 |           |
---------------|------------|------------|-----------|
  Column Total |         91 |        100 |       191 |
               |      0.476 |      0.524 |           |
---------------|------------|------------|-----------|


Fisher's Exact Test for Count Data
------------------------------------------------------------
Sample estimate odds ratio:  1.403724

Alternative hypothesis: true odds ratio is not equal to 1
p =  0.2837612
95% confidence interval:  0.7309261 2.720904

Alternative hypothesis: true odds ratio is less than 1
p =  0.8944841
95% confidence interval:  0 2.461915

Alternative hypothesis: true odds ratio is greater than 1
p =  0.1735619
95% confidence interval:  0.8052523 Inf
```

FIGURE 7.4 Table of rescreen status by severity of hearing loss.

late. One of the easiest ways to do this is by using the **describeBy()** function in the *psych* package. To do this, require the *psych* package by checking the box next to that package in the Packages pane. Once the package is loaded, enter the following in the Console:

```
> describeBy(hear$age, hear$rescreen)
```

The output displayed in Figure 7.5 from this function illustrates that babies who were screened on time were just over a month old (4.92 weeks, sd = 1.67 weeks), on average, at the time of their rescreens, compared to 13.5 weeks (sd = 7.83) for the babies screened late.

We can also use **describeBy()** to determine the age at which babies are rescreened based upon the nursery they were admitted to at birth.

```
> describeBy(hear$age, hear$nursery)
```

We see in Figure 7.6 that, on average, babies admitted to the well-baby nursery were rescreened at 5.35 weeks (sd = 2.32) while babies admitted to the NICU were rescreened at 8.41 weeks (sd = 7.05). Not only are babies from the NICU rescreened later, but there is more variation in their ages at rescreen.

```
group: On Time
  vars  n mean   sd median trimmed  mad min  max range skew kurtosis   se
1    1 58 4.92 1.67   4.35    4.82 0.89   1 8.69  7.69  0.6     0.56 0.22
------------------------------------------------------------------------
group: Late
  vars  n mean   sd median trimmed  mad  min   max range skew kurtosis   se
1    1 10 13.5 7.83  11.95   11.44 4.63 8.69 34.76 26.07 1.91     2.48 2.48
```

FIGURE 7.5 Description of mean age by rescreening status.

```
group: Well
  vars  n mean   sd median trimmed  mad  min   max range skew kurtosis   se
1    1 48 5.35 2.32   4.35    5.08 1.28 1.29 13.04 11.75 1.59     2.81 0.34
------------------------------------------------------------------------
group: NICU
  vars  n mean   sd median trimmed  mad min   max range skew kurtosis   se
1    1 21 8.41 7.05   6.52    7.19 3.22   1 34.76 33.76 2.42     6.45 1.54
```

FIGURE 7.6 Mean age by nursery type.

What Factors Are Related to Different Statuses on Diagnosis Times?

In the first research question, we began by looking at how many and what proportion of babies fell into the *on time* and *late* rescreen categories. We will begin looking at diagnosis in the same way: by looking at how big a problem late diagnosis is for the babies in our sample.

Enter the following into the Console:

```
> diagnose<-table(hear$dx)
> diagnose

On time     late
    138       54
```

Again, it looks like most babies are diagnosed on time, but a sizable minority are diagnosed late. To get the exact proportions, enter the following in the Console:

```
>prop.table(diagnose)*100

On time     late
71.875    28.125
```

A slightly larger percentage of babies are diagnosed on time (71.9%) compared to those rescreened on time (67.5%), which we saw in the previous section. Still, more than one-quarter are diagnosed late.

With the current research question, you will want to expand your thinking. After all, diagnosis follows the initial hospital screening and the rescreen. You may want to think about additional factors that were not considered in the rescreen.

- *Age*: are babies' ages at rescreening related to babies' ages at diagnosis?
- *Rescreen*: is late rescreening more likely to be related to late diagnosis?
- *Nursery*: is the nursery that babies were admitted to at birth related to late diagnosis? That is, does the problem that exists at rescreening still present at diagnosis?
- Medicaid (corresponds to the variable called *mcd*): we might hypothesize that babies with Medicaid coverage may be more likely to be diagnosed late. Our thinking here could be that parents may be very concerned about costly treatment if the child does, in fact, have a hearing loss. While this was not significant at rescreening, it may become more important to parents when a real hearing loss is identified.
- Type of hearing loss (corresponds to the variable called *hltype*): we might hypothesize that babies who are ultimately diagnosed with a sensorineural loss are more likely to be diagnosed on time than babies with conductive losses since conductive losses are often considered temporary and sensorineural losses are considered permanent.
- Laterality of loss (corresponds to the variable called *hleffect*): similarly to the severity of hearing loss, we might suppose that babies who are ultimately

diagnosed with a unilateral loss (i.e., effecting only one ear) may be less obviously impaired than those whose losses occur in both ears.

We can begin this analysis in much the same way as we did when our outcome variable was rescreening.

Age

To begin, we will look to see if there is a significant correlation between babies' ages at rescreen and at diagnosis. The first step here is to determine if there is a linear relationship between these variables, and the best way to do this is by looking at these variables on a scatterplot.

To visualize this, we can use the *car* package to draw a scatterplot with a regression line. If you have not already done so, install and require the *car* package. Instructions for doing this are provided in Chapter 3. Then, enter the following in the Console:

```
>scatterplot(hear$age, hear$dxage, xlab="Age at
Rescreen (weeks)", ylab="Age at Diagnosis (weeks)",
main="Relationship Between Ages at Rescreen and
Diagnosis", smooth=F)
```

The resulting graph is displayed in Figure 7.7.

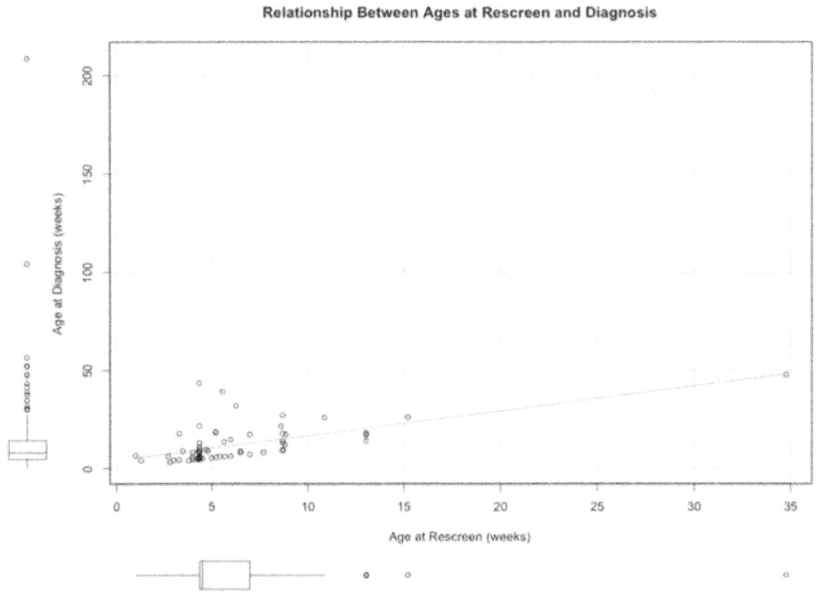

FIGURE 7.7 Scatterplot displaying relationship between age at rescreen and diagnosis.

From this, we can visualize the relationship between age at rescreen and age at diagnosis. We also notice that there are children rescreened from about 13 weeks on that are outliers. Also notice that the scale for age at diagnosis is quite large. However, the relationship between age at rescreen and age at diagnosis is a linear one.

Since the relationship between age at rescreen and age at diagnosis is linear, we can proceed with the correlation. To do this, we will use the *Hmisc* package, as the correlation function in that package provides valuable information. Once you have installed and required that package (see Chapter 3 for more details), enter the following in the Console:

```
> rcorr(hear$age, hear$dxage)
```

The results shown in Figure 7.8 will be displayed in the Console.

The output from this function displays three pieces of important information. At the top, we see the correlation between the variables. Next, we see the number of observations included in the analysis. Finally, the chance of making a Type I is reported. In the case of our question, we see a moderate and significant relationship between age at rescreen and age at diagnosis, and 69 cases were included in the analysis. This number includes only observations in which values for both variables were reported.

```
     x    y
x 1.00 0.61     ---> Correlation between x and y
y 0.61 1.00

n
    x   y
x 192  69       ---> The number of observations
y  69 192            included in the analysis

P
  x y
x   0           ---> The significance of the
y 0                  correlation
```

FIGURE 7.8 Correlation of age at rescreen with age at diagnosis using *Hmisc* package.

Rescreen

As we consider whether late rescreening is related to late diagnosis, notice that both of these are factor variables with two categories each. In order to assess this relationship, then, it is appropriate to do a Fisher's exact test. We can use the `CrossTable()` function, as we did in the previous section:

```
> CrossTable(hear$dx, hear$rescreen,prop.t=TRUE,
fisher=TRUE)
```

```
   Cell Contents
|-------------------------|
|                       N |
| Chi-square contribution |
|           N / Row Total |
|           N / Col Total |
|         N / Table Total |
|-------------------------|


Total Observations in Table:  191


             | hear$rescreen
    hear$dx  |   On Time |      Late | Row Total |
-------------|-----------|-----------|-----------|
     On time |       116 |        22 |       138 |
             |     5.575 |    11.600 |           |
             |     0.841 |     0.159 |     0.723 |
             |     0.899 |     0.355 |           |
             |     0.607 |     0.115 |           |
-------------|-----------|-----------|-----------|
        late |        13 |        40 |        53 |
             |    14.517 |    30.205 |           |
             |     0.245 |     0.755 |     0.277 |
             |     0.101 |     0.645 |           |
             |     0.068 |     0.209 |           |
-------------|-----------|-----------|-----------|
Column Total |       129 |        62 |       191 |
             |     0.675 |     0.325 |           |
-------------|-----------|-----------|-----------|


Fisher's Exact Test for Count Data
------------------------------------------------------------
Sample estimate odds ratio:  15.88622

Alternative hypothesis: true odds ratio is not equal to 1
p =  1.373318e-14
95% confidence interval:  7.036483 38.1411

Alternative hypothesis: true odds ratio is less than 1
p =  1
95% confidence interval:  0 33.33413

Alternative hypothesis: true odds ratio is greater than 1
p =  1.373318e-14
95% confidence interval:  7.890856 Inf
```

FIGURE 7.9 Rescreening status by on time for diagnosis.

By examining the output in Figure 7.9, it is apparent that most children who are rescreened on time are diagnosed on time (116, or 89.9% of children rescreened on time), and most children who are rescreened late are diagnosed late (40, or 64.5% of children rescreened late). Note that the calculated *p*-value for the Fisher's exact is displayed in scientific notation. To turn off scientific notation for your entire *R* session, enter the following in the Console:

```
> options(scipen=999)
```

Now you can rerun the **CrossTable()** function, if you wish, and you will notice that these findings are statistically significant ($p = 0.00000000000001373$). We can reject the null hypothesis that there is no relationship between rescreen status and diagnosis status and accept the alternate.

Since these findings are significant, it might be helpful to visualize them with a simple bar graph. To begin, you will have to create a table:

```
> rescreen<-table(hear$dx, hear$rescreen)
> rescreen

              On Time Late
    On time       116   22
    late           13   40
```

Notice that we are listing the dependent variable first, followed by the independent variable. Also notice that the output in the Console corresponds exactly to the output produced by the **CrossTable()** function. Now we can enter to the following command to produce the bar graph:

```
>barplot(rescreen, col=c("lightgray", "darkgray"),
legend=rownames(rescreen), ylab="Infants rescreened
(count)", xlab="Diagnosis Status", main = "Infant
Rescreen-Diagnosis Status",beside=T)
```

The results of this command are displayed in Figure 7.10.

We can see from this graph that, by far, the largest group of babies was both rescreened and diagnosed on time. Similarly, the next largest group was rescreened late and diagnosed late.

Another way to assess this is to compare the mean ages of babies at rescreen to the diagnosis statuses. That is, is the diagnosis status of the babies related to their age at rescreen? Since age at rescreen is a numeric variable and *dx* is a factor variable with two categories, we will need to do a *t*-test to compare these groups.

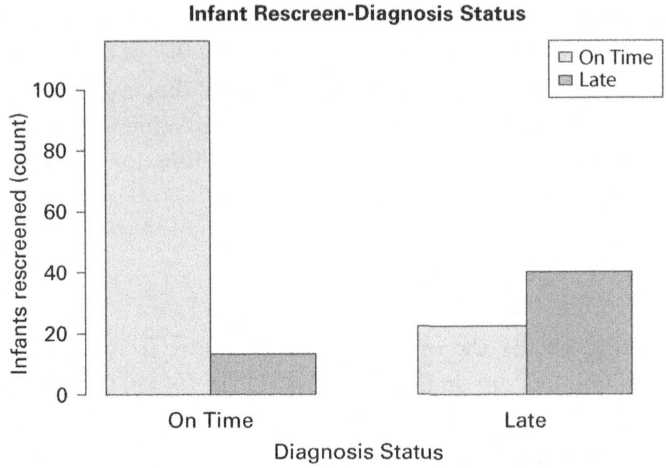

FIGURE 7.10 Barplot displaying counts of rescreen status by diagnosis status.

To choose the most appropriate form of the *t*-test, we first need to determine whether the variances in each of the groups are equal. To do this, enter the following in the Console:

```
> var.test(hear$age~hear$dx)

    F test to compare two variances
data: hear$age by hear$dx
F = 0.0665, num df = 46, denom df = 21,
p-value = 0.00000000000007593
alternative hypothesis: true ratio of variances is
not equal to 1
95 percent confidence interval:
 0.02995177 0.13319610
sample estimates:
ratio of variances
         0.0665404
```

The results of this test indicate that the variances between the groups are significantly different. Because of this, we will run the version of the *t*-test that accounts for these differences.

```
> t.test(hear$age~hear$dx)
```

```
        Welch Two Sample t-test

data: hear$age by hear$dx
t = -3.3291, df = 22.319, p-value = 0.003003
alternative hypothesis: true difference in means is
not equal to 0
95 percent confidence interval:
 -7.711025 -1.794449
sample estimates:
mean in group On time    mean in group late
             4.766809              9.519545
```

The output shows that the mean age at rescreen of babies diagnosed on time was 4.77 weeks, compared to 9.52 weeks for babies who were diagnosed late. As noted by the calculated *p*-value (0.003003), these differences are statistically significant.

It is often helpful to quantify the extent of a difference that exists between two independent groups, as this can suggest the clinical or practical significance of observed differences. As mentioned, Cohen's *d*, a measure of effect size, can be calculated with the *effsize* package's function, **cohen.d()**. You will need to install and load the package. The syntax comparing independent groups is displayed here.

```
>cohen.d(hear$age~as.factor(hear$dx),na.rm=T)
Cohen's d

d estimate: -1.202699 (large)
95 percent confidence interval:
       inf          sup

-1.7666903 -0.6387072
```

In the command above, the numeric variable is entered first and the grouping variable is entered after the "~." Also note that the grouping variable must be a factor variable. The safest approach is to always use the **as.factor()** function to ensure that the grouping variable is seen as a factor.

The effect size produced by the command is –1.202699, indicating a large degree of difference in age between the on-time-diagnosis and the late-for-diagnosis groups. The 95% confidence interval is also displayed, indicating that it is likely that the value ranges between –1.7666903 and –0.6387072.

The interpretation of Cohen's *d* is based upon z-scores. The score represents the degree of difference in age for the on-time-for-diagnosis group compared to the late-for-diagnosis group. An effect size of 1.2 denotes a little over one standard deviation difference in the on-time group scores as compared to the late group. Therefore, an effect size of 0 shows no improvement, while an effect size of 1 indicates a 34.13%

increase in improvement in the first group compared to the second group (Bloom, Fischer, & Orme, 2009). The degree of difference can be expressed as a percentage by using the following syntax:

```
>dchange=(pnorm(-1.202699)-.5)*100
```

Typing **dchange** in the Console displays a percentage of –38.54536 in the Console. This indicates a –38.5% difference in age between those on time for diagnosis compared to those late for diagnosis. The **pnorm()** function provides the area under the normal curve based upon a *z*-score/effect size.

Nursery

At this point we turn our attention back to the nursery the babies were admitted to at birth. We can again use the **CrossTable()** function to gather the necessary information for comparison. We can begin by building a contingency table:

```
> CrossTable(hear$dx, hear$nursery,prop.t=TRUE,
fisher=TRUE)
```

We can look at the results of this table displayed in Figure 7.11.

As displayed in Figure 7.11, slightly more than three out of five babies (n = 86; 62.3%) who were diagnosed on time were admitted to the well-baby nursery, compared to 52 babies (37.7%) who were admitted to the NICU. Of those babies diagnosed late, 51.9% (n = 28) had been admitted to the well-baby nursery, compared to 48.1% admitted to the NICU.

We see, however, that our chances of making a Type I error are too high ($p = 0.195$), so we are unable to reject the null hypothesis that there is no difference in diagnosis status based upon nursery admission. It seems as if the problem at rescreen may have disappeared by the time babies reach diagnosis.

Medicaid

Previously, we had found no statistical difference between rescreen status and whether or not the child had Medicaid; however, with a calculated *p*-value of 0.074, we were approaching significance. Therefore, we may want to continue to consider whether there is a relationship between insurance status and follow-up testing. We can test this hypothesis again, this time using diagnosis status as our outcome variable and the **CrossTable()** function.

```
> CrossTable(hear$dx, hear$mcd,prop.t=TRUE,
fisher=TRUE)
```

```
   Cell Contents
|-------------------------|
|                       N |
| Chi-square contribution |
|           N / Row Total |
|           N / Col Total |
|         N / Table Total |
|-------------------------|


Total Observations in Table:  192


             | hear$nursery
    hear$dx  |      Well |      NICU | Row Total |
-------------|-----------|-----------|-----------|
     On time |        86 |        52 |       138 |
             |     0.201 |     0.294 |           |
             |     0.623 |     0.377 |     0.719 |
             |     0.754 |     0.667 |           |
             |     0.448 |     0.271 |           |
-------------|-----------|-----------|-----------|
        late |        28 |        26 |        54 |
             |     0.515 |     0.752 |           |
             |     0.519 |     0.481 |     0.281 |
             |     0.246 |     0.333 |           |
             |     0.146 |     0.135 |           |
-------------|-----------|-----------|-----------|
Column Total |       114 |        78 |       192 |
             |     0.594 |     0.406 |           |
-------------|-----------|-----------|-----------|


Fisher's Exact Test for Count Data
------------------------------------------------------------
Sample estimate odds ratio:  1.532161

Alternative hypothesis: true odds ratio is not equal to 1
p =  0.1949708
95% confidence interval:  0.7724653 3.03991

Alternative hypothesis: true odds ratio is less than 1
p =  0.9315385
95% confidence interval:  0 2.744055

Alternative hypothesis: true odds ratio is greater than 1
p =  0.1223882
95% confidence interval:  0.8556641 Inf
```

FIGURE 7.11 Diagnosis status by type of nursery.

As displayed in Figure 7.12, it seems as if there are significant differences in diagnosis status between those with Medicaid and those with private insurance ($p = 0.025$). The proportion table indicates that only 58.3% of children with Medicaid coverage were diagnosed on time, while 41.7% of babies diagnosed late had Medicaid.

```
   Cell Contents
|-------------------------|
|                       N |
| Chi-square contribution |
|           N / Row Total |
|           N / Col Total |
|         N / Table Total |
|-------------------------|


Total Observations in Table:  192


             | hear$mcd
     hear$dx |        no |       yes | Row Total |
-------------|-----------|-----------|-----------|
     On time |       110 |        28 |       138 |
             |     0.408 |     1.225 |           |
             |     0.797 |     0.203 |     0.719 |
             |     0.764 |     0.583 |           |
             |     0.573 |     0.146 |           |
-------------|-----------|-----------|-----------|
        late |        34 |        20 |        54 |
             |     1.043 |     3.130 |           |
             |     0.630 |     0.370 |     0.281 |
             |     0.236 |     0.417 |           |
             |     0.177 |     0.104 |           |
-------------|-----------|-----------|-----------|
Column Total |       144 |        48 |       192 |
             |     0.750 |     0.250 |           |
-------------|-----------|-----------|-----------|


Fisher's Exact Test for Count Data
------------------------------------------------------------
Sample estimate odds ratio:  2.299863

Alternative hypothesis: true odds ratio is not equal to 1
p =  0.02517809
95% confidence interval:  1.083944 4.85455

Alternative hypothesis: true odds ratio is less than 1
p =  0.9944659
95% confidence interval:  0 4.346145

Alternative hypothesis: true odds ratio is greater than 1
p =  0.01444537
95% confidence interval:  1.212824 Inf
```

FIGURE 7.12 Diagnosis status by type of insurance.

To think about this slightly differently, we could look at the proportions by diagnosis status. We see that of all the babies diagnosed on time, 79.7% had private insurance, while the remainder (20.3%) had Medicaid coverage.

Since the Fisher's exact showed statistically significant differences in diagnosis status between the groups based on insurance type, it may be useful to make a bar graph depicting these differences. Start by creating a table:

```
> insure<-table(hear$dx, hear$mcd)
> insure

            no yes
  On time  110  28
  late      34  20
```

Again, notice that the counts from the insure table exactly match the counts produced in the output from the **CrossTable()** function. Now enter the following in the Console. The bar graph is shown in Figure 7.13.

```
> barplot(insure, col=c("lightgray", "darkgray"),
legend=rownames(insure), ylab="count", xlab="Medicaid
Status", main="Diagnosis Status By Whether Child Has
Medicaid", beside=T)
```

This illustration makes it abundantly clear that the vast majority of those children diagnosed on time have private insurance.

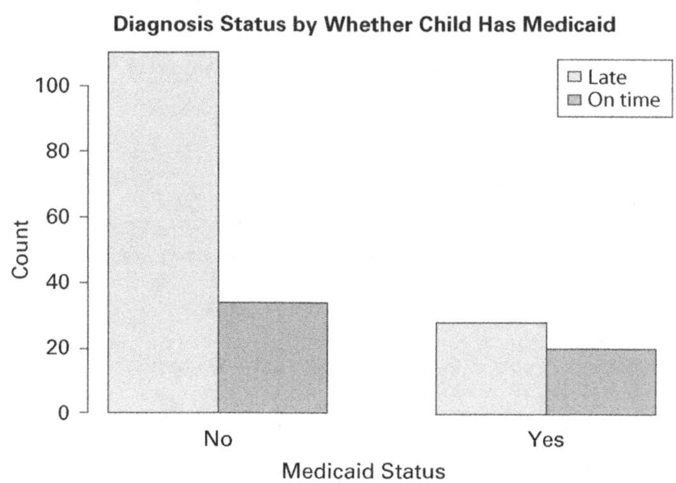

FIGURE 7.13 Diagnosis status by whether child has Medicaid.

Type of Hearing Loss

To test the hypothesis that type of hearing loss, conductive or sensorineural, is related to diagnosis status, we will analyze the data in the same manner as we did in the other cases where both variables were factor variables:

```
   Cell Contents
|-------------------------|
|                       N |
| Chi-square contribution |
|           N / Row Total |
|           N / Col Total |
|         N / Table Total |
|-------------------------|


Total Observations in Table:  192


             | hear$hltype
     hear$dx | Sensorineural |    Conductive |     Row Total |
-------------|---------------|---------------|---------------|
     On time |           122 |            16 |           138 |
             |         0.098 |         0.598 |               |
             |         0.884 |         0.116 |         0.719 |
             |         0.739 |         0.593 |               |
             |         0.635 |         0.083 |               |
-------------|---------------|---------------|---------------|
        late |            43 |            11 |            54 |
             |         0.250 |         1.528 |               |
             |         0.796 |         0.204 |         0.281 |
             |         0.261 |         0.407 |               |
             |         0.224 |         0.057 |               |
-------------|---------------|---------------|---------------|
Column Total |           165 |            27 |           192 |
             |         0.859 |         0.141 |               |
-------------|---------------|---------------|---------------|


Fisher's Exact Test for Count Data
------------------------------------------------------------
Sample estimate odds ratio:  1.943172

Alternative hypothesis: true odds ratio is not equal to 1
p =  0.1640187
95% confidence interval:  0.7525074 4.870367

Alternative hypothesis: true odds ratio is less than 1
p =  0.9611222
95% confidence interval:  0 4.264071

Alternative hypothesis: true odds ratio is greater than 1
p =  0.09219841
95% confidence interval:  0.8678105 Inf
```

FIGURE 7.14 Diagnosis status by type of hearing loss.

```
> CrossTable(hear$dx, hear$hltype,prop.t=TRUE,
fisher=TRUE)
```

As displayed by Figure 7.14, in this sample, 88.4% of babies diagnosed on time had a sensorineural loss, while 11.6% had a conductive loss. Of those babies diagnosed late, 79.6% were diagnosed with a sensorineural loss, while 20.4% had a conductive loss.

With a *p*-value of 0.164 for Fisher's exact, we have to conclude that there are no differences in diagnosis status by type of hearing loss, and we cannot reject the null hypothesis.

Laterality of Hearing Loss

To test the hypothesis that those with bilateral losses are different from those with unilateral losses, we will use the **CrossTable()** function once again. Enter the following into the Console:

```
> CrossTable(hear$dx, hear$hleffect,prop.t=TRUE,
fisher=TRUE)
```

As displayed in Figure 7.15, we see that of those babies diagnosed on time, 105, or 76.1%, had bilateral losses, compared to 33, or 23.9%, with unilateral losses. Of those diagnosed late, a very high percentage, 90.7%, had bilateral losses, while 9.3% had unilateral losses.

In general, many more children had bilateral losses compared to unilateral losses; therefore, it may be interesting to look at this slightly differently. By looking only at the bilateral losses, 68.2% were diagnosed on time, compared to 86.8% of children with unilateral losses.

For the Fisher's exact test, we see that those differences are statistically significant ($p = 0.026$). Since these differences are significantly different, you may want to illustrate this visually with a bar graph. Since the differences are illustrated most dramatically, we will want to emphasize this. Again, you will need to build a table first, but this time we will list laterality first. The actual bar graph is displayed in Figure 7.16.

```
> laterality<-table(hear$hleffect, hear$dx)
> laterality

             On time late
Bilateral        105   49
Unilateral        33    5
```

```
   Cell Contents
|-------------------------|
|                       N |
| Chi-square contribution |
|           N / Row Total |
|           N / Col Total |
|         N / Table Total |
|-------------------------|


Total Observations in Table:  192


             | hear$hleffect
     hear$dx |  Bilateral | Unilateral |  Row Total |
-------------|------------|------------|------------|
     On time |        105 |         33 |        138 |
             |      0.292 |      1.184 |            |
             |      0.761 |      0.239 |      0.719 |
             |      0.682 |      0.868 |            |
             |      0.547 |      0.172 |            |
-------------|------------|------------|------------|
        late |         49 |          5 |         54 |
             |      0.747 |      3.027 |            |
             |      0.907 |      0.093 |      0.281 |
             |      0.318 |      0.132 |            |
             |      0.255 |      0.026 |            |
-------------|------------|------------|------------|
Column Total |        154 |         38 |        192 |
             |      0.802 |      0.198 |            |
-------------|------------|------------|------------|


Fisher's Exact Test for Count Data
------------------------------------------------------------
Sample estimate odds ratio:  0.3262916

Alternative hypothesis: true odds ratio is not equal to 1
p =  0.0259442
95% confidence interval:  0.09369366 0.9131439

Alternative hypothesis: true odds ratio is less than 1
p =  0.01478443
95% confidence interval:  0 0.798247

Alternative hypothesis: true odds ratio is greater than 1
p =  0.9958215
95% confidence interval:  0.1148227 Inf
```

FIGURE 7.15 Diagnosis status by laterality.

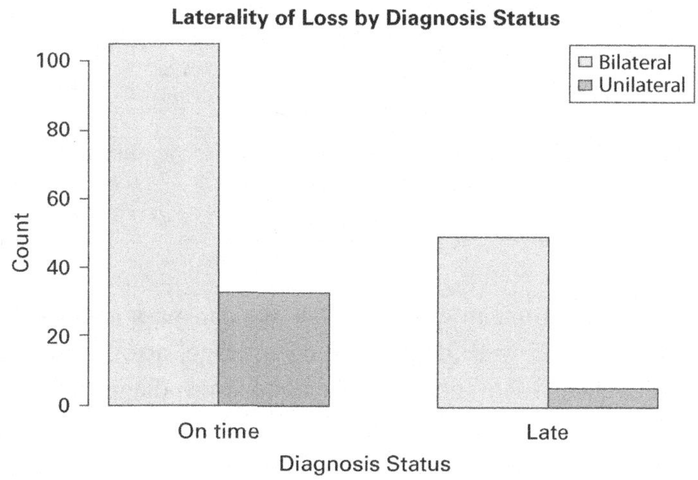

FIGURE 7.16 Laterality of loss by diagnosis status.

```
> barplot(laterality, col=c("lightgray", "dark-
gray"), legend=rownames(laterality), ylab="count",
xlab="Diagnosis Status", main="Laterality of Loss By
Diagnosis Status", beside=T)
```

This graph illustrates that, in either case, more babies were diagnosed on time when they had bilateral losses compared to unilateral losses. We can clearly see this in comparing the heights of each of the *Bilateral* bars compared to the *Unilateral* bars.

Some Additional Analysis

In our analysis above, we determined that there was a relationship between the age at rescreen and the age at diagnosis. We also learned that there were statistically significant differences between diagnosis status and the following independent variables: insurance status and laterality of loss. From a program evaluation and remediation standpoint, it may be helpful to find out the ages of the babies when they are diagnosed for each of these conditions.

Begin by requiring the *psych* package by entering the following into the Console:

```
> require(psych)
```

Alternatively, you can check the box next to the *psych* package in the Packages pane in the lower right corner of *RStudio*.

```
> describeBy(hear$dxage, hear$dx)
```

```
group: On time
  vars   n mean   sd median trimmed  mad  min   max range skew kurtosis   se
1    1 138 6.39 3.09    5.7    6.17 2.51 0.42 17.82  17.4 0.76      0.7 0.26
------------------------------------------------------------------------------
group: late
  vars  n  mean    sd median trimmed  mad min    max  range skew kurtosis se
1    1 54 29.79 29.41  21.73   24.58 8.67 9.4 208.57 199.17 4.44    23.11  4
```

FIGURE 7.17 Mean age at diagnosis by diagnosis status.

Now we have a bit more information that we can pass on (see Figure 7.17). Babies diagnosed on time were diagnosed, on average, at 6.39 weeks (sd = 3.09 weeks). Babies diagnosed late, on the other hand, were diagnosed, on average, at 29.41 weeks (sd = 21.73 weeks).

We can do this same analysis for diagnostic age by insurance status by entering the following into the Console:

```
> describeBy(hear$dxage, hear$mcd)
```

Here we notice from Figure 7.18 that, on average, babies with Medicaid are diagnosed at 15.32 weeks (sd = 18.09) compared to babies with private insurance, who are diagnosed at 12.18 weeks (sd = 19.19). Since these ages are somewhat close, we may want to compare those means to see if they are significantly different.

```
group: no
  vars   n  mean    sd median trimmed mad  min    max  range skew kurtosis  se
1    1 144 12.18 19.19   7.86    8.94 5.2 0.42 208.57 208.15 7.69    73.63 1.6
------------------------------------------------------------------------------
group: yes
  vars  n  mean    sd median trimmed  mad min    max  range skew kurtosis   se
1    1 48 15.32 18.09   8.69   11.93 7.48   1 104.29 103.29 2.82    10.07 2.61
```

FIGURE 7.18 Mean age at diagnosis by diagnosis status.

Since insurance status is a factor variable with two factors and diagnostic age is a numeric variable, a *t*-test is the most appropriate way to compare those means. To choose the most appropriate form of the t-test, we first need to determine whether the variances in each of the groups is equal. To do this, enter the following in the Console:

```
> var.test(hear$dxage~hear$mcd)
```

```
        F test to compare two variances

data:  hear$dxage by hear$mcd
F = 1.1255, num df = 143, denom df = 47, p-value = 0.6523
alternative hypothesis: true ratio of variances is not equal to 1
95 percent confidence interval:
 0.6835121 1.7516013
sample estimates:
ratio of variances
          1.125475
```

FIGURE 7.19 Equality of variance test for age at diagnosis by type of insurance.

As Figure 7.19 displays, since the calculated *p*-value is greater than 0.05 (0.6523), we can conclude that the variance between the groups is not significantly different, and we can proceed with the *t*-test for equal variances by entering the following into the Console:

```
> t.test(hear$dxage~hear$mcd, var.equal=TRUE)
```

Notice that with the **t.test()** function we specified the test for equal variances. Unlike most statistical packages, the default in *R* is for unequal variances, thus you must specify if your preference is the test for equal variances.

As Figure 7.20 shows, this output displays the means for the groups as **describeBy()** function did; however, this time we see the calculated *t*-value ($t = -0.9952$), the degrees of freedom ($df = 190$), and the *p*-value ($p = 0.3209$), which is not significant.

Adding to what we learned earlier, we can conclude that, while babies with Medicaid are diagnosed later than those with private insurance, their actual ages at diagnosis are not statistically different from one another.

To confirm the small difference between types of insurance and age at diagnosis, an effect size can be run using the following syntax:

```
        Two Sample t-test

data:  hear$dxage by hear$mcd
t = -0.9952, df = 190, p-value = 0.3209
alternative hypothesis: true difference in means is not equal to 0
95 percent confidence interval:
 -9.361699  3.083088
sample estimates:
 mean in group no mean in group yes
         12.18465          15.32396
```

FIGURE 7.20 *t*-test of age at diagnosis by insurance type.

```
>cohen.d(hear$dxage~as.factor(hear$mcd),na.rm=T)
Cohen's d

d estimate: -0.1658625 (negligible)
95 percent confidence interval:
       inf         sup
-0.4967733  0.1650484
```

The effect size produced by the command is –0.1658625, which indicates a negligible degree of difference in age between the on-time-for-diagnosis and the late-for-diagnosis groups. The degree of change can be expressed as a percentage by using the following syntax:

```
>dchange=(pnorm(-0.1658625 )-.5)*100.
```

Typing **dchange** into the Console produces a value of –6.586742, which indicates a very small difference between groups, one of only 6.59%.

We can apply this same type of analysis to the age of babies by laterality of loss by entering the following command into the Console:

```
> describeBy(hear$dxage, hear$hleffect)
```

What we observe in Figure 7.21 is interesting. Babies with bilateral losses are diagnosed about a month later than those with unilateral losses. Note, however, that the standard deviation, which is the square root of the variance, is much higher for the bilateral babies (20.52) compared to the unilateral babies (9.71). In order to choose the correct *t*-test, we first need to look at the equality of the variances by conducting a `var.test()`:

```
group: Bilateral
  vars   n  mean    sd median trimmed  mad min    max  range skew kurtosis   se
1    1 154 13.78 20.52   8.69   10.17 6.45 0.7 208.57 207.87 6.32    52.63 1.65
------------------------------------------------------------------------------
group: Unilateral
  vars  n mean   sd median trimmed  mad  min  max range skew kurtosis   se
1    1 38  9.7 9.71    7.5    7.67 2.74 0.42 47.8 47.38 2.59      6.3 1.58
```

FIGURE 7.21 Mean age at diagnosis by laterality of loss.

```
> var.test(hear$dxage~hear$hleffect)
```

Not surprisingly, as shown in Figure 7.22, the variances of the groups are significantly different, so the *t*-test we conduct will have to account for the unequal variances.

```
        F test to compare two variances

data:  hear$dxage by hear$hleffect
F = 4.4641, num df = 153, denom df = 37, p-value = 1.207e-06
alternative hypothesis: true ratio of variances is not equal to 1
95 percent confidence interval:
 2.563814 7.167428
sample estimates:
ratio of variances
          4.464111
```

FIGURE 7.22 Test of equality of variance for age at diagnosis by laterality of hearing loss.

```
> t.test(hear$dxage~hear$hleffect)

Welch Two Sample t-test
data: hear$dxage by hear$hleffect
t = 1.7859, df = 126.337, p-value = 0.07652
alternative hypothesis: true difference in means is
not equal to 0
95 percent confidence interval:
 -0.4408604  8.5985774
sample estimates:
mean in group Bilateral mean in group Unilateral

                13.776753                 9.697895
```

While there is an observed 4-week difference in diagnosis between infants with unilateral and bilateral loss, our chances of making a Type I error are greater than 0.05, although we are approaching significance ($p = 0.07652$).

Once again, using the following syntax, Cohen's *d* is used to confirm these findings.

```
>cohen.d(hear$dxage~as.factor(hear$hleffect),na.rm=T)
Cohen's d

d estimate: 0.2157444 (small)
95 percent confidence interval:
inf         sup
-0.1440916  0.5755805
```

Here we have an example of a small difference between groups with an effect size of .2157444. The percentage of difference is calculated using the following syntax:

```
>dchange=(pnorm(.2157444)-.5)*100
```

Typing **dchange** in the Console displays the percentage of 8.540651, which confirms that a 4-week difference in diagnosis age between bilateral and unilateral is small.

The practical implications for these results could result in a recommendation for administrators running the Hearing and Speech Center. For instance, since we have observed that babies with bilateral loss are diagnosed later than those with unilateral losses, the Center may want to call parents whose babies present with bilateral loss when they are approximately 2 months old to encourage them to return to the Center for diagnostic testing and/or to remind them of existing appointments. This may have an impact on the age at which babies presenting with bilateral loss are actually diagnosed.

What Factors Are Related to Different Statuses on Treatment Times?

The final research question is related to treatment status. To begin, it would be helpful to learn about the various statuses related to treatment and the numbers and percentages of babies falling into each category. Enter the following into the Console:

```
> treat<-table(hear$tx)
> treat
```

```
          on time              Late did not follow-up
               75                32                 85
```

We see that, unlike rescreen and diagnosis, there are three categories for treatment. Seventy-five were treated *on time*, 32 were treated *late*, and 85 *did not follow up* at all. To view these as proportions, enter the following into the Console:

```
>prop.table(treat)
```

```
          on time              Late did not follow-up
        0.3906250         0.1666667          0.4427083
```

These results are alarming to the Hearing and Speech Center, as 44% of babies needing treatment did not follow up at all. Thirty-nine percent were treated on time, and 17% were late to be treated. Both the late-to-treat and the did-not-follow-up groups need intervention, which constitutes about three out of five babies requiring treatment at the Hearing and Speech Center.

Because late or no follow-up is such a serious problem, it would make sense to cast a wide net in looking at this problem, and we may want to consider all of the following variables to determine which are related to being late or not following up with treatment:

- Insurance type
- Diagnosis status
- Severity of hearing loss
- Laterality of hearing loss.

As we move through this analysis, we will do it as we did when we were looking at rescreen status and diagnosis status.

Insurance Type

To see if there are significant differences between the groups based upon insurance status, we will create a table and then do a chi-square test, since the table we create is a 3 × 2 table: *mcd* has two categories while *tx* has three.

To accomplish this, we can use the **CrossTable()** function, but instead of selecting the **fisher** option, we will specify **chisq**. Enter the following into the Console:

```
>CrossTable(hear$tx, hear$mcd,prop.t=TRUE, chisq=TRUE)
```

As displayed in Figure 7.23, the largest group of babies had private insurance (*mcd* = *no*) and were treated on time (n = 62), which is 32.3% of the sample (see the bottom value in the *no/on time* cell). There is, however, another large group that also had private insurance but did not follow up at all (n = 59, or 30.7% of the sample).

As the *p*-value for the chi-square is above 0.05 ($p = 0.14$), we can conclude that there are no differences between the three treatment groups based upon insurance type.

Diagnosis Status

We have previously seen that late rescreening is related to late diagnosis. We are now hypothesizing that late diagnosis is related to late treatment. Enter the following into the Console:

```
>CrossTable(hear$tx, hear$dx,prop.t=TRUE, chisq=TRUE)
```

Since there is a significant difference in the groups (Figure 7.24) based upon diagnosis status ($p = 0.009$), we should take a close look at where these differences lie.

We can clearly see that the largest group was both diagnosed on time and followed up on time (n = 63, or 32.8% of the sample); however, the next largest group was diagnosed on time, but did not follow up at all (n = 56, or 29.2% of the sample). Interestingly, most of the infants who were diagnosed late either did not follow up

```
   Cell Contents
|-------------------------|
|                       N |
| Chi-square contribution |
|           N / Row Total |
|           N / Col Total |
|         N / Table Total |
|-------------------------|


Total Observations in Table:  192


                  | hear$mcd
         hear$tx  |        no  |       yes  | Row Total  |
------------------|------------|------------|------------|
         on time  |        62  |        13  |        75  |
                  |     0.588  |     1.763  |            |
                  |     0.827  |     0.173  |     0.391  |
                  |     0.431  |     0.271  |            |
                  |     0.323  |     0.068  |            |
------------------|------------|------------|------------|
            Late  |        23  |         9  |        32  |
                  |     0.042  |     0.125  |            |
                  |     0.719  |     0.281  |     0.167  |
                  |     0.160  |     0.188  |            |
                  |     0.120  |     0.047  |            |
------------------|------------|------------|------------|
did not follow-up |        59  |        26  |        85  |
                  |     0.354  |     1.062  |            |
                  |     0.694  |     0.306  |     0.443  |
                  |     0.410  |     0.542  |            |
                  |     0.307  |     0.135  |            |
------------------|------------|------------|------------|
    Column Total  |       144  |        48  |       192  |
                  |     0.750  |     0.250  |            |
------------------|------------|------------|------------|


Statistics for All Table Factors


Pearson's Chi-squared test
------------------------------------------------------------
Chi^2 =  3.933464     d.f. =  2     p =  0.1399133
```

FIGURE 7.23 Diagnosis by insurance type.

at all (n = 29, or 15.1% of the sample) or were late to follow up (n = 13, or 6.8% of the sample).

Of all the babies diagnosed on time, 45.7% were treated on time, 13.8% were treated late, and 40.6% did not follow up at all. Of all the babies diagnosed late,

```
   Cell Contents
|-------------------------|
|                       N |
| Chi-square contribution |
|           N / Row Total |
|           N / Col Total |
|         N / Table Total |
|-------------------------|


Total Observations in Table:  192


                  | hear$dx
          hear$tx |   On time |      late | Row Total |
------------------|-----------|-----------|-----------|
          on time |        63 |        12 |        75 |
                  |     1.534 |     3.920 |           |
                  |     0.840 |     0.160 |     0.391 |
                  |     0.457 |     0.222 |           |
                  |     0.328 |     0.062 |           |
------------------|-----------|-----------|-----------|
             Late |        19 |        13 |        32 |
                  |     0.696 |     1.778 |           |
                  |     0.594 |     0.406 |     0.167 |
                  |     0.138 |     0.241 |           |
                  |     0.099 |     0.068 |           |
------------------|-----------|-----------|-----------|
did not follow-up |        56 |        29 |        85 |
                  |     0.425 |     1.085 |           |
                  |     0.659 |     0.341 |     0.443 |
                  |     0.406 |     0.537 |           |
                  |     0.292 |     0.151 |           |
------------------|-----------|-----------|-----------|
     Column Total |       138 |        54 |       192 |
                  |     0.719 |     0.281 |           |
------------------|-----------|-----------|-----------|


Statistics for All Table Factors


Pearson's Chi-squared test
------------------------------------------------------------
Chi^2 =  9.437954     d.f. =  2     p =  0.008924304
```

FIGURE 7.24 Diagnosis status by treatment status.

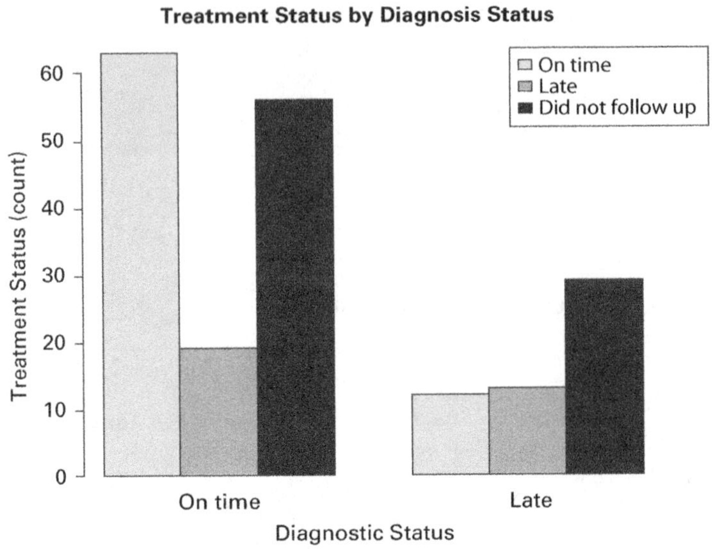

FIGURE 7.25 Treatment status by diagnosis status.

22.2% were treated on time, 24.1% were treated late, and 53.7% did not follow up at all. Therefore, we can conclude that while *all* babies who go through the diagnosis process are at risk for not following up, those who were diagnosed late were most likely to be lost to follow-up.

Graphing this could be helpful, but first we will need to create a table. Enter the following in the Console to create the bar graph in Figure 7.25.

```
> diag<-table(hear$tx, hear$dx)
> diag
                         On time late
  on time                     63   12
  Late                        19   13
  did not follow-up           56   29

> barplot(diag, col=c("lightgray", "darkgray",
"black"), legend=rownames(diag), ylab="Treatment
status (count)", xlab="Diagnostic Status",
main="Treatment Status By Diagnosis Status",
beside=T)
```

Here, it is easy to see that for both diagnosis groups, loss to follow-up is a large problem.

Severity of Hearing Loss

Here we are hypothesizing that those babies with more severe losses may have different treatment patterns from those with less severe losses.

Begin this analysis by entering the following into the Console:

```
> CrossTable(hear$tx, hear$hlsev,prop.t=TRUE,
chisq=TRUE)
```

By simply examining the table in Figure 7.26, we notice that for each treatment category, there are nearly equal numbers of babies with mild and severe hearing losses. It does not look likely that there will be significant differences based upon severity of the loss. Not surprisingly, the chances of making a Type I error are very high, at 79.6%, and we cannot reject the null hypothesis that there is no differences in treatment status based upon severity of the loss.

Laterality of Hearing Loss

Recall that previously we noted statistically significant differences in diagnosis status based upon whether a baby had a unilateral or bilateral loss. A similar hypothesis can be tested with regard to treatment status.

```
> CrossTable(hear$tx, hear$hleffect,prop.t=TRUE,
chisq=TRUE)
```

Here, as shown in Figure 7.27, we see fairly dramatic differences just looking at the counts of the babies in each group. There were far more babies with bilateral losses needing treatment than unilateral losses. Note that only one baby with unilateral loss was treated on time compared to the largest overall group of 74 babies with bilateral losses who were treated on time. Note also that the largest group of unilateral losses was lost to follow-up.

Note that the *p*-value for the chi-square is so low that it is written in scientific notation. When the scientific notation is turned off, you can observe a calculated p-value of 0.00000005269, which is far less than the accepted threshold of 0.05.

As we look at the contingency table more closely, notice that two of the cells (unilateral/on-time and unilateral/late) have very small counts. Under these conditions, the *p*-value for the chi-square may not be reliable. It may be a good idea, then, to run the Fisher's exact, which would provide a more reliable *p*-value. Enter the following in the Console:

```
> fisher.test(hear$tx, hear$hleffect)

    Fisher's Exact Test for Count Data

data: hear$tx and hear$hleffect
p-value = 2.583e-09
alternative hypothesis: two.sided
```

```
   Cell Contents
|-------------------------|
|                       N |
| Chi-square contribution |
|           N / Row Total |
|           N / Col Total |
|         N / Table Total |
|-------------------------|


Total Observations in Table:  192


                  | hear$hlsev
          hear$tx |      Mild |    Severe | Row Total |
------------------|-----------|-----------|-----------|
          on time |        34 |        41 |        75 |
                  |     0.104 |     0.096 |           |
                  |     0.453 |     0.547 |     0.391 |
                  |     0.370 |     0.410 |           |
                  |     0.177 |     0.214 |           |
------------------|-----------|-----------|-----------|
             Late |        15 |        17 |        32 |
                  |     0.007 |     0.007 |           |
                  |     0.469 |     0.531 |     0.167 |
                  |     0.163 |     0.170 |           |
                  |     0.078 |     0.089 |           |
------------------|-----------|-----------|-----------|
did not follow-up |        43 |        42 |        85 |
                  |     0.127 |     0.116 |           |
                  |     0.506 |     0.494 |     0.443 |
                  |     0.467 |     0.420 |           |
                  |     0.224 |     0.219 |           |
------------------|-----------|-----------|-----------|
     Column Total |        92 |       100 |       192 |
                  |     0.479 |     0.521 |           |
------------------|-----------|-----------|-----------|


Statistics for All Table Factors


Pearson's Chi-squared test
------------------------------------------------------------
Chi^2 =  0.4575591     d.f. =  2     p =  0.7955039
```

FIGURE 7.26 Table of treatment status by severity.

The output here confirms what we saw previously. We now have more assurance that the differences we observe are not unduly influenced by the small cell sizes we observed. We can accept the hypothesis that there is a relationship between treatment status and laterality of loss.

```
   Cell Contents
|-------------------------|
|                       N |
| Chi-square contribution |
|           N / Row Total |
|           N / Col Total |
|         N / Table Total |
|-------------------------|


Total Observations in Table:  192


                  | hear$hleffect
          hear$tx |  Bilateral | Unilateral |  Row Total |
------------------|------------|------------|------------|
          on time |         74 |          1 |         75 |
                  |      3.186 |     12.911 |            |
                  |      0.987 |      0.013 |      0.391 |
                  |      0.481 |      0.026 |            |
                  |      0.385 |      0.005 |            |
------------------|------------|------------|------------|
             Late |         27 |          5 |         32 |
                  |      0.069 |      0.281 |            |
                  |      0.844 |      0.156 |      0.167 |
                  |      0.175 |      0.132 |            |
                  |      0.141 |      0.026 |            |
------------------|------------|------------|------------|
did not follow-up |         53 |         32 |         85 |
                  |      3.379 |     13.692 |            |
                  |      0.624 |      0.376 |      0.443 |
                  |      0.344 |      0.842 |            |
                  |      0.276 |      0.167 |            |
------------------|------------|------------|------------|
     Column Total |        154 |         38 |        192 |
                  |      0.802 |      0.198 |            |
------------------|------------|------------|------------|


Statistics for All Table Factors


Pearson's Chi-squared test
------------------------------------------------------------
Chi^2 =  33.51782     d.f. =  2     p =  5.268626e-08
```

FIGURE 7.27 Table of treatment status by laterality of loss.

Referring back to the contingency table, produced earlier, we should note where these relationships lie. Of the babies treated on time, over 98% had bilateral losses, and only 1.3% had unilateral losses. Similar yet less dramatic differences are noted in the late-to-treat group (84.4% of babies treated late had bilateral losses, compared to 15.6% of babies with unilateral losses). In terms of being lost to follow-up, 62.4% had bilateral losses and 37.6% had unilateral losses.

To illustrate this most dramatically, we could create a bar chart, as we have done previously, but instead of putting the bars side by side, we could stack them (Figure 7.28). Enter the following in the Console:

```
> lat1<-table(hear$tx, hear$hleffect)
> lat1

                      Bilateral Unilateral
on time                      74          1
Late                         27          5
did not follow-up            53         32

> barplot (lat1, col=c("lightgray", "darkgray",
"black"), legend=rownames(lat1), ylab="count",
xlab="Treatment Status", main="Treatment Status By
Laterality of Loss")
```

It is easy to see that those who were lost to follow-up made up a substantial number of those in each group. Additionally, in the unilateral group, those lost to follow-up were by far the largest group.

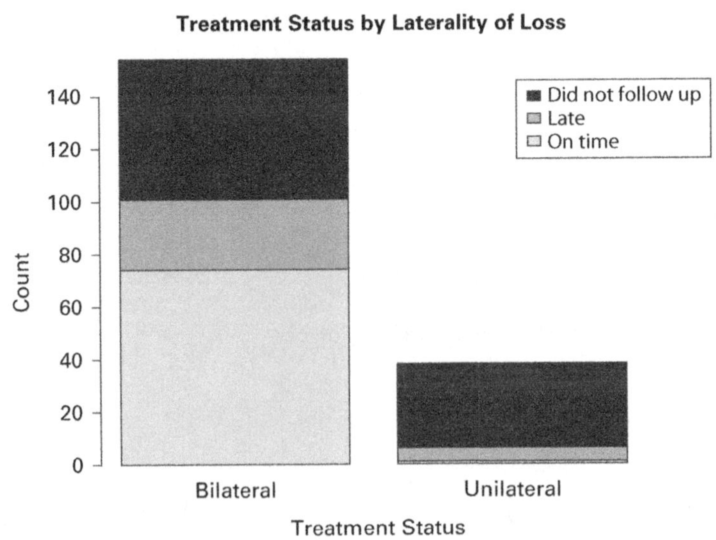

FIGURE 7.28 Treatment status by laterality of loss.

A Little More Analysis

In the chi-square analysis, we found that both diagnosis status and laterality of loss were significantly related to treatment status. It could be helpful to get additional information that might be useful in making recommendations to the Hearing and Speech Center.

We can look for significant differences between the groups based upon the ages of the babies at treatment; that is, are the ages for the babies in each group different from one another? Since there are three categories, a *t*-test is inappropriate and we need to use a one-way analysis of variance (ANOVA) as described in Table 7.2. Enter the following in the Console:

```
> a1<-aov(hear$txage~hear$tx)
```

The above function creates a vector holding the values for the ANOVA. The numeric variable is entered first and the factor variable is entered after the tilde (~). To view the results of the ANOVA, enter the following:

```
> summary(a1)
             Df Sum Sq Mean Sq F value                Pr(>F)
hear$tx       2  62794   31397   45.84 0.00000000000000531 ***
Residuals   104  71229     685
---
Signif. codes:  0 '***' 0.001 '**' 0.01 '*' 0.05 '.' 0.1 ' ' 1
85 observations deleted due to missingness
```

As we see, these findings are statistically significant, as noted in Pr(> F) being less than 0.05. Note also that *R* places three asterisks next to this value, noting that the significance level is very close to zero, as shown in the key to the significance codes, listed under the output.

Now we know that there are significant differences between the groups, but there are actually three combinations of groups, and we are not sure where these differences actually lie. The three combinations are the following:

- *On time* compared to *late*
- *On time* compared to *did not follow up*
- *Late* compared to *did not follow up.*

In order to see where the differences are, we can follow the ANOVA with a Tukey *post hoc* analysis. To do this, enter the following in the Console:

```
> TukeyHSD(a1)
```

```
  Tukey multiple comparisons of means
      95% family-wise confidence level

Fit: aov(formula = hear$txage ~ hear$tx)

$`hear$tx`
                                   diff       lwr      upr     p adj
Late-on time                 51.5759722  38.35543 64.79651  0.0000000
did not follow-up-on time 52.2655556  15.59837 88.93274  0.0028277
did not follow-up-Late      0.6895833 -36.88310 38.26227  0.9989506
```

The output here allows you to view the difference in the means between each of the groups and the level of significance for each pair. For example, the mean difference between the *late* group and the *on time* group was 51.58, and that difference is significant ($p = 0.000$). Similar differences are noted between the *did not follow up* group with those *on time*. Notice, however, the very small and nonsignificant difference between those who *did not follow up* and those who were *late* to treatment. To actually view those means, we can use the **describeBy()** function in the *psych* package.

```
> describeBy(hear$txage, hear$tx)
```

As displayed in Figure 7.29, the average age of babies treated on time was 17.26 weeks (sd = 6.38); the average age of babies treated late is 68.83 weeks (sd = 46.94 weeks), and the average age for babies not receiving follow up treatment is 69.52 weeks (sd = 4.35). Note, however, that for the *did not follow up* group, there are only three babies! That is because the rest of the data are missing for this group, probably because of the lack of follow-up.

Because of the similarities of the ages of the babies in the late and did not follow up treatment groups, we might want to combine them for future analysis. That is, we could then compare babies with problematic treatment statuses to those without. We could do this by generating a new variable, *probtx*, that reduces the three categories

```
group: on time
  vars  n  mean   sd median trimmed  mad min   max range  skew kurtosis   se
1    1 72 17.26 6.38  18.05    17.6 7.44 3.1 26.07 22.97 -0.35    -0.84 0.75
------------------------------------------------------------------------
group: Late
  vars  n  mean    sd median trimmed   mad   min    max  range skew kurtosis  se
1    1 32 68.83 46.94  52.14   60.06 20.82 30.42 247.68 217.26 2.09     4.45 8.3
------------------------------------------------------------------------
group: did not follow-up
  vars n  mean   sd median trimmed  mad   min   max range skew kurtosis   se
1    1 3 69.52 4.35  69.52   69.52 6.43 65.18 73.87  8.69    0    -2.33 2.51
```

FIGURE 7.29 Treatment status by treatment age.

in the *tx* variable to two. Perhaps the easiest way to do this in *R* is by using the **ifelse()** function. Enter the following in the Console:

```
> hear$probtx<-ifelse(hear$tx=="on time",
c("On time"), c("Late/Lost"))
```

In dissecting this statement, we can see that we are instructing *R* as follows:

- Create a vector/variable called *probtx* in the data frame called *hear*. This is the current data frame, so this variable will be appended to the end of the variables list.
- If the value of *tx* is "on time," assign *probtx* the value "On time."
- Otherwise assign *probtx* the value of "Late/Lost."

Note that there are two equal signs following *hear$tx*. This tells *R* to assign a value of "On time" if, and only if, the value for *tx* is EXACTLY "on time." Notice, also, that the value assigned to the *if* portion of the **ifelse()** is listed immediately after the conditions under which the value is assigned, and the value for the *else* portion of the function is listed last.

Now, it might make more sense to use a *t*-test to compare the means of the babies in the *On time* group to those in the *Late/Lost* group. Begin by testing for equality of variances:

```
> var.test(hear$txage~hear$probtx)

F test to compare two variances

data: hear$txage by hear$probtx
F = 49.4175, num df = 34, denom df = 71, p-value <
0.00000000000000022
alternative hypothesis: true ratio of variances is
not equal to 1
95 percent confidence interval:
 28.35535 91.53804
sample estimates:
ratio of variances
          49.41753
```

Since the variances between these groups is significantly different, we will want to use a *t*-test for unequal variances:

```
> t.test(hear$txage~hear$probtx)
```

```
    Welch Two Sample t-test

data: hear$txage by hear$probtx
t = 6.7803, df = 34.671, p-value = 0.00000007711
alternative hypothesis: true difference in means is
not equal to 0
95 percent confidence interval:
 36.16962 67.10053
sample estimates:
mean in group Late/Lost   mean in group On time
               68.89286                17.25778
```

The output here shows that the mean age of babies in the *Late/Lost* group was 68.89 weeks, compared to 17.26 weeks for babies in the *On time* group, and those differences, as noted by the low *p*-value, are statistically significant.

As in the previous example, a Cohen's *d* is calculated to quantify how large a difference there is in *txage* between the two independent groups (late for follow-up and on time for follow-up).

```
cohen.d(hear$txage~as.factor(hear$probtx),na.rm=T)
Cohen's d

d estimate: 1.982477 (large)
95 percent confidence interval:
     inf      sup
1.487405 2.477549
```

The findings indicate a large difference between groups with an effect size of 1.982477. The 95% confidence interval ranges between 1.48705 and 2.477549. Typing the following syntax calculates the percentage of change.

```
>dchange=(pnorm(1.982477)-.5)*100
```

Typing **dchange** into the Console displays the result of 47.62871, which indicates a large degree of difference between groups at the age they began treatment.

It may also be interesting to do a similar analysis based on laterality of loss. Since many more babies with unilateral losses are late or lost to follow-up, it would be reasonable to test whether babies with unilateral losses and bilateral losses are treated at different ages. Again, this analysis should begin with a test to check for equality of variances:

```
>var.test(hear$txage~hear$hleffect)
```

```
F test to compare two variances

data: hear$txage by hear$hleffect
F = 0.3231, num df = 100, denom df = 5,
p-value = 0.02442
alternative hypothesis: true ratio of variances is
not equal to 1
95 percent confidence interval:
 0.05313896 0.87105572
sample estimates:
ratio of variances
         0.3230848
```

This output shows that the variances are significantly different ($p = 0.02442$), so it is most appropriate to use a t-test for unequal variances.

```
> t.test(hear$txage~hear$hleffect)

   Welch Two Sample t-test
data: hear$txage by hear$hleffect
t = -1.9272, df = 5.194, p-value = 0.1097
alternative hypothesis: true difference in means is
not equal to 0
95 percent confidence interval:
 -105.46423   14.50948
sample estimates:
 mean in group Bilateral mean in group Unilateral
               31.59762                 77.07500
```

As shown in Figure 7.30, the mean age of babies at treatment with bilateral losses is 31.6 weeks, compared to 77.1 weeks for babies with unilateral losses; however, with a *p*-value of 0.1097, this is not considered statistically significant. To gather more information, it would be helpful to use the **describeBy()** function.

```
group: Bilateral
  vars   n mean    sd median trimmed   mad min    max  range skew kurtosis   se
1    1 101 31.6 32.54  21.73   25.68 12.88 3.1 247.68 244.58 3.71    18.83 3.24
------------------------------------------------------------------
group: Unilateral
  vars n  mean    sd median trimmed   mad   min    max range skew kurtosis    se
1    1 6 77.08 57.26   63.8   77.08 62.19 13.14 156.44 143.3 0.28    -1.88 23.37
```

FIGURE 7.30 Mean treatment age by laterality.

```
> describeBy(hear$txage, hear$hleffect)
```

With only six babies in the unilateral category (there are more, but the treatment age data for those babies are missing) and a lot of variation for both the bilateral and unilateral groups, it would have been difficult to achieve statistical significance.

Once again, the following syntax calculates a Cohen's *d* to quantify how large a difference there is in *txage* between the two independent groups of infants with bilateral and unilateral hearing loss:

```
>cohen.d(hear$txage~as.factor(hear$hleffect),na.rm=T)
Cohen's d

d estimate: -1.332481 (large)
95 percent confidence interval:
        inf          sup
-2.1934580 -0.4715034
```

As in the previous example, these findings indicate a large difference between groups, with an effect size of –1.332481. The 95% confidence interval ranges between –2.1934580 and –0.4715034. Typing the following syntax calculates the percentage of change:

```
dchange=(pnorm(-1.332481)-.5)*100
```

Typing **dchange** into the Console displays the result of 47.62871, which indicates a large degree of difference between groups.

Although there was no statistically significant difference between the groups, the large effect size shows that there was a large difference in *txage* between them. Effect size is not a measure of significance; instead, it is a way to quantify the degree of difference between groups. Even though there are only six infants with unilateral hearing loss, the average difference in the age of treatment differs greatly from those infants with bilateral hearing loss.

SUMMARY

In our overall analysis, we noted different factors that were related to rescreen status, diagnosis status, and treatment status. At rescreen, only nursery type was a significant predictor of late rescreening. At diagnosis, being late for rescreen, insurance type, and laterality of loss were all significant predictors of being diagnosed late. Finally, being late for diagnosis and laterality of losses were significant predictors of being late for treatment or lost to follow-up.

This provides some interesting information that could be helpful to the Hearing and Speech Center. For example, we now understand that babies who are late for rescreening are more likely to be late for diagnosis, which, in turn, makes these babies more likely to be treated late. Additionally, unilateral losses were problematic at both diagnosis and treatment. This, then, provides support for developing creative interventions at all points of contact with patients' families. It might be helpful, for instance, to provide opportunities to rescreen babies, particularly those who had been in the NICU, as soon as possible. Perhaps additional rescreening could be done in the hospital prior to discharge or in a primary care physician's office, with the office reporting findings to the Hearing and Speech Center. Additional intervention is needed for babies who have unilateral losses, and parent education may be helpful.

Whatever the Hearing and Speech Center ultimately decides to do to address these issues, more information is needed. As interventions are developed, data can continue to be collected for those who have received these additional interventions and those who have not. Once sufficient data for those receiving the interventions have been collected, more evaluation can be conducted to determine if these are having the desired effect of reducing late diagnosis and treatment or being completely lost to treatment altogether.

ANOTHER FORM OF THE *t*-TEST

Throughout this chapter we have talked about independent sample *t*-tests. In these cases, as described above, we were comparing the means of two separate groups across a given measure. Individuals in the sample could either belong to one group or the other, but not both.

In some cases, however, you may be interested in comparing measures within a given observation. For example, you may measure depression using the Beck Depression Inventory (BDI) in a sample of clients at intake and then introduce an intervention such as cognitive behavioral therapy. Because you want to evaluate the effectiveness of your program, you measure client depression upon completion of the intervention. In a situation like this, you may be most interested in seeing if individual scores on the BDI change over time. In this case, you would have to pair the individual BDI scores at intake (pre-test) and after the intervention is complete (post-test). This method of the t-test is called a *paired samples t-test.*

As an example, we will consider an evaluation of an intervention done to help address symptoms of depression in women with lupus. Open the data set entitled *lupus*. Variables included in this data set are listed in Table 7.3.

Use the **describe()** function in the *psych* package to get descriptive statistics for both *beck1* and *beck2*:

```
> describe(lupus$beck1)

>describe(lupus$beck2)
```

TABLE 7.3 Lupus Client Data

Variable	Description	Indicators	Variable Type
id	Client id number	This is a unique identifier for each patient.	Numeric
gender	Gender of the client	Female or male	Factor
age	Age of the client	< 21, 21–35, 36–45, 40–60, 61+	Factor
marital	Marital status of client	Single, married, with partner, living separate, divorced, widowed	Factor
ethnicity	Race/ethnicity of client	Asian, African American, Hispanic, white, American Indian, other	Factor
children	Number of dependent children in the household	Actual number reported by client	Factor
educ	Highest level of education of client	HS, some college, college grad, advanced degree	Factor
employ	Employment status of client	Part-time, full-time, unemployed, disability	Factor
insure	Type of insurance held by client	Medicaid, Medicare, private insurance, no insurance	Factor
dxage	Age at which client was diagnosed with lupus	Age reported by client	Numeric
admit	Number of hospital admissions in the previous year	Actual number reported by client	Numeric
beck1	Score on BDI at intake	Actual BDI score	Numeric
beck2	Score on BDI after group CBT	Actual BDI score	Numeric

As seen in Figures 7.31 and 7.32, the output in the Console indicates that there are 76 observations for each variable, and the mean level of depression at intake ranges from zero to 51. The mean score on the BDI at intake is 13.51 (sd = 9.45). After the intervention, the range of scores is reduced to between 2 and 20. The mean also drops to 9.8 (sd = 5.24).

To describe this visually, we can create side-by-side boxplots, which are displayed in Figure 7.33.

```
  vars  n  mean   sd median trimmed  mad min max range skew kurtosis   se
1    1 76 13.51 9.45   11.5   12.58 9.64   0  51    51 1.14     1.73 1.08
```

FIGURE 7.31 Description of *beck1*.

```
  vars  n mean   sd median trimmed  mad min max range skew kurtosis  se
1    1 76  9.8 5.24    8.5    9.53 5.19   2  20    18 0.47    -0.96 0.6
```

FIGURE 7.32 Description of *beck2*.

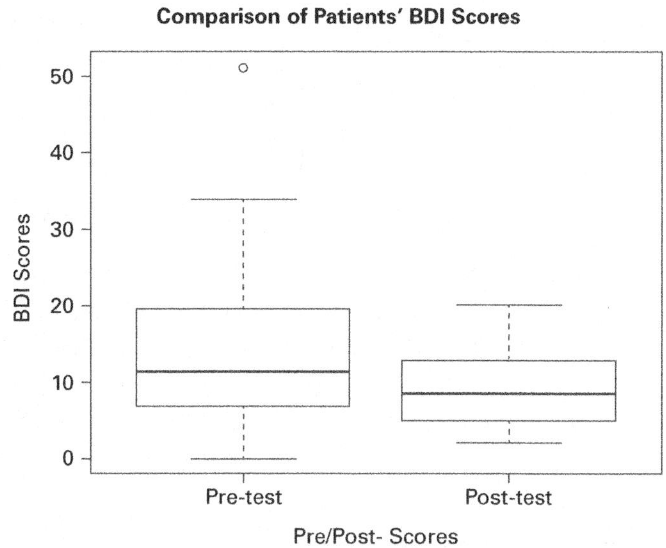

FIGURE 7.33 Boxplot example.

```
> boxplot(lupus$beck1, lupus$beck2, ylab="BDI
Scores", xlab="Pre-/Post- Scores", main="Comparison
of Patients' BDI Scores", names=c("Pre-test",
"Post-test"))
```

In this command, notice that we placed the variables in the order in which we want them to appear in the final boxplot. Also notice that we used the **names** option because we wanted to actually label each boxplot separately. The output provides a visual description showing the reduced range in BDI scores after the intervention and a slight drop in median scores from the baselines.

To test for Type I error in this case, it would be most appropriate to do a paired samples *t*-test since we will be comparing the pre-intervention BDI scores for each individual with their post-intervention BDI scores.

In *R*, the paired sample t-test is invoked as an option on the **t.test()** function introduced earlier. Additionally, since there is no grouping variable, the variables listed are separated by a comma instead of a tilde. Enter the following in the Console:

```
> t.test(lupus$beck1, lupus$beck2, paired=TRUE)
```

```
    Paired t-test


data:  lupus$beck1 and lupus$beck2
t = 4.0691, df = 75, p-value = 0.0001156
```

```
alternative hypothesis: true difference in means is
not equal to 0
95 percent confidence interval:
 1.893980 5.527073
sample estimates:
mean of the differences
               3.710526
```

The output displayed in the Console does not show the means for *beck1* and *beck2*, but it does display the difference in the means (3.710526). These differences are statistically significant, as the calculated *p*-value is 0.0001156. It appears as if there was a significant reduction in BDI scores of clients after the intervention.

A MORE DETAILED DISCUSSION ON COHEN'S *d*

In the example above, there were statistically significant differences between intake and post-intervention in terms of individuals' scores on the BDI, but in program evaluation we may want to expand our thinking to determine if the differences that are observed are having a qualitative effect on clients. After all, does a 3.7-point reduction in BDI score actually make a difference in clients' lives? One way to quantify this is through a descriptive statistic called *effect size*. Effect size calculations are most concerned with how much change is observed.

To compute and interpret Cohen's *d*, a common measure of effect size, in *R* you will need to install and require the *effsize* package available on CRAN. Once this is done, enter the following in the Console:

```
> cohen.d(lupus$beck1, lupus$beck2, na.rm=T)
```

In this function, you are instructing *R* to calculate effect size based upon paired samples. The output for this is shown in the Console:

```
Cohen's d

d estimate: 0.4855715 (small)
95 percent confidence interval:
      inf       sup
0.1581248 0.8130183
```

Notice that the syntax is different from the examples discussed in the previous section. In this example, independent groups are not being compared. Instead, the degree of change before and after an intervention is being compared.

In this case, the calculated value for Cohen's *d* is 0.4855715. The 95% confidence intervals indicate that it is 95% likely that the true effect size is between 0.1581248 and 0.8130183.

As mentioned, the interpretation of Cohen's *d* is based upon z-scores. The score then represents the degree of average improvement in the post-intervention period over the pre-intervention period. An effect size of 0.4855715 denotes less than one standard deviation improvement in the post-intervention scores over the pre-intervention scores. An effect size of 0 shows no improvement, while an effect size of 1 indicates a 34. 13% increase in improvement in the post-intervention phase over the pre-intervention phase (Bloom et al., 2009). The degree of change can be expressed as a percentage by using the following syntax:

```
>dchange=(pnorm(.4855715)-.5)*100
```

Typing **dchange** in the Console yields a percentage of 18.63645. This indicates an 18.6% reduction in the Beck's BDI. The **pnorm()** function provides the area under the normal curve for a given value.

NON-PARAMETRIC TESTS OF TYPE I ERROR

As previously stated, in most cases the parametric tests discussed throughout this chapter will be appropriate for bivariate analysis; however, in cases of small data sets in which you can not assume normality, it may be necessary to conduct non-parametric tests.

In cases where it would have been appropriate to do a paired sample *t*-test, but where normality cannot be assumed, a Wilcoxson Signed Rank Test can be completed to test for Type I error. Using the example of looking at change in BDI scores illustrated above, we can do this test by entering the following in the Console:

```
>wilcox.test(lupus$beck1, lupus$beck2, paired=TRUE)

    Wilcoxon signed rank test with continuity
correction

data:  lupus$beck1 and lupus$beck2
V = 2056.5, p-value = 0.0001026
alternative hypothesis: true location shift is not
equal to 0
```

Notice that instead of a calculated *t* value, this test computes *V*. Using this non-parametric test, we still find significant differences for the sample after the introduction of the intervention ($p = 0.0001026$).

Earlier in the chapter, we examined the relationship between diagnosis status of newborns, which has only two categories, and age at rescreen, with a *t*-test. If we were assuming non-normality, we could conduct a Mann-Whitney U Test. If the *newborn hearing.rdata* file is not open, you will need to open it in order to work through this example. Then, enter the following in the Console:

```
>wilcox.test(hear$age~hear$dx)

Wilcoxon rank sum test with continuity correction

data: hear$age by hear$dx
W = 174.5, p-value = 0.000009029
alternative hypothesis: true location shift is not
equal to 0
```

The *p*-value (0.000009029) in this case shows statistical differences between the diagnosis groups based upon age at rescreen.

Note that the output for this version of the **wilcox.test()** function is slightly different with the paired option invoked; the calculated test statistic is *W* in this situation.

In some cases, you may want to compare means across groups, but the factor variable will have more than two categories. As an example, we can test the hypothesis that there is a relationship between age at rescreen and treatment status (with three categories: on time, late, and lost to follow-up). Enter the following in the Console:

```
>kruskal.test(hear$age~hear$tx)

    Kruskal-Wallis rank sum test

data: hear$age by hear$tx
Kruskal-Wallis chi-squared = 0.1815, df = 2,
p-value = 0.9132
```

In this case, we note no differences between the ages by treatment group as the calculated *p*-value is greater than 0.05 ($p = 0.9132$).

We also examined the relationship between age at rescreen and age at diagnosis using the *Hmisc* command **rcorr()** with two numeric variables. If we wanted to conduct a non-parametric correlation, we could use Spearman's rho. Using the same **rcorr()** function, we could add an option that specifies this type of correlation. Enter the following in the Console:

```
>rcorr(hear$age, hear$dxage, type=c("spearman"))
```

```
      x    y
x 1.00 0.62
y 0.62 1.00

n
     x   y
x 192   69
y  69 192

P
   x  y
x       0
y  0
```

Note that the command is the same as for calculating Pearson's *r* with the addition of the option **type=c("spearman")**. The output that you see in the Console is formatted the same as for Pearson's *r* and should be interpreted in the same way.

MCNEMAR'S TEST

There is often a need to test change in a dichotomous variable (yes/no) before and after an intervention. A standard chi-square cannot be used because it assumes that the groups are independent. Obviously, this is not the case when you are testing clients' pre- and post-intervention scores. The McNemar test can be used in this type of situation. Once again, it can only be used to compare two dichotomous variables.

An Example

An outpatient clinic treating patients diagnosed with lupus develops an intervention to help increase medication compliance. Twenty clients are selected to receive daily texts from the clinic reminding them to take their medication. Prior to the intervention, the patients are asked a simple yes/no question, "Are you taking your medication on a daily basis?" They are asked the same question 6 weeks later. The question to test is as follows: Is the patient's rate of daily compliance (answering yes to the question) higher after the intervention?

In *RStudio*, open the data set titled *rxcomply.RData*. Note that there are two variables (*pre* and *post*) and 20 observations. Each patient has a pre- and post- answer to the question "Are you taking your medication on a daily basis?" The *yes* responses were coded as 1 and *no* as 0.

The easiest way to perform the McNemar test is to create a table vector using the following syntax:

```
t<-table(rxcomply$pre,rxcomply$post)
```

It is easier to view the table using the **CrossTable()** function in the gmodels package. Load the package and use the following syntax:

```
>CrossTable(rxcomply$pre,rxcomply$post)
```

The results in Figure 7.34 are displayed in the Console.

The results indicate that three patients who answered "no" pre-intervention answered "no" post-intervention. Thirteen patients who answered "no" pre-intervention changed their responses to "yes" during the intervention.

```
   Cell Contents
|-------------------------|
|                       N |
| Chi-square contribution |
|           N / Row Total |
|           N / Col Total |
|         N / Table Total |
|-------------------------|


Total Observations in Table:  20


             | rxcomply$post
rxcomply$pre |         0 |         1 | Row Total |
-------------|-----------|-----------|-----------|
           0 |         3 |        13 |        16 |
             |     0.250 |     0.083 |           |
             |     0.188 |     0.812 |     0.800 |
             |     0.600 |     0.867 |           |
             |     0.150 |     0.650 |           |
-------------|-----------|-----------|-----------|
           1 |         2 |         2 |         4 |
             |     1.000 |     0.333 |           |
             |     0.500 |     0.500 |     0.200 |
             |     0.400 |     0.133 |           |
             |     0.100 |     0.100 |           |
-------------|-----------|-----------|-----------|
Column Total |         5 |        15 |        20 |
             |     0.250 |     0.750 |           |
-------------|-----------|-----------|-----------|
```

FIGURE 7.34 Table comparing Rx compliance pre- and post-intervention.

The next step is to test the hypothesis that the increase in "yes" responses from pre-intervention to post-intervention did not occur by chance. The following syntax will produce a McNemar chi-square:

```
>mcnemar.test(t)
```

The results displayed in the Console are show below.

```
McNemar's Chi-squared test with continuity correction

data: tp
McNemar's chi-squared = 6.6667, df = 1,
p-value = 0.009823
```

The results show a significant increase in the rate of "yes" responses from pre- to post-intervention with a p-value of 0.009823.

Although the McNemar test uses a continuity correction for small sample sizes, the *exact2x2* package has a function that provides an exact form of the test for small sample sizes. Install the package and load it. The syntax is shown below.

```
mcnemar.exact(t)
Exact McNemar test (with central confidence intervals)

data:  t
b = 13, c = 2, p-value = 0.007385
alternative hypothesis: true odds ratio is not
equal to 1
95 percent confidence interval:
  1.47156 59.32850
sample estimates:
odds ratio
       6.5
```

The results of the test are below and confirm the previous findings with a *p*-value of 0.007385.

CONCLUSION

Bivariate analysis, examining the relationship of a predictor variable to an outcome, is a powerful way to uncover potentially valuable information in the evaluation process. This type of inquiry builds upon the univariate analysis conducted in the previous chapter by adding an additional dimension. Similarly, findings from the results of bivariate analyses can be used to build more complex analyses, which will be discussed in the following chapters. For example, when looking at the factors related to treatment status, we found that both diagnosis status and laterality of hearing loss were significant predictors. But what happens if we want to identify a constellation of factors that are predictive of diagnosis status? Significant predictors identified from bivariate analyses can be used to develop multivariate models in which we can examine the influence of a predictor variable while holding others constant.

/// 8 /// MAKING YOUR CASE USING LINEAR REGRESSION WITH *R*

In order to work through the examples in this chapter, you will need to *install* and *load* the following packages:

- *car*
- *aod*

For more information on how to do this, refer to the Packages section in Chapter 3.

INTRODUCTION

In simple terms, regression is a set of statistical methods to predict an outcome variable from one or more explanatory variables. The outcome variable is referred to as a dependent variable (DV), and the explanatory variables are independent variables (IV). Regression allows for the development of the best possible equation to predict the values of a dependent variable from one or more independent variables.

There are a number of situations in which regression can be used to test a research question. For example, a director of social work at an acute care hospital wants to predict the number of days it takes to discharge a patient. The dependent variable would be the length of stay (LOS), measured in days. The independent variables include everything that he can measure that he thinks contributes to length of stay. This could include activities of daily living (ADL), age, gender, and having a spouse.

Another example of this method's use would be to test for the degree of gender gap in income at a large social service agency. The dependent variable could be beginning salary, and the independent variables could include gender, education in years, experience in months, and age in years. Using regression, in this scenario you could acquire an estimate of the gender gap in salaries between male and females of equal education, experience, and age.

SIMPLE REGRESSION

The most basic type of regression would be the prediction of a single dependent variable from a single independent variable. The following equation represents this simple regression model:

$$\hat{Y} = \beta_0 + \beta_1 X_1$$

In this equation

- $\hat{Y}$ is the predicted value for a particular observation
- β_0 is the constant/y-intercept (the predicted value of Y when all independent variables, in this case just one, are zero).
- X_1 is an independent/predictor variable
- β_1 is the slope (the degree of change in *Y* for each unit increase in *X*, the predictor variable).

The objective of regression is to find the best equation that minimizes the difference between what is observed in the data from what is predicted by the model.

The constant and slope need some more explanation, as they are the two coefficients derived from the model. As an example, we can look at salary (Y) predicted from education in years (X). Assume that the constant in this model is $6,000 and the slope is $950. The constant in this example can be interpreted as follows: when education is 0 (i.e., the person has had NO education), the predicted income would be $6,000. The slope can be interpreted in this example as follows: for every one-year increase in education (this is a unit increase), salary increases by $950. The final equation for this model would be:

$$\hat{Y} = 6000 + 950X_1$$

An employee with 12 years of education, then, would have a predicted salary of $17,400, which is ($6,000 + (12 x $950)).

Throughout the rest of this chapter, we will take a look at increasingly complex regression concepts through the use of a case study.

CASE STUDY # 3: SOCIAL WORK SERVICES IN A HOSPITAL

St. Luke's Hospital is a mid-sized medical center located in Freehold, a small city. Hospital administration is concerned, as referenced earlier in this chapter, about patients' length of stay.

While everyone recognizes that there is a need for inpatient hospital stays, administrators would like to ensure timely discharges when patients' acute care needs have been met. Specifically, the administrator has asked you to identify what the main, non-medical factors are that are related to patients' length of stay. The hope is that if the hospital could identify a profile for those most at risk for lengthy hospital stays, social work services could try to intervene with these patients early in their admissions. In this way, safe discharge plans could hopefully be arranged in a timely and expedient manner.

The data you have is located in the file called *hospital1.rdata*, which you created in Chapter 3. If you did not create the file, it can be found at www.ssdanalysis.com, where it can be downloaded from the *Datasets* tab.

In *RStudio* click **File / Open** from the menu bar, and navigate to the folder in which the file was saved. Once the file is open, use the **`names()`** command to list the variables in the data set as displayed below.

```
>names(hospital1)

 [1] "admit"     "gender"    "marital"   "katz1"     "katz2"     "katz3"
 [7] "katz4"     "katz5"     "katz6"     "iad1"      "iad2"      "iad3"
[13] "iad4"      "iad5"      "iad6"      "iad7"      "disdate"   "return30"
[19] "age"       "spouse"    "agecat"    "age80"     "tkatzsum"  "tkatzmean"
[25] "tiadlmean" "los"
```

A table defining the variables in this data set is available in Chapter 3. In the data set we have length of stay in days (*los*) and activities of daily living (*tkatzmean*).

USING `lm()` TO FIT A REGRESSION MODEL

Using simple regression, we can examine how well length of stay can be predicted from activities of daily living. Use the **`lm()`** function by typing the following in the Console and pressing <Return>:

```
>simple<-lm(los~tkatzmean,data=hospital1)
```

In this command, the dependent variable, *los*, is entered first, followed by a tilde (~). The independent variable, *tkatzmean*, follows. Including *hospital$* in front of the variables was unnecessary in this case because the option "**`data=hospital1`**" was included. To see the results of the regression, shown in Figure 8.1, enter the following in the Console:

```
>summary(simple)
```

The coefficients are displayed under the column labeled "Estimate." The intercept/constant is 57.906. Since the Katz ADL cannot be 0 (the range of possible

```
Call:
lm(formula = los ~ tkatzmean, data = hospital1)

Residuals:
    Min      1Q  Median      3Q     Max
-32.529  -7.400  -3.902   5.347  66.600

Coefficients:
            Estimate Std. Error t value Pr(>|t|)
(Intercept)   57.906      5.291   10.94  < 2e-16 ***
tkatzmean    -15.502      1.967   -7.88 4.86e-13 ***
---
Signif. codes:  0 '***' 0.001 '**' 0.01 '*' 0.05 '.' 0.1 ' ' 1

Residual standard error: 15.05 on 159 degrees of freedom
Multiple R-squared:  0.2809,    Adjusted R-squared:  0.2763
F-statistic: 62.09 on 1 and 159 DF,  p-value: 4.861e-13
```

FIGURE 8.1 Summary of model *simple.*

values for the *tkatzmean* goes from 1 to 3), the constant becomes a correction. The second row of the first column is the slope, which is –15.502. The slope indicates that for every one-point increase in ADL, there is a 15.502-day decrease in LOS. The calculated *t*-value is –7.88 and is the value used to determine statistical significance based upon the degrees of freedom. In this case, the slope is statistically significant ($p < 0.001$).

The prediction equation is then: LOS = 57.906 + (–15.502 x ADL).

Output from the **summary()** function provides us with additional information about the regression model. The Multiple R-squared is a measure of the amount of variance that is accounted for by the model. The Multiple R-squared can vary from 0 to 1. A value of 1 would be a perfectly predictive model. In this case, a value of 0.2809 indicates that the model (in this case, inclusion of only the predictor *tkatzmean*) explains 28% of the variance in LOS. The residual standard error of 15.05 is the average amount of the difference in error in predicting LOS from ADL. The F-statistic is a test of the overall model; that is, how likely is it that the collective impact of the independent variables' prediction of the dependent variable occurs by chance? This F-statistic is used to determine the *p*-value for the overall model. In this case, the *p*-value is very low and the overall model is statistically significant. This becomes more important when the model includes more than one independent variable. The R-squared and the residual standard error indicate that there is a large amount of error in this model's predictability.

The 95% confidence interval of the slope can be obtained using the **confint()** function as follows:

```
>confint(simple)

                 2.5 %     97.5 %
(Intercept)  47.45635  68.35606
tkatzmean   -19.38748 -11.61678
```

The confidence interval indicates that it is 95% likely that the true change in LOS for a unit increases in Katz ADL is between –19.38748 and –11.61678 days.

To visualize this, require the *car* package, and enter the following in the Console to create the plot in Figure 8.2.

```
> scatterplot(hospital1$tkatzmean, hospital1$los,
xlab="Katz ADL", ylab="length of stay (days)",
boxplots=F)
```

Each dot represents a patient's ADL score relative to his or her LOS. The line is the regression line, which represents the predicted values from the model. If the R-squared was 1 and the standard error of the residual was 0, all the dots would be on the line and there would be no difference between the observed and predicted values.

The **fitted()** function calculates the predicted values for each observation based on the model. The **residuals()** function is used to calculate the residuals

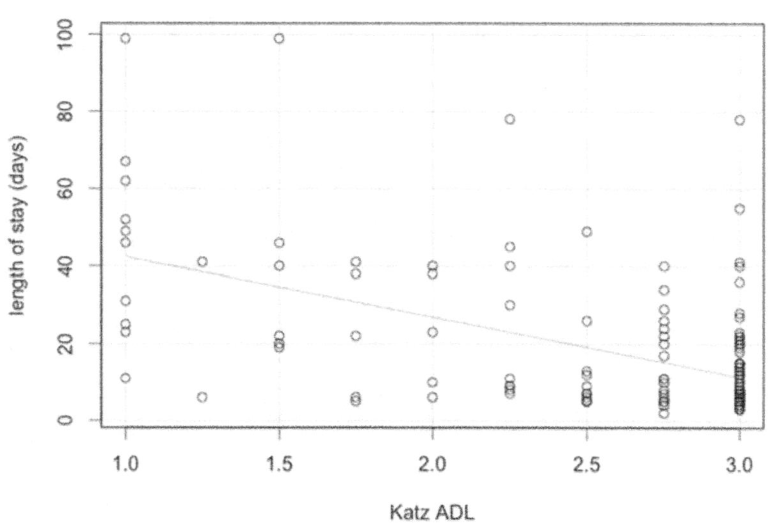

FIGURE 8.2 Scatterplot of Katz ADL by LOS.

(defined as the value for an observation less the value that is predicted by the model). To do this, use the following commands:

```
>pred<-fitted(simple)
>resid<-residuals(simple)
```

Notice that the model vector *simple* is put into the parentheses and two new vectors, *pred* and *resid*, are created. For the purpose of demonstration, create a data frame that includes three variables—the observed LOS, predicted LOS (based upon the regression model), and the residual—with the following command:

```
>simpmodel<-data.frame(hospital1$los,pred,resid)
```

Click on the spreadsheet icon next to the *simpmodel* data frame in the Environment tab. A spreadsheet will appear in the top right pane. Figure 8.3 displays the first 20

simpmodel ×

	hospital1.los	pred	resid
1	15	11.39981	3.6001858
2	7	15.27535	-8.2753466
3	6	11.39981	-5.3998142
4	7	11.39981	-4.3998142
5	8	11.39981	-3.3998142
6	6	30.77748	-24.7774763
7	20	11.39981	8.6001858
8	10	11.39981	-1.3998142
9	6	11.39981	-5.3998142
10	4	11.39981	-7.3998142
11	10	11.39981	-1.3998142
12	20	15.27535	4.7246534
13	41	11.39981	29.6001858
14	22	15.27535	6.7246534
15	3	11.39981	-8.3998142
16	10	11.39981	-1.3998142
17	19	34.65301	-15.6530087
18	40	11.39981	28.6001858
19	5	11.39981	-6.3998142
20	8	11.39981	-3.3998142

FIGURE 8.3 Twenty observations from *simpmodel* dataframe.

observations in this data frame. For observation 8, the observed score in the first column was 10 days and the predicted score based upon the model was 11.39981, which is displayed in the second column. The residual, or the amount of difference between the observed value and the predicated value, was –1.3998142. This is pretty good; it was off by only a little more than a day. In observation 18, on the other hand, the observed value is 40, the predicted value is 11.39981, and the residual is 28.6001858. In this case, the model is off by over 28 days. Recall that the standard error of the residuals was 15 days, indicating that on average the residuals vary from case to case by 15 days.

When conducting regression analysis, there are certain statistical assumptions that must be met, otherwise the findings are suspect. They are as follows: normality, independence, linearity, and homoscedasticity. Normality means that the dependent variable is normally distributed around the independent variables. Independence suggests that observations (e.g., cases) are independent of each other. Linearity is met when there is a linear relationship between the independent and the dependent variable. Finally, the assumption of homoscedasticity is met when the variance of the residuals is constant across values of the independent variable(s).

FACTOR VARIABLES IN REGRESSION MODELS

So far, we have considered regression when both the independent and dependent variables were numeric. Often it is necessary to include categorical variables as predictors in a regression. These could include, for example, gender, ethnicity, and whether someone was admitted or not admitted to the hospital. To include categorical variables in a regression model, it is necessary to express them as one or more dichotomies.

We can look at the example of gender using the *hospital1* data. Enter the following command into the Console to produce the output depicted in Figure 8.4:

```
>d1<-lm(los~gender, data=hospital1)
>summary(d1)
```

Because gender is a factor variable, *R* automatically expresses gender as a dichotomous factor variable (*males* = 1, compared to *females* = 0). The nonsignificant "Estimate"/slope for male patients is –3.125, which describes an average of a 3-day shorter stay than female patents. The intercept is the mean of the dependent variable when all predictors (i.e., independent variables) are zero. In this case, it represents the mean length of stay for women. To calculate the mean length of stay for males, add the slope to the intercept (–3.125 + 19.156 = 16.031). As displayed in the following, this regression is identical to a two-sample *t*-test.

```
Call:
lm(formula = los ~ gender, data = hospital1)

Residuals:
    Min      1Q  Median      3Q     Max
-16.156 -11.031  -7.031   3.969  79.844

Coefficients:
            Estimate Std. Error t value Pr(>|t|)
(Intercept)   19.156      2.210   8.669 4.77e-15 ***
genderMale    -3.125      2.847  -1.098    0.274
---
Signif. codes:  0 '***' 0.001 '**' 0.01 '*' 0.05 '.' 0.1 ' ' 1

Residual standard error: 17.68 on 159 degrees of freedom
Multiple R-squared:  0.007522,  Adjusted R-squared:  0.00128
F-statistic: 1.205 on 1 and 159 DF,  p-value: 0.274
```

FIGURE 8.4 Summary of model *d1*.

```
>t.test(los~gender,data=hospital1)

    Welch Two Sample t-test

data:  los by gender
t = 1.0704, df = 123.246, p-value = 0.2865
alternative hypothesis: true difference in means is
not equal to 0
95 percent confidence interval:
 -2.654023  8.904667
sample estimates:
mean in group Female      mean in group Male
            19.15625                16.03093
```

Categorical variables can have more than two categories. Marital status or ethnicity, for example, can have three or more categories associated with them. To include a categorical variable with more than two categories as a predictor, a *k* –1 dummy variable must be created. For example, we can examine the variable *agecat* in the *hospital1* data by typing:

```
>table(hospital1$agecat)
```

The following output is produced in the Console:

```
65-69          70-74          75-79 80 or older
   41             32             35          46
```

```
Call:
lm(formula = los ~ agecat, data = hospital1)

Residuals:
    Min      1Q  Median      3Q     Max
-21.087  -9.317  -6.244   3.600  82.829

Coefficients:
                  Estimate Std. Error t value Pr(>|t|)
(Intercept)         14.317      2.626   5.451 2.01e-07 ***
agecat70-74         -1.942      3.967  -0.490  0.62515
agecat75-79          1.854      3.870   0.479  0.63254
agecat80 or older    9.770      3.612   2.705  0.00762 **
---
Signif. codes:  0 '***' 0.001 '**' 0.01 '*' 0.05 '.' 0.1 ' ' 1

Residual standard error: 16.82 on 150 degrees of freedom
  (7 observations deleted due to missingness)
Multiple R-squared:  0.07226,   Adjusted R-squared:  0.0537
F-statistic: 3.894 on 3 and 150 DF,  p-value: 0.01027
```

FIGURE 8.5 Summary of model *d2*.

There are four categories and three dummy variables that will need to be created ($k = 4; 4 - 1 = 3$). Because *agecat* is a factor variable, this will be done automatically by *R*. The first category of *agecat* will be left out of the equation and all of the newly created categories will be compared to it. Type the following into the Console to produce the necessary output in Figure 8.5:

```
>d2<-lm(los ~agecat,data=hospital1)
>summary(d2)
```

In interpreting the coefficients, remember that the first category *agecat65-69* is not included and is used as the basis for comparison. In this example, the only significant category is *agecat80 or older* ($p = 0.00762$). On average, the length of stay of patients 80 years or older is 9.77 days longer than 65- to 69-year-old patients. The other two categories, *agecat70-74* and *agecat75-79,* are not statistically different from *agecat65-69* category.

When regressing $k - 1$ dummy variables, it is important to test for the overall effect of the variable and to compare the categories included in the model to each other. To do this, install the package *aod* by typing the following command in the Console:

```
> install.packages("aod")
```

After it is installed, you will need to load it by typing **require(aod)** in the Console. The package includes the function **wald.test()**, which can be used to test for significance between coefficients. Type the following command in the Console:

```
>wald.test(b = coef(d2), Sigma = vcov(d2), Terms=2:4)
```

The following output will be produced:

```
Wald test:
----------

Chi-squared test:
X2 = 11.7, df = 3, P(> X2) = 0.0086
```

In entering the command, notice that the model vector name is used after **coef** and **vcov**. The **Terms** option needs some explanation; in the model *d2*, estimates of *agecat70-74, agecat75-79*, and *agecat80 or older* are coefficients 2, 3, and 4, while the intercept is coefficient 1. In the command, we are specifying that the entire variable *agecat* comprises coefficients 2 through 4.

In considering the results of this test, the significant X^2 indicates that the overall effect of *agecat* is statistically significant.

To compare *agecat70-74* to *agecat80 or older* is more complicated. You need to create a comparison vector as follows in the Console:

```
>L2<- cbind(0, 1, 0, -1)
```

The intercept and *agecat75-79* are assigned 0 because they are excluded. The category *agecat80 or older* is assigned a –1 because it is being compared to *agecat70-74*, which is assigned a value of 1. Type the following command into the Console to obtain the results that follow:

```
>wald.test(b = coef(d2), Sigma = vcov(d2), L = L2)

Wald test:
----------

Chi-squared test:
X2 = 9.2, df = 1, P(> X2) = 0.0025
```

To compare *agecat75-79* to *agecat80 or older*, create the following vector:

```
>L3<- cbind(0, 0, 1, -1)
>wald.test(b = coef(d2), Sigma = vcov(d2), L = L3)
```

```
Wald test:
----------

Chi-squared test:
X2 = 4.4, df = 1, P(> X2) = 0.036
```

These results indicate that *agecat80 or older* is statistically different from *agecat70-74* and *agecat75-79*. To be thorough, compare *agecat70-74* to *agecat75-79* by first creating the vector **`L4 <- cbind(0, 1, -1, 0)`**. Then, type the following into the Console to obtain the results:

```
>wald.test(b = coef(d2), Sigma = vcov(d2), L = L4)

Wald test:
----------

Chi-squared test:
X2 = 0.85, df = 1, P(> X2) = 0.36
```

In this case, the differences between *agecat70-74* and *agecat75-79* are not significant but again, *agecat80 or older* is significantly different from all other categories.

MULTIPLE LINEAR REGRESSION

As displayed by the following equation, multiple linear regression is an extension of simple regression with the inclusion of multiple independent variables. Because there are multiple independent variables, the interpretation of the coefficients is more complex. The slope of X_1, defined as β_1, is the amount of increase in $\hat{Y}$ when all the other independent variables ($X_2 \ldots X_n$) equal zero.

$$\hat{Y} = \beta_0 + \beta_1 X_1 + \beta_2 X_2 + \cdots + \beta_n X_n$$

In continuing to look at hospital length of stay, we may want to include in our analysis numerous factors that we believe to be influential. In our simple regression, we created two models. The first looked at the influence of ADLs on length of stay, while the second looked at patient age. Perhaps we are interested in a more complex model and want to understand the cumulative effect of ADLs, age, having a spouse, and gender on length of stay. The *hospital1* data set has two variables related to ADLs: *tkatzmean* (which we used in our simple regression example) and *tiadlmean*. We can use the *age* variable, which measured patients' ages in years.

It is good practice to begin the analysis by looking at the interrelationship between variables in the proposed model by using simple bivariate correlations. To do this, first create a vector that contains the dependent variable and all numeric independent variables. Factor variables cannot be included. Create a vector *ADL* as displayed in the following command:

```
>ADL<-
data.frame(hospital1$los,hospital1$tkatzmean,hospital
1$tiadlmean,hospital1$age)
```

The next step is to use the **cor()** function to produce a correlation matrix from the *ADL* vector. Enter the following in the Console:

```
>cor(ADL,use="complete.obs")
```

Notice the inclusion of the option **use="complete.obs"**, which instructs *R* to not include observations in the analysis with missing data using list-wise deletion. If your choice was to use pair-wise deletion, you would simply replace **use="complete.obs"** with **use="pairwise.complete.obs"**.

As shown in Figure 8.6, the correlation matrix is displayed in the Console:

	hospital1.los	hospital1.tkatzmean	hospital1.tiadlmean	hospital1.age
hospital1.los	1.0000000	-0.5659560	-0.5204377	0.2499748
hospital1.tkatzmean	-0.5659560	1.0000000	0.8555508	-0.2851664
hospital1.tiadlmean	-0.5204377	0.8555508	1.0000000	-0.3948662
hospital1.age	0.2499748	-0.2851664	-0.3948662	1.0000000

FIGURE 8.6 Correlation matrix of *hospital1* data.

This matrix displays the correlations between variables. Both measures of ADL have a moderately strong correlation with LOS, while age has a weaker correlation with it. Notice the 0.85555508 correlation between the two measures of ADL (*tkatzmean* and *tiadlmean*). The strong correlation between these independent variables could be a sign of multicollinearity, which can lead to large confidence intervals being produced for coefficients in the regression model. This happens because the coefficient is a measure of the impact of an independent variable on the dependent variables when all other independent variables are held constant. Holding *tiadlmean* constant while measuring *tkatzmean* would be confounding since patients' level on one measure is highly predictive of the other. The negative correlation between both measures of ADL and LOS indicates that as ADL increases, LOS decreases. The positive correlation, although weaker, between age and LOS indicates that as age increases, so does LOS.

Another good practice is to produce scatterplots to depict the relationship between variables to be included in the equation. It is very helpful to see all the variables plotted at once. The *car* package provides a function, **scatterplotMatrix()**, which produces a matrix of scatterplots. First, remember to load the package by using the **require()** function, shown below.

The **scatterplotMatrix()** function will accept factor variables; as a result, we can include *gender* in this analysis. The syntax of the command is very similar to the **lm()** syntax. Observe that the tilde (~) is entered before the first variable in the command. The results of the command are displayed in Figure 8.7.

```
>require(car)
>scatterplotMatrix(~los + tkatzmean + tiadlmean +
age + spouse + gender,data=hospital1,smooth=F)
```

Note that the scatterplots for each independent variable compared with length of stay go down the first column and across the first row. By examining the scatterplot matrix, both the *tkatzmean* and *tiadlmean* have a negative linear relationship with LOS, with the regression line sloping downward. The regression line for the variable *spouse* and *los* indicates that patients without a spouse have longer lengths of stay. The statistically significant results of a two-sample *t*-test ($p = 0.0003957$), shown below, displays that patients with no spouse remain, on average, 10 days longer in the hospital.

```
>t.test(los~spouse,data=hospital1)

    Welch Two Sample t-test

data:  los by spouse
t = -3.6477, df = 117.547, p-value = 0.0003957
alternative hypothesis: true difference in means is
not equal to 0
95 percent confidence interval:
 -15.61699  -4.62673
sample estimates:
mean in group yes  mean in group no
         12.55814          22.68000
```

On the other hand, the scatterplot for the variable *gender* shows a weak decrease in days stayed for men, as noted by the flatter regression line. The *t*-test displayed below indicates a statistically nonsignificant difference of 3 days in length of stay between men and women.

```
>t.test(los~gender,data=hospital1)

    Welch Two Sample t-test
```

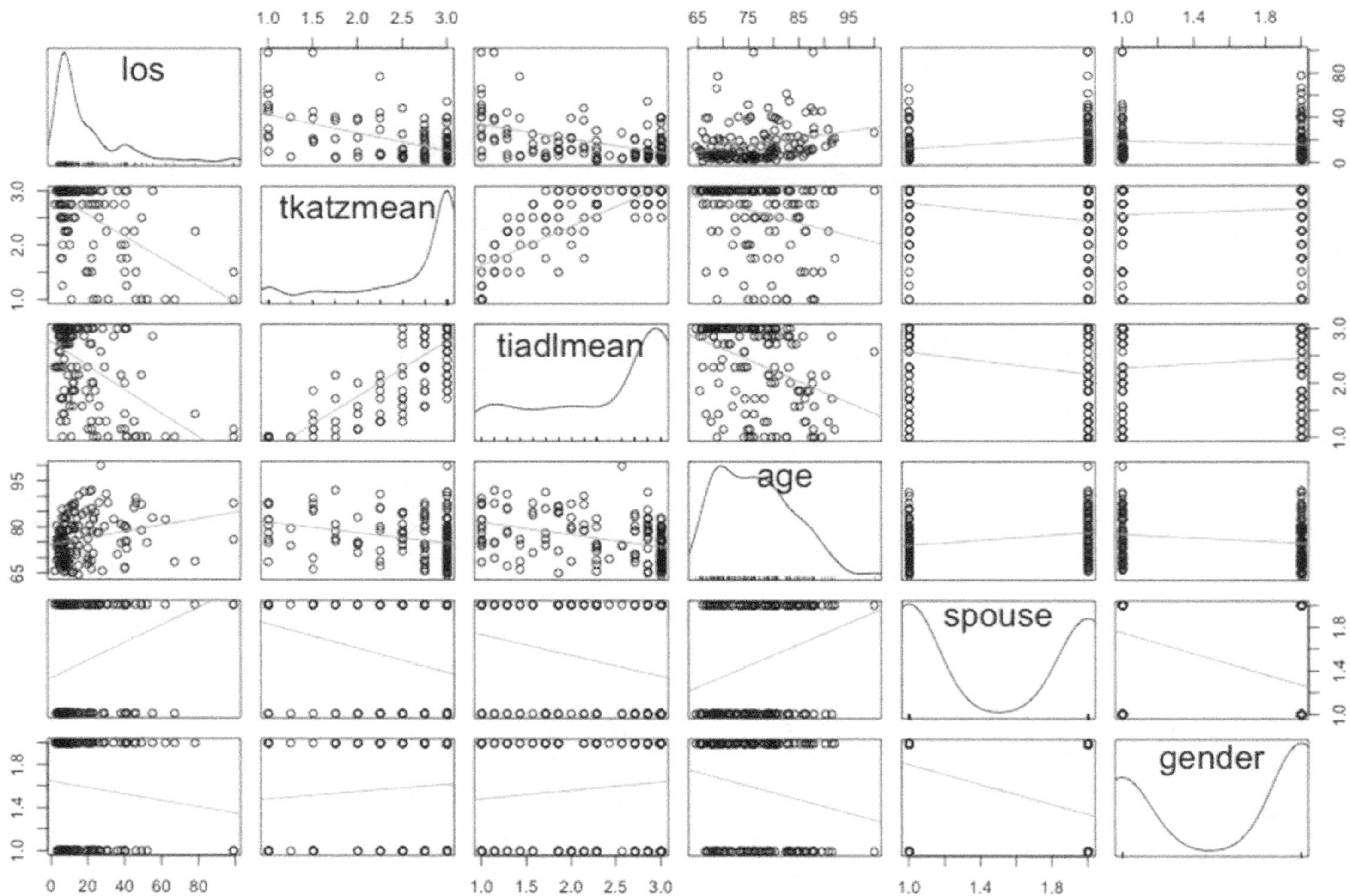

FIGURE 8.7 Scatterplot matrix for dependent and independent variables.

```
data:   los by gender
t = 1.0704, df = 123.246, p-value = 0.2865
alternative hypothesis: true difference in means is
not equal to 0
95 percent confidence interval:
 -2.654023  8.904667
sample estimates:
mean in group Female   mean in group Male
  19.15625                    16.03093
```

The scatterplot of *age* and *los* shows a rapid increase in LOS around age 80. We can use the *car* package's **scatterplot()** function, displayed in Figure 8.8, to expand our view.

```
>scatterplot(los~age,boxplots=FALSE,xlab="AGE",ylab="
Length of Stay (days)",smoother=FALSE,data=hospital1)
```

The scatterplot confirms the results of the analysis of *agecat* on LOS in the section on factor variables in regression models. In that analysis, the age category of 80 and above was significantly different from all other age groups. This is a good reason to include the *age80* variable in the regression model, which is a factor variable comparing those 80 years or older to all other age groups.

The syntax to run the regression and the output produced by the function is displayed below. Because *spouse* is a factor variable, *R* automatically expresses spouse as a dichotomous factor variable (*no* = 1, compared to *yes* = 0). The results are saved

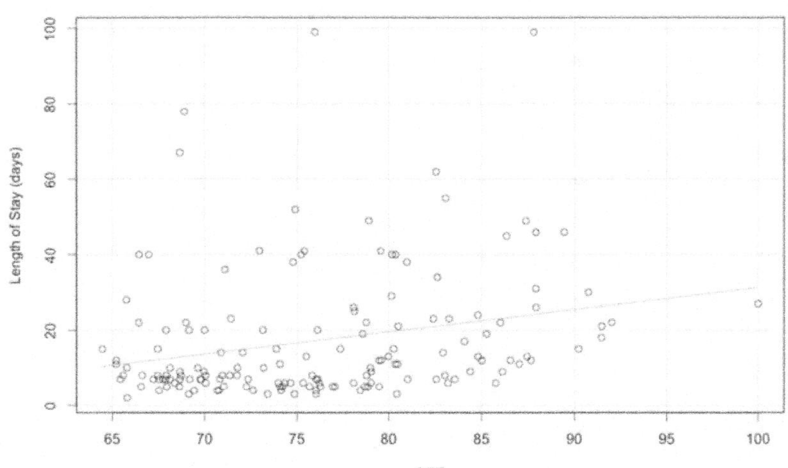

FIGURE 8.8 Scatterplot of LOS and age.

in the vector *m1,* and then the **`summary()`** function is used to display the results in the Console (see Figure 8.9).

```
>m1<-lm(los ~ tkatzmean + spouse +
age80,data=hospital1)
>summary(m1)
```

Note that, like simple regression, the dependent variable is listed first in the `lm()` command, followed by the independent variables separated from each other with a plus sign (+). Also note that we chose to leave *tiadlmean* out of the equation because of its high correlation with *tkatzmean,* thus addressing the issue of multicollinearity.

The only statistically significant independent variable in this model is *tkatzmean,* with a coefficient of –14.372. The coefficient can be interpreted as follows: for patients with a spouse (*spouse* = 0) and who are younger than 80 (*age80* = 0), for each one unit increase in ADL, as measured by *tkatzmean,* there is a 14.372-day decrease in LOS. Although not statistically significant, when *tkatzmean* and *age80* are held constant, not having a spouse increases a patient's LOS by nearly 4 days. Similarly, a patient's LOS increases, on average, by almost 4 days for patients 80 years or older when *spouse* and *tkatzmean* are held constant. The model explains almost 35% of variance as indicated by the Multiple R-squared of 0.3474. The model is also statistically significant as displayed by the *p*-value of 7.335e-14 for the F-statistic.

```
Call:
lm(formula = los ~ tkatzmean + spouse + age80, data = hospital1)

Residuals:
    Min      1Q  Median      3Q     Max
-34.227  -7.559  -1.670   4.551  60.959

Coefficients:
            Estimate Std. Error t value Pr(>|t|)
(Intercept)   51.787      5.755   8.999  9.4e-16 ***
tkatzmean    -14.372      1.963  -7.320  1.4e-11 ***
spouseno       3.987      2.422   1.646    0.102
age80          3.825      2.626   1.457    0.147
---
Signif. codes:  0 '***' 0.001 '**' 0.01 '*' 0.05 '.' 0.1 ' ' 1

Residual standard error: 14.1 on 150 degrees of freedom
  (7 observations deleted due to missingness)
Multiple R-squared:  0.3474,    Adjusted R-squared:  0.3344
F-statistic: 26.62 on 3 and 150 DF,  p-value: 7.335e-14
```

FIGURE 8.9 Summary of model *m1.*

REGRESSION DIAGNOSTICS

The output from the **summary()** function does not tell you if the model fit is a good one. It is advisable, then, to perform some diagnostics on the overall model fit, as misspecification of a model can lead to incorrect conclusions. For example, you could erroneously conclude that the independent variables are related to the outcome when they are not. On the other hand, it could also be incorrectly concluded that the independent variables are unrelated to the outcome when they are.

Begin with obtaining 95% confidence intervals for the coefficients. This provides an estimate of the true change in the dependent variable for a one-unit change in the independent variable. Enter the following into the Console to obtain this:

```
>confint(m1)
```

```
                    2.5 %      97.5 %
(Intercept)   40.4162968   63.157009
tkatzmean    -18.2514411  -10.492828
spouseno      -0.7991218    8.773944
age80         -1.3638974    9.014026
```

Here we see that for a one-unit change in the variable *tkatzmean*, the true change in *los* when all other independent variables are held constant is between −18.2514411 and −10.492828. Wide confidence intervals for coefficients make their interpretation difficult.

R has a number of built-in diagnostic graphs that can help identify problematic models. To produce them, we will first want to allow the graphic environment to accept four graphs in a 2 × 2 configuration. To do this, run the **par()** function as follows. Next simply use the **plot()** function with the model vector shown below to produce the graphs in Figure 8.10. The final command will reset the graphics environment for future graphs.

```
>par(mfrow=c(2,2))
>plot(m1)
>par(mfrow=c(1,1))
```

The first plot, Residuals vs. Fitted, is a diagnostic of linearity. If the relationship between the independent and dependent variables is linear, there will be no systematic relationship between the residuals and the fitted, or predicted, values. In this case the relationship is not systematic (i.e., it is random), with an almost flat line dividing the points.

The Normal Q-Q plot is a measure of the normality of the residuals of the dependent variable. The straight dotted line depicts the normal distribution. When all the dots are on this straight line, the assumption of normality of the dependent variable

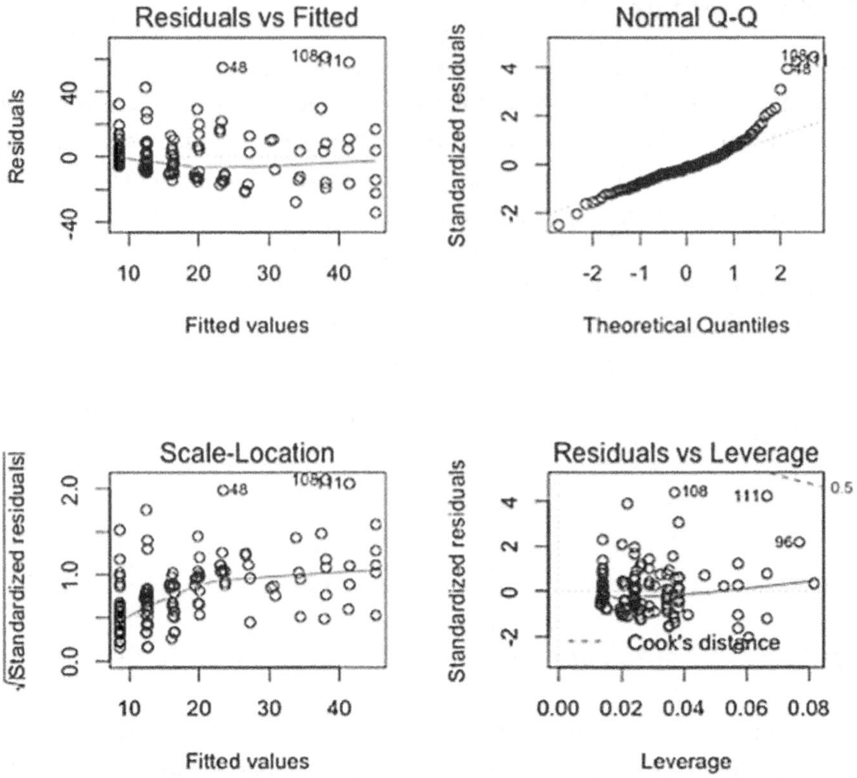

FIGURE 8.10 Diagnostic plots for multiple regression, *m1*.

is met. Because the dots in the graph are off the line at the top right, *los* is skewed positively. This skew may possibly be addressed by transforming the dependent variable.

The Scale-Location plot is a measure of homoscedasticity/variance of residuals. When looking at this plot, there should be a random band around the line with no clear pattern. This assumption appears not to have been met, as there is rapid increase between values 10 and 30, as noted by the cluster of dots around the line along those values.

The final plot, Residuals vs. Leverage, identifies outliers, which may be highly influential points. In the plot there are three cases with heavy influence (high leverage): observations 96, 108, and 110.

The *car* package contains a number of important enhancements for the purpose of regression diagnostics. For example, the **ncvTest()** function is a test of homoscedasticity. This function tests the hypothesis that the residuals have a constant variance against an alternate hypothesis that the residual variance changes with the levels of the predicted/fitted values. A nonsignificant result is desired signifying homoscedasticity, while a significant difference indicates a non-constant variance of the residuals (i.e., heteroscedasticity).

Enter the following command in the Console to view this diagnostic:

```
>ncvTest(m1)

Non-constant Variance Score Test
Variance formula: ~ fitted.values
Chisquare = 70.5791     Df = 1      p = 4.42176e-17
```

The *p*-value of the Non-constant Variance Score Test is statistically significant, indicating that the variance is non-constant and heteroscedasticity is problematic. This had been suggested in the Scale-Location plot illustrated in Figure 8.10.

The **spreadLevelPlot()** function produces a scatterplot of the absolute studentized residuals by the fitted/predicted values. The following syntax, **spreadLevelPlot(m1)** will produce the graph in Figure 8.11 and the following output in the Console:

```
Suggested power transformation: -0.2123061
```

A fit line is overlaid on the graph. A straight horizontal line indicates a good fit, while a non-horizontal line, such as the one displayed in Figure 8.11, suggests a poorer fit.

A suggested power transformation is displayed in the Console to help address this issue. Table 8.1 provides a listing of **spreadLevelPlot()** power transformation

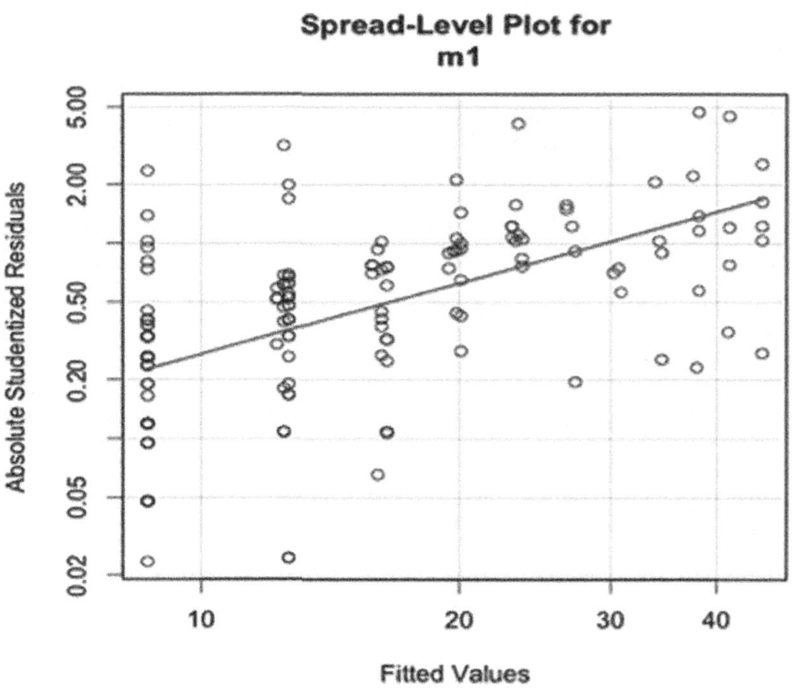

FIGURE 8.11 Spread-level plot for multiple regression, *m1*.

TABLE 8.1 Transformations Based Upon `spreadLevelPlot` Values

spreadLevelPlot() Values	Transformation	Purpose
–2	$1/Y^2$	Reduce severe negative skew
–1	1/Y	Reduce very severe positive skew
–0.5	$1/\sqrt{Y}$	Reduce severe positive skew
0	Log(Y)	Reduce positive skew
0.5	$\sqrt{Y}$	Reduce mild positive skew
1	None	No change raw data
2	Y^2	Reduce mild negative skew

values in the first column of the table that may be helpful in addressing problematic data. The type of transformation is displayed in the second column, and the purpose of the transformation is described in the last column. The value 0 is the closest to –0.2123061, suggesting a log-transformation of the dependent variable due to the positive skew we first observed in the Normal Q-Q plot.

Another function, the **`vif()`**, is a test of multicollinearity discussed earlier in the this chapter. A variance inflation factor (VIF) with a square root greater than 2 is indicative of multicollinearity. Enter the following into the Console with the *car* package loaded:

```
> vif(m1)

tkatzmean     spouse       age80
 1.116632  1.130887  1.118338
```

The low VIF values for the independent variables indicate that multicollinearity is not an issue in this model.

TRANSFORMING DATA

As detected by the diagnostics tests of the model, *m1*, the assumption of a normally distributed dependent variable and homoscedasticity have not been met. Using a log-transformation of the dependent variable, *los*, can normalize a positively skewed distribution.

To do this with the *hospital1* data open, we will create a new variable that will be the log of *los* using the following syntax:

```
>loglos<-log(hospital1$los)
```

```
Call:
lm(formula = loglos ~ tkatzmean + spouse + age80, data = hospital1)

Residuals:
     Min       1Q   Median       3Q      Max 
-1.73628 -0.50662 -0.07184  0.46380  1.69582 

Coefficients:
            Estimate Std. Error t value Pr(>|t|)    
(Intercept)  3.72000    0.27997  13.287  < 2e-16 ***
tkatzmean   -0.56742    0.09552  -5.940 1.91e-08 ***
spouseno     0.26982    0.11786   2.289  0.02346 *  
age80        0.37493    0.12777   2.934  0.00387 ** 
---
Signif. codes:  0 '***' 0.001 '**' 0.01 '*' 0.05 '.' 0.1 ' ' 1

Residual standard error: 0.6862 on 150 degrees of freedom
  (7 observations deleted due to missingness)
Multiple R-squared:  0.3387,	Adjusted R-squared:  0.3255 
F-statistic: 25.61 on 3 and 150 DF,  p-value: 1.956e-13
```

FIGURE 8.12 Linear regression with log-transformed dependent variable.

We can now rerun the model using the log-transformed dependent variable as follows. The results are displayed in Figure 8.12.

```
>trans1<-lm(loglos~tkatzmean + spouse +
age80,data=hospital1)
>summary(trans1)
```

As can be observed, transforming the dependent variable generated a different model with different metrics. All three independent variables are now significant.

We can now test to see if this model has met the criteria of homoscedasticity and a normally distributed dependent variable. Type the following in the Console to produce Figure 8.13:

```
>par(mfrow=c(2,2))
>plot(trans1)
>par(mfrow=c(1,1))
```

As Figure 8.13 illustrates, for the Normal Q-Q plot, all the dots are now on the line, indicating a normal distribution. Furthermore, in the Scale-Location plot, the dots are more randomly distributed around the superimposed line than they were previously. This is indicative of homoscedasticity of the error variance.

Now with the *car* package loaded, enter the following to further test for homoscedasticity:

```
>ncvTest(trans1)
```

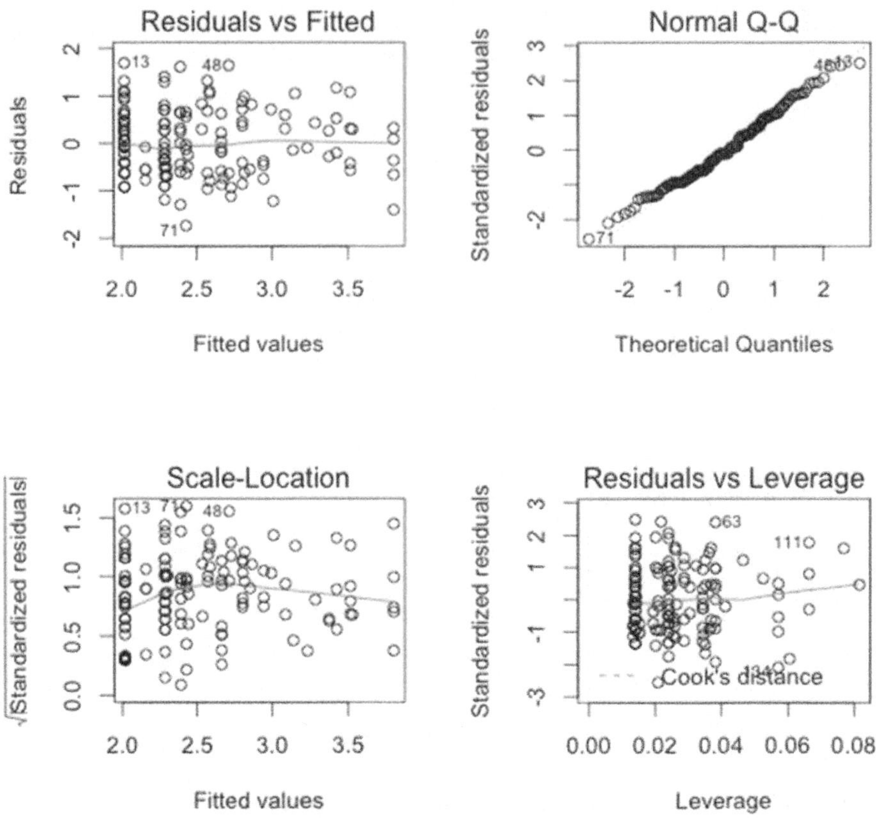

FIGURE 8.13 Diagnostic plots for multiple regression, *trans1.*

```
Non-constant Variance Score Test
Variance formula: ~ fitted.values
Chisquare = 0.5585293    Df = 1      p = 0.4548534
```

Because the score test is not significant (p = 0.4548534), we can conclude that there is a constant error variance, and, therefore, the assumption of homoscedasticity is now met.

INTERPRETATION OF FINDINGS

When a data transformation is done, the interpretation must be based upon it and not upon the original model with the untransformed data. In the *trans1* model, the dependent variable was log-transformed, but the independent variables are in their original form. Comparing this model to the original untransformed model for *los*, there is an obvious difference in coefficients because the scale of the dependent variable was altered.

Because a log-transformation was used, the results should be interpreted as a percentage of change in the dependent variable due to a one-unit change in an independent variable when all other variables are held constant. To do this, first use the exponential function (i.e., e^x) where x is the slope of the independent variable, then subtract it from 1. For example, to interpret the *tkatzmean* coefficient, do the following multiplication in the Console:

```
>1-(exp(-.56742))
```

and the following is displayed is displayed in the Console: **.4330136**. Because the slope is negative, 1 is subtracted from the exponent of the coefficient.

The interpretation of this coefficient would be that for a one-unit increase in Katz ADL, there is a 43.30% decrease in the length of stay when all other independent variables are held constant. To calculate the impact of a three-unit increase in the coefficient of *tkatzmean* upon LOS, you would have to multiply the exponent of the coefficient of *tkatzmean* by 3. Type the following syntax into the Console: **>1-(exp(-.56742*3))**.

The following result is displayed in the Console: **0.8177289**. This indicates a 81.77% decrease in LOS for a 3-unit increase in Katz ADL.

For the variable *spouse*, because the slope is positive, use the following syntax: **>exp(0.26982)-1**.

The result of 0.3097287 indicates a 31% increase in LOS for patients with no spouse when all other independent variables are held constant.

```
Call:
lm(formula = loglos ~ tkatzmean + spouse + age80 + age80:tkatzmean,
    data = hospital1)

Residuals:
     Min       1Q   Median       3Q      Max
-1.73569 -0.51188 -0.04674  0.47389  1.72092

Coefficients:
                Estimate Std. Error t value Pr(>|t|)
(Intercept)       3.9386     0.3535  11.143  < 2e-16 ***
tkatzmean        -0.6486     0.1247  -5.201 6.44e-07 ***
spouseno          0.2740     0.1179   2.324   0.0215 *
age80            -0.1079     0.4934  -0.219   0.8273
tkatzmean:age80   0.1910     0.1886   1.013   0.3127
---
Signif. codes:  0 '***' 0.001 '**' 0.01 '*' 0.05 '.' 0.1 ' ' 1

Residual standard error: 0.6862 on 149 degrees of freedom
  (7 observations deleted due to missingness)
Multiple R-squared:  0.3432,	Adjusted R-squared:  0.3256
F-statistic: 19.47 on 4 and 149 DF,  p-value: 6.622e-13
```

FIGURE 8.14 Summary of model *trans2*.

INTERACTIONS

Often we are interested in how two independent variables interact. For example, it would be interesting to determine if there was a significant interaction between *age80* and *tkatzmean* in our model. This will examine the combined effects between *tkatzmean* and *age80*, as if it were a single variable. To do this, enter the following syntax in the Console:

```
>trans2<-lm(loglos~tkatzmean + spouse + age80 +
age80:tkatzmean,data=hospital1)
>summary(trans2)
```

Notice the addition of the interaction term *age80:tkatzmean*. A colon(:) between independent variables denotes the interaction. The output from the command is shown in Figure 8.14.

The interaction is not significant, indicating that ADL impacts LOS regardless of age.

CONCLUSION

As you think about reporting your findings to hospital administration, you will want to consider a good-fitting regression model in which the most variables are significant predictors of the dependent variable. You will want to select a model that is statistically significant overall and that explains as much variance as possible.

In our analysis, we would consider the best-fitting model the one described in Figure 8.14. Here we were able to identify a strong model that identified nearly 34% in the variance in length of stay with three independent variables, all of which could be used to create a profile of patients at risk for extended hospital stays based on psychosocial factors. This model provides a way to identify patients most at risk for longer hospital stays: patients who have low ADLs, older patients, and those without a spouse are more likely to have longer lengths of stay.

What would this mean for hospital administration? First, the social work department should consider using a functional assessment, such as the Katz ADL, for patients early in their hospital stays, particularly for patients aged 80 and over and for those without a spouse (Auerbach & Mason, 2010; Rock et al., 1996). This provides a rationale for the early intervention of social work services among patients with this at-risk profile.

/// 9 ///

MAKING YOUR CASE USING LOGISTIC REGRESSION WITH *R*

In order to work through the examples in this chapter, you will need to *install* and *load* the following packages:

- *car*
- *gmodels*
- *ResourceSelection*
- *aod*
- *effects*

For more information on how to do this, refer to the Packages section in Chapter 3.

INTRODUCTION

In the previous chapter on regression, the dependent variable was required to be a numeric measure. There are a number of situations in which the outcome variable is binary. In those cases, it may be more appropriate to use logistic regression. Logistic regression is included within the class of structure of the generalized linear model (GLM), which is appropriate to use in predicting different types of dependent variables from a set of independent variables, including binary outcomes.

Here are some examples of binary dependent variables: admitted or not admitted to a hospital, accepted or not accepted to a college, and voting or not voting in an election. The binary outcome is coded as 1 = present; 0 = absent. For the admitted to hospital example, admitted would be coded as 1 and not admitted as 0. A binary outcome is suited to logistic regression because its probability of occurring lies between 0 and 1. In logistic regression, we estimate the log-odds. This can be defined as the log of the probability of success divided by the probability of failure. The log-odds of the dependent variable is calculated for each observation. By performing this transformation, the dependent variable can be predicted using a linear model.

This chapter is a practical overview of using logistic regression. For an in-depth discussion of the topic, you can refer to one of the following authors, whose texts are listed in Appendix A: Fox, Weisberg, & Fox, 2011; Hamilton, 1991; and Faraway, 2004.

We start with an example from the *hospital1* data. In Chapter 8, we discussed how the hospital administrator was interested in factors associated with length of stay. Now that the report is complete, you have been given a new task: exploring what factors increase the likelihood a patient will return within 30 days of discharge.

To begin, open the *hospital1* data file in *RStudio* by clicking on **File / Open** in the menu bar and navigate to the directory in which it is stored. We can take a look at the dependent variable, *return30*, by typing:

```
>table(hospital1$return30
```

The following will be displayed in the Console:

```
no yes
133  28
```

The odds of a patient returning within 30 days is calculated as follows: yes/no = 28/133 = 0.2105263.

The log-odds is equal to: log(28/133) = –1.558145.

glm() is the general linear model function in *R*. The **glm()** function can be used to replicate the above example. To accomplish this, run a constant-only model (i.e., one that does not include any predictor variables) using the following syntax:

```
>cons<-glm(return30~1,
family="binomial",data=hospital1)
>summary(cons)
```

The results in Figure 9.1 are displayed in the Console.

A constant of "1" is entered in place of an independent variable when deriving a constant-only model. Because the outcome is binary, **family=** was set to **"binomial"**. Notice that the Estimate (i.e., coefficient of the intercept) in the constant-only model is the log-odds for *return30*. To obtain the odds of returning within 30 days, the following syntax is used:

```
>exp(coef(cons))
```

The following results are displayed in the Console:

```
(Intercept)
  0.2105263
```

```
Call:
glm(formula = return30 ~ 1, family = "binomial", data = hospital1)

Deviance Residuals:
    Min       1Q   Median       3Q      Max
-0.6181  -0.6181  -0.6181  -0.6181   1.8704

Coefficients:
            Estimate Std. Error z value Pr(>|z|)
(Intercept)  -1.5581     0.2079  -7.494 6.69e-14 ***
---
Signif. codes:  0 '***' 0.001 '**' 0.01 '*' 0.05 '.' 0.1 ' ' 1

(Dispersion parameter for binomial family taken to be 1)

    Null deviance: 148.78  on 160  degrees of freedom
Residual deviance: 148.78  on 160  degrees of freedom
AIC: 150.78

Number of Fisher Scoring iterations: 4
```

FIGURE 9.1 Constant only model using `glm()` function.

The constant-only model is interesting, but to improve our prediction, other independent variables, such as having a spouse (a dichotomous "yes" or "no" variable), can be added to the model. The table in Figure 9.2 is a 2-way contingency table of returned within 30 days by having a spouse (*yes* or *no*). The table was produced by the **`CrossTable()`** function from the *gmodels* package. The syntax used to create the table in Figure 9.2 is as follows:

```
>require(gmodels)
>CrossTable( hospital1$spouse, hospital1$return30,
prop.chisq=F, prop.r=F, prop.c=F, resid=F,
prop.t=F, )
```

Here, we are displaying the counts of the relationship between two variables: *return30* (no/yes) and *spouse* (no/yes). We can calculate the odds of returning within 30 days as follows:

- The odds of returning if the patient has a spouse are calculated as follows: 5/81 = 0.0617284.
- The odds of returning if the patient does not have a spouse are calculated as follows: 23/52 = 0.4423077.

```
    Cell Contents
|-------------------------|
|                       N |
|-------------------------|


Total Observations in Table:  161


                 | hospital1$return30
hospital1$spouse |        no |       yes | Row Total |
-----------------|-----------|-----------|-----------|
             yes |        81 |         5 |        86 |
-----------------|-----------|-----------|-----------|
              no |        52 |        23 |        75 |
-----------------|-----------|-----------|-----------|
    Column Total |       133 |        28 |       161 |
-----------------|-----------|-----------|-----------|
```

FIGURE 9.2 Contingency table of readmission to St. Luke's Hospital within 30 days by spouse.

As observed, patients without a spouse are much more likely to return within 30 days compared to those who have a spouse. The odds can be combined into a single coefficient called an odds ratio by dividing the odds of returning within 30 days if a patient does not have a spouse by the odds of returning within 30 days if a patient does have a spouse. The calculation is as follows:

```
0.4423077/0.0617284 = 7.165384
```

What this indicates is that the odds of a patient with no spouse returning within 30 days is more than 7 times greater than those with a spouse. This can also be replicated using the **glm()** and **exp()** functions as follows:

```
>sp<-glm(return30~  spouse ,
family="binomial",data=hospital1)
>exp(coef(sp))

(Intercept)     spouseno
  0.0617284    7.1653846
```

The 95% confidence intervals can be calculated with the following command:

```
>exp(confint.default(sp))
```

The following results are displayed in the Console:

```
      2.5 %       97.5 %
(Intercept) 0.02501775  0.1523076
spouseno    2.56345626 20.0287157
```

The confidence interval indicates that it is 95% likely that the true odds of returning within 30 days for patients with no spouse are between 2.56345626 and 20.0287157. The odds ratio is easier to interpret than the log-odds because it makes much more sense intuitively. The odds ratio is not used as a score of the outcome variable because its distribution is not normal.

An odds ratio of 1 would indicate that the independent variable makes no difference with regard to the outcome. For example, if the odds ratio for spouse were 1, then patients with and without spouses would be equally likely to return to the hospital within 30 days. Odds of 2 would suggest that patients without a spouse are twice as likely, or 100% more likely, to return within 30 days than those with a spouse.

A major drawback with the odds ratio is that it has a skewed distribution, which is not normal. Odds ratios above 1 can vary between 1 and infinity. On the other hand, odds ratios below 1 can only vary between 0 and 1. This can make the interpretation of odds ratios below 1 more difficult to interpret.

Now we add two more independent variables to the model, *tkatzmean* and *age80*, by utilizing the following syntax:

```
>logit1 <- glm(return30 ~ tkatzmean  + spouse + age80 ,
family = "binomial",data=hospital1)
```

The results of the model are saved into the vector *logit1* and the **summary()** function displays the results in Figure 9.3 in the Console.

```
>summary(logit1)
```

The log-odds for the intercept and the three independent variables are listed under the column labeled "Estimate." The standard errors, *z* values and *p*-values, are also listed. Notice that all the independent variables except for *age80* in this model are statistically significant.

Now, the **confint.default()** function can be used to produce the 95% confidence intervals for the log-odds. The syntax is as follows, and the results displayed in the Console are presented as follows.

```
Call:
glm(formula = return30 ~ tkatzmean + spouse + age80, family = "binomial",
    data = hospital1)

Deviance Residuals:
    Min       1Q   Median       3Q      Max
-1.9507  -0.3727  -0.1747  -0.1496   2.5540

Coefficients:
            Estimate Std. Error z value Pr(>|z|)
(Intercept)   3.6966     1.2014   3.077 0.00209 **
tkatzmean    -2.7278     0.4967  -5.491 3.99e-08 ***
spouseno      1.5536     0.7182   2.163 0.03052 *
age80         0.5825     0.6481   0.899 0.36878
---
Signif. codes:  0 '***' 0.001 '**' 0.01 '*' 0.05 '.' 0.1 ' ' 1

(Dispersion parameter for binomial family taken to be 1)

    Null deviance: 142.983  on 153  degrees of freedom
Residual deviance:  73.055  on 150  degrees of freedom
  (7 observations deleted due to missingness)
AIC: 81.055

Number of Fisher Scoring iterations: 6
```

FIGURE 9.3 Summary results of model *logit1*.

```
>confint.default(logit1)

                  2.5 %      97.5 %
(Intercept)   1.3419446    6.051256
tkatzmean    -3.7014442   -1.754254
spouseno      0.1460177    2.961199
age80        -0.6878212    1.852878
```

The **exp()** function calculates odds ratios from the log-odds of an independent variable. The interpretation, however, is more complex when there is more than one independent variable in the equation.

To obtain the odds ratios from the results of the *logit1* model, enter the following syntax into the Console. The results are displayed as follows:

```
>exp(coef(logit1))
(Intercept)   tkatzmean    spouseno        age80
40.31003163  0.06535972  4.72850246  1.79056012
```

The odds ratio for *spouse* can be interpreted as follows: the odds of a patient with no spouse of returning within 30 days increase 4.7 times when all other independent variables are held constant. This is equal to (4.7 – 1)*100 = 370%, which is a 370% increase in the odds of returning within 30 days. For a one-unit increase in the Katz ADL, *tkatzmean*, there is a 93.5% decrease in the odds of a patient returning within 30 days when all other independent variables are held constant (i.e., (1 – 0.06535972)*100 = 93.5%).

As mentioned earlier, odds ratios less than 1 can be difficult to interpret. We know that a one-point increase in *tkatzmean* decreases the odds of being admitted within 30 days by 93.5%. You might conclude that calculating a three-unit increase is a simple multiplication problem; however, the change is geometric; that is, the previous units are compounded. To calculate the impact of a three-unit increase, then, you would have to take the odds ratio to the third power, as follows:

$$\left(1 - 0.06535972^{3}\right) * 100 = 99.97208$$

The formula for an odds ratio below 1 would be as follows:

$$\left(1 - \text{odds}^{\times}\right) * 100$$

Now we can look at an example for interpreting an increase in odds ratios with more than a one-unit increase in an independent variable. In predicting admittance, we can consider a hypothetical odds ratio for age in years at 1.005. This would be interpreted as follows: for a one-year increase in age, there is a 0.5% increase in the odds of returning within 30 days. This values is calculated as follows:

$$\left(\text{odds}^{\times} - 1\right) * 100$$

To calculate the odds ratio for an 80-year-old, you would do the following:

$$\left(1.005^{80} - 1\right) * 100 = 49.03386\%$$

The odds of being admitted increases to a little over 49%. To compare the difference in odds between a 60-year-old and an 80-year-old, you would first calculate the difference in age, which is 20 years. This difference is used as the exponent in the calculation:

$$\left(1.005^{20} - 1\right) * 100 = 10.48956\%$$

The result illustrates that an 80-year-old's likelihood of returning within 30 days would be almost 10.5% higher than a 60-year-old's.

The **exp()** function can be used to calculate the 95% percent confidence intervals.

```
>exp(confint.default(logit1))
```

```
                  2.5 %       97.5 %
(Intercept) 3.82647711 424.6461174
tkatzmean   0.02468785   0.1730363
spouseno    1.15721667  19.3211316
age80       0.50267009   6.3781505
```

ASSESSING MODEL FIT

One method used to assess the overall fit of a model is to compare the null-model/intercept-only model (i.e., the model with no predictors/no independent variables) to the full model (i.e., model containing all predictors/independent variables). This is very helpful when comparing models.

The question tested is as follows: Does the model with predictors significantly improve the fit of the model compared to the model with no predictors? The test statistic is X^2, which is the difference between the residual deviance of the null-model from the residual deviance of the full model. Stated simply, the residual deviance is a measure of how poorly the model fits the data. The smaller the deviance, the better the fit of the model. The following are the steps for calculating the model X^2. The output shown in the Console is included with each step:

Step 1. First, subtract the deviance of the full model from the null model using the following statement:

```
>chi<-logit1$null.deviance -logit1$deviance
>chi
```

```
[1] 69.92781
```

Step 2. Next, subtract the degrees of freedom of the residuals from the degrees of freedom of the null model, as follows:

```
>df<-logit1$df.null-logit1$df.residual
>df
```

```
[1] 3
```

Step 3. The vectors *chi* and *df* are entered into the **pchisq()** function to obtain a *p*-value as follows:

```
>pchisq(chi,df, lower.tail = FALSE)
```

```
[1] 4.423e-15
```

In the first two steps, you calculated the model X^2, which is stored in a vector we called *chi*, and the degrees of freedom, which is stored in a vector we called *df*. The **pchisq()** function is used in Step 3 to calculate the significance of X^2. The X^2 in Step 3 is below 0.05; as a result, it is concluded that the model with predictors significantly improves the fit of the model as compared to the model with no predictors.

Another test of model fit is the Hosmer and Lemeshow's goodness-of-fit test. This test of goodness-of-fit compares the predicted frequency to the observed frequency. The closer they match, the better the fit. The test statistic for this test is a Pearson's X^2. If there is no significant difference between the observed and predicted frequency, the X^2 will be statistically nonsignificant.

To run the Hosmer and Lemeshow's goodness-of-fit test, the *ResourceSelection* package needs to be installed and loaded. This package contains the needed function **hoslem.test()**. The syntax for doing this is as follows. Remember the package needs to be installed only once, but loaded before using in each *R* session.

```
>install.packages("ResourceSelection")
>require(ResourceSelection)
```

To run the **hoslem.test()**, complete the following steps:

Step 1. A new data frame needs to be created that excludes missing values. The code for doing this is as follows:

```
>m1<-data.frame(na.omit(hospital1))
```

Step 2. The dependent variable must be numeric, but our variable, *return30,* is a factor variable. The **ifelse()** function can be utilized to create a new numeric variable, which we will call *return*. The following syntax will accomplish this:

```
>return<-ifelse(m1$return30=="yes",1,0)
```

Step 3. The next step is to rerun the **glm()** with the following syntax. Notice that the *hospital1* was replaced with *m1*:

```
>gof<- glm(return30 ~ tkatzmean  + spouse + age80 ,
family = "binomial",data=m1)
```

Step 4. The final step is to run the **hoslem.test()** function using the following syntax:

```
>hoslem.test(return,gof$fit)
```

The variable *return* was created in Step 2, and *gof* is the vector to which the results of the logistic regression were saved. The results of the test are as follows.

```
        Hosmer and Lemeshow goodness of fit (GOF) test

data:   return, gof$fit
X-squared = 7.8402, df = 8, p-value = 0.4492
```

The nonsignificant p-value of the [use existing symbol] (p = 0.4492) supports the hypothesis that the observed frequencies are equal to the predicted frequencies.

Diagnostics

The variable *age80* was the only statistically nonsignificant independent variable in the model *logit1*. As a result, the model *logit2* was run excluding *age80*. The syntax and the results are displayed in Figure 9.4.

```
>logit2<-glm(return30~ tkatzmean + spouse, family="bi
nomial",data=hospital1)
>summary(logit2)
```

To calculate the odds ratios for the independent variables, enter the following into the Console:

```
>exp(coef(logit2))

(Intercept)    tkatzmean     spouseno
38.27817282  0.06957032   6.21903948
```

And to obtain the 95% confidence intervals, enter the following syntax:

```
>exp(confint(logit2))

                    2.5 %       97.5 %
(Intercept) 4.54660058 421.6971751
tkatzmean   0.02471119   0.1626051
spouseno    1.80886491  26.7587586
```

The independent variables *spouse* and *tkatzmean* are both statistically significant. Their odds ratio is somewhat different as compared to the *logit1* model. The calculation of the model X^2 follows:

```
Call:
glm(formula = return30 ~ tkatzmean + spouse, family = "binomial",
    data = hospital1)

Deviance Residuals:
    Min       1Q   Median       3Q      Max
-1.8333  -0.3927  -0.1600  -0.1600   2.7239

Coefficients:
            Estimate Std. Error z value Pr(>|z|)
(Intercept)   3.6449     1.1381   3.203  0.00136 **
tkatzmean    -2.6654     0.4741  -5.621 1.89e-08 ***
spouseno      1.8276     0.6739   2.712  0.00669 **
---
Signif. codes:  0 '***' 0.001 '**' 0.01 '*' 0.05 '.' 0.1 ' ' 1

(Dispersion parameter for binomial family taken to be 1)

    Null deviance: 148.776  on 160  degrees of freedom
Residual deviance:  80.102  on 158  degrees of freedom
AIC: 86.102

Number of Fisher Scoring iterations: 6
```

FIGURE 9.4 Summary of model *logit2*.

```
>chi<-logit2$null.deviance -logit2$deviance
>chi

[1] 68.67358

> df<-logit2$df.null-logit2$df.residual
> df

[1] 2

>pchisq(chi,df, lower.tail = FALSE)

[1] 1.22383e-15
```

The model X^2 is statistically significant, indicating that, compared to the constant-only model, the model with independent variables improves the predictability of the dependent variable.

The *car* package contains a number of functions that provide helpful diagnostics for logistic regression. If you have not installed the car package, do so before proceeding, by typing **install.packages("car")** in the Console or downloading it from CRAN through the Packages tab. Next, the package needs to be loaded using the **require(car)** command or by clicking the check box next to the package in the Packages tab.

The **residualPlots()** function in the *car* package provides useful graphs of residuals versus predictors. Run the function to assess the *logit2* model by using the following syntax:

```
>residualPlots(logit2)
```

The lack-of-fit-test results for numeric variables are displayed in the Console. *Spouse* is a binary, so "NA" is listed in the results section for it. The graph in Figure 9.5 is displayed in the Plots pane.

```
Test          stat    Pr(>|t|)
tkatzmean     0.015     0.904
spouse           NA        NA
```

The lack-of-fit test has a nonsignificant *p*-value of 0.904 for *tkatzmean,* which confirms what we see in the graph.

logit2 fits the data well for the variable *tkatzmean*, as the dots move around both sides of the horizontal line in a fairly constant fashion. Also, the smoother in the

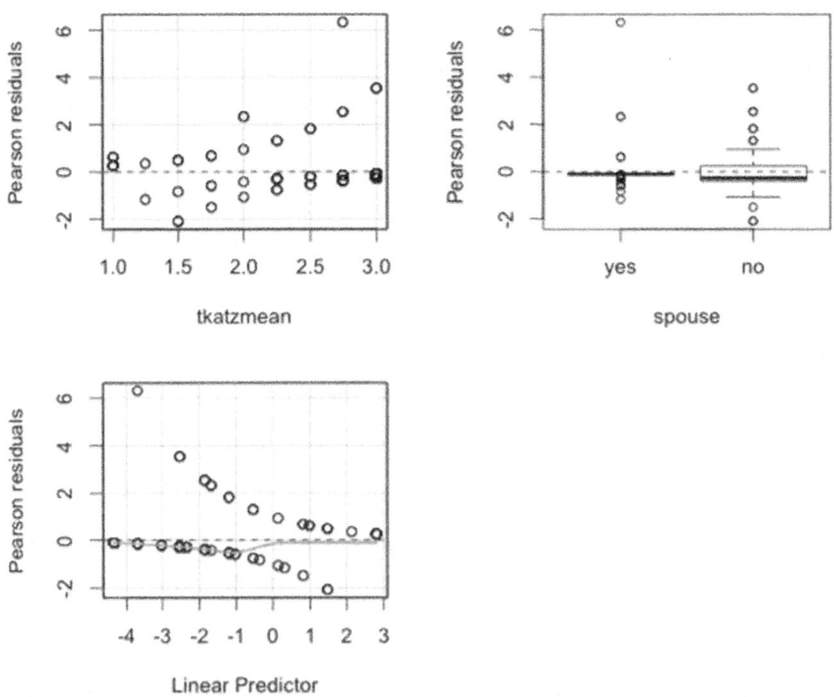

FIGURE 9.5 Residual plots for *logit2* model.

Linear Predictor is fairly straight, indicating a good fit. A boxplot is displayed for the variable *spouse* because it is a binary variable. The dark line in the boxplot is the median and is similar for both categories, *yes* and *no*, which is indicative of a good fit.

Another helpful function provided by the *car* package is **avPlots()**. Added value plots display the influence of an independent variable when all other independent variables are held constant. Type **avPlots(logit2)** in the Console to obtain the graph in Figure 9.6. The figure displays that, as a patient's ADL score increases, there is a strong decrease in the likelihood of returning within 30 days. Just the opposite is true for *spouse,* where not having a spouse increases a patient's chances of returning within 30 days.

For some cases, interpreting of probabilities is easier than odds ratios. The **predict()** function can be used to compare probabilities between categories. For example, if we hold constant the impact of ADL, what is the difference in the probability of returning within 30 days between patients with and without a spouse?

The first step in this analysis is to create a data frame with the two independent variables from the *logit2* model (i.e., *tkatzmean* and *spouse*) using the same names as in the original model. To control for ADL, *tkatzmean* is set to its mean, while *spouse* is allowed to vary. This is accomplished with the following syntax:

```
>return.prob<-
data.frame(tkatzmean=mean(hospital1$tkatzmean),spouse=(1:2))
```

Type **return.prob** in the Console to display the data frame as follows:

```
  tkatzmean       spouse
  1  2.621118        1
  2  2.621118        2
```

The mean of *tkatzmean* is displayed for both levels of *spouse* and will be used to control for its impact. *Spouse* needs to be a factor variable with the levels *yes/no*. It has to match the levels used in the *logit2* model. Use the following syntax to create this factor variable:

```
>return.prob$spouse<-
factor(return.prob$spouse,level=c(1,2),labels=c("yes","no"))
```

Now the probabilities can be calculated for spouse, both *yes* and *no*. To do this, use the following syntax:

```
>return.prob$prob<-predict(logit2,newdata=return.
prob,type="response")
```

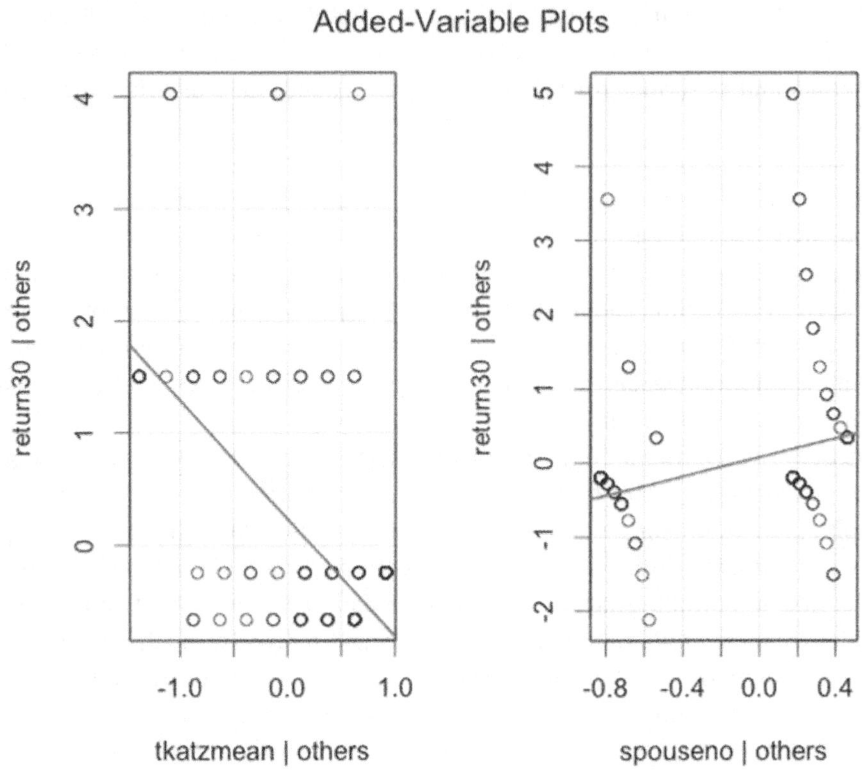

FIGURE 9.6 Added variable plots for *logit2* model.

This command instructs *R* to place the probabilities into a vector called *prob* and append it to the data frame *return.prob*. A file with the result is temporarily stored in *newdata*. Finally, because *spouse* is a response variable, the **type="response"** option is used.

Entering the following into the Console displays the data frame.

```
>return.prob
tkatzmean        spouse      prob
1   2.621118       yes 0.03417483
2   2.621118       no   0.18036479
```

The results indicate that when ADL is held constant at its mean, not having a spouse substantially increases the probability of returning within 30 days. A probability can range between 0 (i.e., the lowest probability of occurring) and 1 (i.e., the highest probability of occurring).

EXAMPLE SUMMARY

We are now ready to report back to hospital administration about the factors related to hospital readmissions within 30 days of discharge. We were able to develop a strong model in which patient ADLs and whether or not they had a spouse were predictive of readmissions within 30 days of discharge.

When this was presented, the hospital chose to implement a community-based intervention: a social worker was assigned to contact all discharged patients with low ADLs within 24 hours of discharge to determine how they are managing with their basic care at home. These discharged patients are asked, for example, about how they are managing getting around their own homes, whether they are having difficulty obtaining food or eating, and if they are having any problems getting to or using the bathroom. Patients who are continuing to have difficulty with these basic activities of daily living receive an evaluation from the local visiting nurse service. Patients who also do not have a spouse are called first and are asked about additional help they may need.

In this way, it is the hospital's intent that patients without an acute medical need are given additional support back in their homes while they recuperate in order to avoid unnecessary readmissions.

ANOTHER EXAMPLE

In this section a new data set is introduced on patients seen in the emergency department (ED) of St. Luke's Hospital. As a follow-up to the previous research you have done, the hospital administrator asked you to examine one more thing: there is interest in understanding what non-medical factors are related to being admitted to the hospital from the ED. The thought is that social work intervention in the ED may be able to avert non-medical admissions.

TABLE 9.1 Description of Variables in the *ed.rdata* File

Variable	Description	Indicators	Variable Type
age	Current age of the patient	The patient's actual age in years	Numeric
adl1	Indicates whether the patient has problems with activities of daily living	0 = no; 1 = yes	Categorical
environment1	Whether the patient has problems in his or her environment outside the hospital. Examples include needing a home health aid, having suitable housing, or financial problems	0 = no environmental problems ; 1 = environmental problems	Categorical
admitted	Whether or not the patient was admitted to the hospital from the ED	0 = not admitted; 1 = admitted	Categorical
race1	The race/ethnicity of the patient	1= white; 2 = Asian; 3 = African American; 4 = Hispanic	Categorical

Open the data file called *ed.rdata* by clicking on **File / Open** in the menu bar and navigating to the folder in which the file is stored. Once the file is open, type **names(ed)** in the Console to obtain a list of variables as shown here:

```
[1] "age"   "adl1"   "environment1" "admitted"
"race1"
```

A description of these variables is provided in Table 9.1.

The major dependent variable in this data set is *admitted.* Using the **table()** function as follows, we can see many fewer patients are admitted than not.

```
>table(ed$admitted)

   0    1
2287  449
```

From this, we can determine that the odds of being admitted are 0.1963271 (admitted/not admitted = 449/2287 = 0.1963271).

Before beginning the logistic regression and to make the analysis easier, we will need to create factor variables for *adl1, enviornment1* and *race1*. Use the following syntax to accomplish this.

```
>adl<-factor(ed$adl1)
>env<-factor(ed$environment1)
>race<-factor(ed$race1)
```

Use the following statement to create the logistic model:

```
>ed1<-glm(admitted~race + age+ env +adl,
data=ed,family="binomial")
```

The **summary(ed1)** function displays the results of the model in the Console, as shown in Figure 9.7.

The confidence intervals are displayed by typing **confint.default(ed1)**.

```
                   2.5 %        97.5 %
(Intercept) -1.31696458 -0.769979841
race2       -1.10818332  0.201990916
race3       -0.85293719 -0.367219228
race4       -0.50283675  0.290291822
age         -0.01094613 -0.003284076
```

```
env1          -0.48004312 -0.050187137
adl1           0.02970981  0.461886176
```

Examinations of the log-odds indicate that all the independent variables except *adl1* decrease the likelihood of a patient being admitted. As defined in the *race1* variable described in Table 9.1, the variable *race2* refers to Asians; *race3*, African Americans; and *race4*, Hispanics. The variable *env1* refers to patients with an environmental problem, and *adl1* refers to patients with ADL problems. Except for *race2* (Asian) and *race4* (Hispanic), all other independent variables in the *ed1* model are statistically significant.

To produce the odds ratios and confidence intervals, enter the following into the Console:

```
>exp(coef(ed1))
```

```
(Intercept)  race2     race3     race4     age       env1      adl1
0.3522295    0.6356570 0.5433084 0.8991796 0.9929102 0.7671176 1.2786413
```

```
Call:
glm(formula = admitted ~ race + age + env + adl, family = "binomial",
    data = ed)

Deviance Residuals:
    Min       1Q   Median       3Q      Max
-0.8623  -0.6418  -0.5672  -0.4632   2.2979

Coefficients:
             Estimate Std. Error z value Pr(>|z|)
(Intercept) -1.043472   0.139539  -7.478 7.55e-14 ***
race2       -0.453096   0.334234  -1.356 0.175219
race3       -0.610078   0.123910  -4.924 8.50e-07 ***
race4       -0.106272   0.202332  -0.525 0.599419
age         -0.007115   0.001955  -3.640 0.000273 ***
env1        -0.265115   0.109659  -2.418 0.015622 *
adl1         0.245798   0.110251   2.229 0.025785 *
---
Signif. codes:  0 '***' 0.001 '**' 0.01 '*' 0.05 '.' 0.1 ' ' 1

(Dispersion parameter for binomial family taken to be 1)

    Null deviance: 2442.8  on 2735  degrees of freedom
Residual deviance: 2399.7  on 2729  degrees of freedom
AIC: 2413.7

Number of Fisher Scoring iterations: 4
```

FIGURE 9.7 Summary results of model *ed1*.

```
>exp(confint.default(ed1))

                2.5 %       97.5 %
Intercept)    0.2679474 0.4630224
race2         0.3301582 1.2238369
race3         0.4261614 0.6926578
race4         0.6048125 1.3368175
age           0.9891136 0.9967213
env1          0.6187567 0.9510514
adl1          1.0301556 1.5870646
```

Because the race variable has four categories, each are compared to whites, the category not included. African Americans (*race3*) are 46% less likely to be admitted compared to whites.

To be comprehensive, the overall effect of race and the differences between categories should be tested. To do this, the *aod* package needs to be installed and then loaded. If you have not already done so, install the package.

The next step is to require the package by entering the following command in the Console:

```
> require(aod)
```

The **`wald.test()`** function will test the overall significance of *race*. The syntax below produces a X^2 test. Notice **`Terms = 2:4`**, which refers to the second, third, and fourth coefficients in the model (i.e., *race2, race3, race4*). The significant X^2 indicates that, overall, race is a significant factor.

```
wald.test(b = coef(ed1), Sigma = vcov(ed1),
Terms = 2:4)

Wald test:
----------

Chi-squared test:
X2 = 25.1, df = 3, P(> X2) = 1.5e-05
```

These results indicate that *race*, overall, is significant in the model; however, we do not know where these differences lie.

Below, African Americans are compared to Hispanics. First, a vector called *L1* is created in which African American is assigned a value of 1 (the third coefficient) and Hispanic (the fourth coefficient) is assigned a value of –1. All other coefficients, including the constant, are assigned a value of 0. The statistically significant X^2

indicates that African Americans are more likely not to be admitted compared to Hispanics.

```
>L1 <- cbind(0, 0, 1, -1, 0, 0, 0)

wald.test(b = coef(ed1), Sigma = vcov(ed1), L = L1)
Wald test:
----------

Chi-squared test:
X2 = 5.5, df = 1, P(> X2) = 0.019
```

To compare Asian patients to African American patients using the **wald.test()** function , a new vector, *L2*, is created. Asian (the second coefficient) is assigned a value of 1 and African American (the third coefficient) a value of –1. All other coefficients are assigned a value of 0.

```
>L2 <- cbind(0, 1, -1, 0, 0, 0, 0)

wald.test(b = coef(ed1), Sigma = vcov(ed1), L = L2)
Wald test:
----------

Chi-squared test:
X2 = 0.21, df = 1, P(> X2) = 0.65
```

The large *p*-value of 0.65 indicates a lack of statistical difference between Asian and African American patients.

To calculate the model X^2, complete the following steps:

Step 1:

```
>chi<-ed1$null.deviance -ed1$deviance
>chi

[1] 43.10193
```

Step 2:

```
> df<-ed1$df.null-ed1$df.residual
>df
```

```
[1] 6
```

Step 3:

```
>pchisq(chi,df, lower.tail = FALSE)
```

```
[1] 1.113497e-07
```

The significant model X^2 of 43.20293 indicates that the model with independent variables improves the prediction of admission from the ED as compared to the constant-only model.

INTERACTIONS

Often an independent variable is dependent on different levels of another predictor variable. In other words, a statistically significant interaction means that one predictor variable's relationship with the outcome variable is dependent on its relationship with another independent variable. As an example, and using the *ed.rdata* data set, we can test the impact of age on environment using the following syntax:

```
>ed2<-glm(admitted~race + age+ env +adl
+env:age,data=ed,family="binomial")
>summary(ed2)
```

The statement **env:age** is the interaction. A colon (:) between two independent variables is recognized as an interaction in *R*.

The results in Figure 9.8 indicate that the interaction is statistically significant. The main effect for *environment* is significant, but *age* is not. This suggests that the impact of age on being admitted to the hospital is dependent upon having an environmental issue. The output shows that the odds of being admitted decrease as age increases for patients with environmental problems (*age:env1*).

The odds ratios are displayed for the interaction using the following syntax:

```
>exp(coef(ed2))
```

```
(Intercept) race2     race3     race4     age       env1      adl1      age:env1
0.2026483   0.6502772 0.5696833 0.9283346 1.0045059 1.8539146 1.2695020 0.9815227
```

The results show that for a one-unit increase in age, the odds of being admitted decreases by 2% (i.e., 1 – 0.9815227) for patients with environmental issues.

```
Call:
glm(formula = admitted ~ race + age + env + adl + env:age, family = "binomial",
    data = ed)

Deviance Residuals:
    Min       1Q   Median       3Q      Max
-0.8831  -0.6419  -0.5342  -0.4444   2.4029

Coefficients:
             Estimate Std. Error z value Pr(>|z|)
(Intercept) -1.596283   0.187730  -8.503  < 2e-16 ***
race2       -0.430357   0.334862  -1.285  0.19873
race3       -0.562675   0.124394  -4.523 6.09e-06 ***
race4       -0.074363   0.202955  -0.366  0.71406
age          0.004496   0.003043   1.477  0.13962
env1         0.617299   0.212430   2.906  0.00366 **
adl1         0.238625   0.110661   2.156  0.03106 *
age:env1    -0.018650   0.003758  -4.963 6.94e-07 ***
---
Signif. codes:  0 '***' 0.001 '**' 0.01 '*' 0.05 '.' 0.1 ' ' 1

(Dispersion parameter for binomial family taken to be 1)

    Null deviance: 2442.8  on 2735  degrees of freedom
Residual deviance: 2374.9  on 2728  degrees of freedom
AIC: 2390.9

Number of Fisher Scoring iterations: 4
```

FIGURE 9.8 Summary of model *ed2*.

Now, we can compare a 30-year-old to an 80-year-old with environmental problems. The age difference is 50 years. Given an odds ratio of 0.9815227, do the following calculation in the Console to obtain this likelihood:

```
>(1-.9815227^50)*100
[1] 60.64342
```

The odds of an 80-year-old with environmental problems being admitted decrease 60.64342% compared to a 30-year-old with environmental problems.

A model with an interaction should be compared to the model without one. The **anova()** function is used to compare models. Entering the following syntax in the Console results in the outcome depicted in Figure 9.9.

```
>anova (ed1,ed2,test="Chisq")
```

The significant X^2 and the lower residual deviance for *ed2* indicate that including the interaction in the model improves the fit.

Another possible interaction to consider is the interaction between ADL and age. Model *ed3* contains a second interaction, *adl:age*. The code for creating model *ed3* is as follows:

```
Analysis of Deviance Table

Model 1: admitted ~ race + age + env + adl
Model 2: admitted ~ race + age + env + adl + env:age
  Resid. Df Resid. Dev Df Deviance  Pr(>Chi)
1      2729     2399.7
2      2728     2374.9  1   24.842 6.222e-07 ***
---
Signif. codes:  0 '***' 0.001 '**' 0.01 '*' 0.05 '.' 0.1 ' ' 1
```

FIGURE 9.9 ANOVA comparing models *ed1* and *ed2*.

```
>ed3<-glm(admitted~race + age+ env +adl +env:age+
adl:age,data=ed,family="binomial")
```

The **summary(ed3)** syntax displays the results of the model in Figure 9.10.

```
>summary(ed3)
```

```
Call:
glm(formula = admitted ~ race + age + env + adl + env:age + adl:age,
    family = "binomial", data = ed)

Deviance Residuals:
    Min       1Q   Median       3Q      Max
-0.9368  -0.6360  -0.5524  -0.4264   2.6273

Coefficients:
             Estimate Std. Error z value Pr(>|z|)
(Intercept) -1.232122   0.201950  -6.101 1.05e-09 ***
race2       -0.418328   0.335766  -1.246  0.21280
race3       -0.557349   0.124822  -4.465 8.00e-06 ***
race4       -0.043815   0.203474  -0.215  0.82950
age         -0.006125   0.004018  -1.524  0.12745
env1         0.635862   0.210877   3.015  0.00257 **
adl1        -0.514457   0.208999  -2.462  0.01383 *
age:env1    -0.018770   0.003732  -5.029 4.92e-07 ***
age:adl1     0.017402   0.004128   4.216 2.49e-05 ***
---
Signif. codes:  0 '***' 0.001 '**' 0.01 '*' 0.05 '.' 0.1 ' ' 1

(Dispersion parameter for binomial family taken to be 1)

    Null deviance: 2442.8  on 2735  degrees of freedom
Residual deviance: 2356.2  on 2727  degrees of freedom
AIC: 2374.2

Number of Fisher Scoring iterations: 5
```

FIGURE 9.10 Summary of model *ed3*.

The results indicate that both interactions are statistically significant. The main effects for both environment and ADL are statistically significant. Once again, age is not significant.

The following command will produce the odds ratios:

```
exp(coef(ed3))
```

```
(Intercept) race2     race3     race4     age       env1      adl1      age:env1  age:adl1
0.2916730  0.6581462 0.5727252 0.9571305 0.9938941 1.8886501 0.5978250 0.9814049 1.0175539
```

The odds ratio for the interaction *env1:age* is 0.9814049. This indicates that for patients with environmental problems, as age goes up, the odds of being admitted decrease by 2% for a one-year increase in age. The odds ratio for *adl1:age* is 1.0175539. This indicates that for patients with ADL problems, as age goes up, their odds of being admitted increases. For example, we can compare a 30-year-old to an 80-year-old with ADL problems. The age difference is 50 years. Do the following calculation in the Console to obtain the likelihood:

```
>(1.0175539^50 -1)*100
[1] 138.7103
```

This indicates that the odds of an 80-year-old with ADL problems being admitted to the hospital are 138.7% greater than for a 30-year-old patient with ADL problems.

A graph of the interaction is helpful in understanding them. To do this, first install the *effects* package with the following syntax:

```
>install.package("effects")
```

Once the package is installed, load it into *R* with the following syntax:

```
>require(effects)
```

Now the interaction can be plotted using the following syntax:

```
>plot(effect("age:env",ed3),multiline=T)
```

The *age:env* is the interaction to be plotted, and *ed3* is the model from which the interaction was derived. The graph produced by the command is provided in Figure 9.11. The dashed line shows the change in the probability of being admitted for a patient with environmental problems. The x-axis contains age in years and the y-axis is the probability of being admitted. A probability can vary between 0 and 1; the closer to 0 a probability is, the less likely it is that a patient will be admitted; the closer to 1, the more likely it is that a patient will be admitted. Figure 9.11 shows

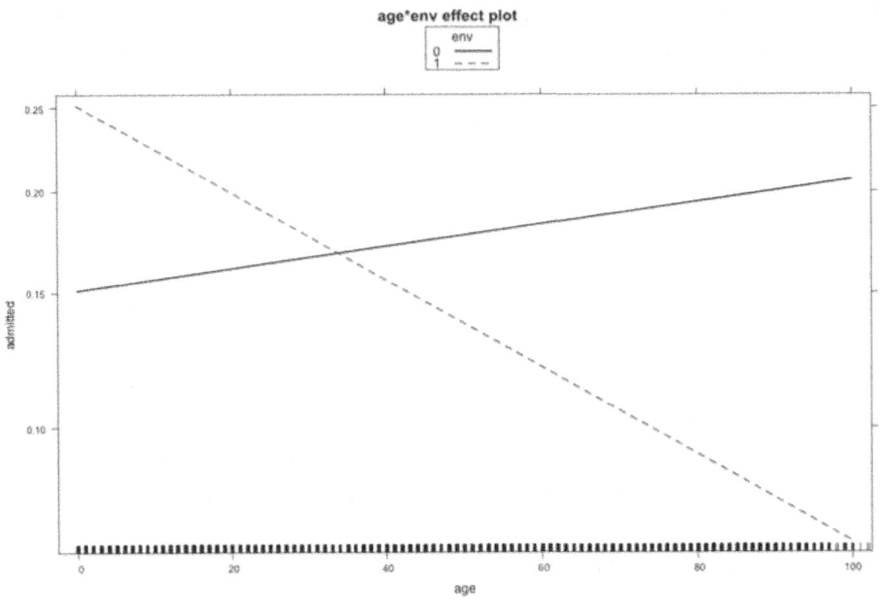

FIGURE 9.11 Interaction plot for age x environment.

that as age increases, the probability of being admitted decreases for those with environmental problems.

Note that the lines cross at about 38 years of age. At this point, and only at this point, does age not matter with regard to hospital admittance based on environment. Also note that people below that age with environmental problems have a higher probability of being admitted than those without environmental problems. Finally, note that the steepness of the two lines is quite different. The steeper negative line for those with environmental problems indicates the faster decrease in the probability of hospital admittance for those with environmental problems as patients age.

An interaction graph for the *age:adl* interaction can be created using the following syntax:

```
>plot(effect("age:adl",ed3),multiline=T)
```

The results are displayed in Figure 9.12. The dashed line represents patients with ADL problems. Note that the line remains relatively flat regardless of age. The solid line represents patients who do not have ADL problems. For patients without an ADL problem, as age increases, the probability of being admitted decreases.

Note that the lines cross at about 36 years of age. At this point, and only at this point, does age not matter with regard to hospital admittance from the ED based on ADL. Also note that for patients above that age who do not have ADL problems, there is a decreasing probability of being admitted compared to those

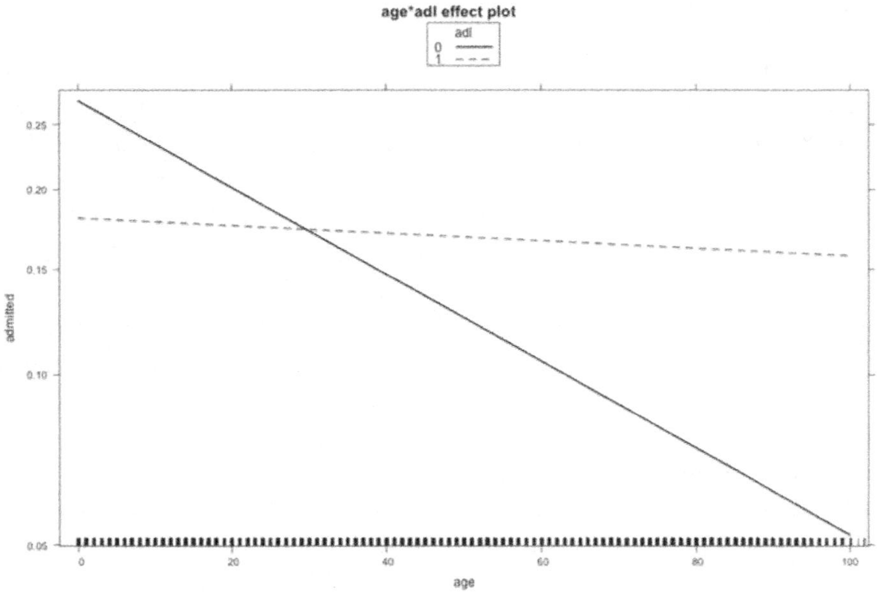

FIGURE 9.12 Interaction plot for age x ADL.

with ADL problems (i.e., the gap between those with and without ADL problems increases with age). Finally, note that the steepness of the two lines is quite different.

To complete our analysis, the **anova()** can be used to test if the addition of the *adl1:age* interaction improves the overall fit of the model. The syntax to enter into the Console is as follows, and the results are displayed in Figure 9.13.

```
>anova (ed2,ed3,test="Chisq")
```

```
Analysis of Deviance Table

Model 1: admitted ~ race + age + env + adl + env:age
Model 2: admitted ~ race + age + env + adl + env:age + adl:age
  Resid. Df Resid. Dev Df Deviance  Pr(>Chi)
1      2728     2374.9
2      2727     2356.2  1   18.626 1.591e-05 ***
---
Signif. codes:  0 '***' 0.001 '**' 0.01 '*' 0.05 '.' 0.1 ' ' 1
```

FIGURE 9.13 ANOVA comparing models *ed2* and *ed3*.

The decrease of the residual deviance by 18.7 and the significant X^2 presented in the results indicate that the addition of this interaction does improve the model fit.

EXAMPLE SUMMARY

The findings from this analysis indicates that patients with ADL problems are more at risk of being admitted to the hospital from the ED, while African American patients and those with environmental problems are less likely to be admitted to the hospital. This study provides further evidence of the usefulness of a systemic method of assessing emergency room patients by offering a model for early identification of patients at risk (Auerbach, Rock, Goldstein, Kaminsky, & Heft-Laporte, 2001; Auerbach et al., 2007).

Additionally, more questions arise that warrant follow-up study; namely, for what reasons are African American patients less likely to be admitted than other patients, and is this a desirable condition? As an evaluator at St. Luke's, you would likely bring this to the attention of hospital administration and collect additional data that might provide insight into this finding.

With an emphasis on cost containment in hospitals, the findings of this current analysis support the cost-effective nature of social work in the emergency service setting. Preventing unnecessary admissions helps to alleviate the growing problem of bed availability. Keeping patients out of the hospital and providing community-based supports, which will be promoted under the Affordable Care Act, can help prevent many patients from experiencing deteriorating health (National Coalition on Care Coordination, n.d.).

Furthermore, the results of the logistic regression suggest that the criteria used by social work to assess patients are based on sound psychosocial factors. Patients who are assessed as having environmental problems are much less likely to be admitted. On the other hand, patients with ADL problems have a heightened chance of being admitted (Auerbach et al., 2007).

/// 10 /// BRINGING IT ALL TOGETHER

Using *The Clinical Record* to Evaluate a Program

In order to work through the examples in this chapter, you will need to *install* and *load* the following packages:

- *psych*
- *Hmisc*
- *gmodels*
- *effsize*
- *ggplot2*

For more information on how to do this, refer to the Packages section in Chapter 3.

INTRODUCTION

In this chapter, we will bring together many of the concepts described throughout this book in a comprehensive example. To begin, however, we will introduce you to *The Clinical Record*, our free downloadable software package that can be used to track clients. We will then provide detailed instructions for importing data into *R* for analysis, and then we will demonstrate a program evaluation based upon the case study presented in this chapter.

This chapter, then, should provide you with an end-to-end example of conducting a simple program evaluation in an agency setting.

GETTING STARTED WITH *THE CLINICAL RECORD*

Instructions for downloading *The Clinical Record* can be found on our website at www.ssdanalysis.com. On the Home Page, click on the "Supporting Docs" tab, and select the *readme* file on installing *The Clinical Record*. There are separate instructions for Mac and Window versions.

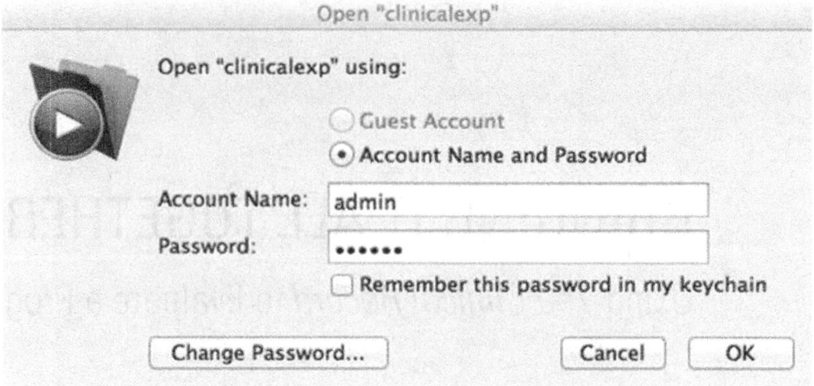

FIGURE 10.1 Sign-in screen.

FIGURE 10.2 Opening splash screen.

The first time you open the application after installing it, you will see the following dialogue, illustrated in Figure 10.1.

Enter *admin* as your account name and *newpass* as your password. You have just entered the system as the administrator, which allows you access to all aspects of the program. Later you will learn how to add users and allocate different levels of access to the system.

After clicking *OK* you will see the splash screen (shown in Figure 10.2) at the top left corner of your screen.

From here, you can go directly to the authors' website for technical support, to view additional resources, and to request any new information on *The Clinical Record*. Clicking *Close* will open the screen displayed in Figure 10.3.

For security reasons, it is extremely important that you change your password immediately. To do this, as shown in Figure 10.4, click on the *File* option and select *Change Password*.

Simply fill in the information in the *Change Password* dialogue, as displayed in Figure 10.5.

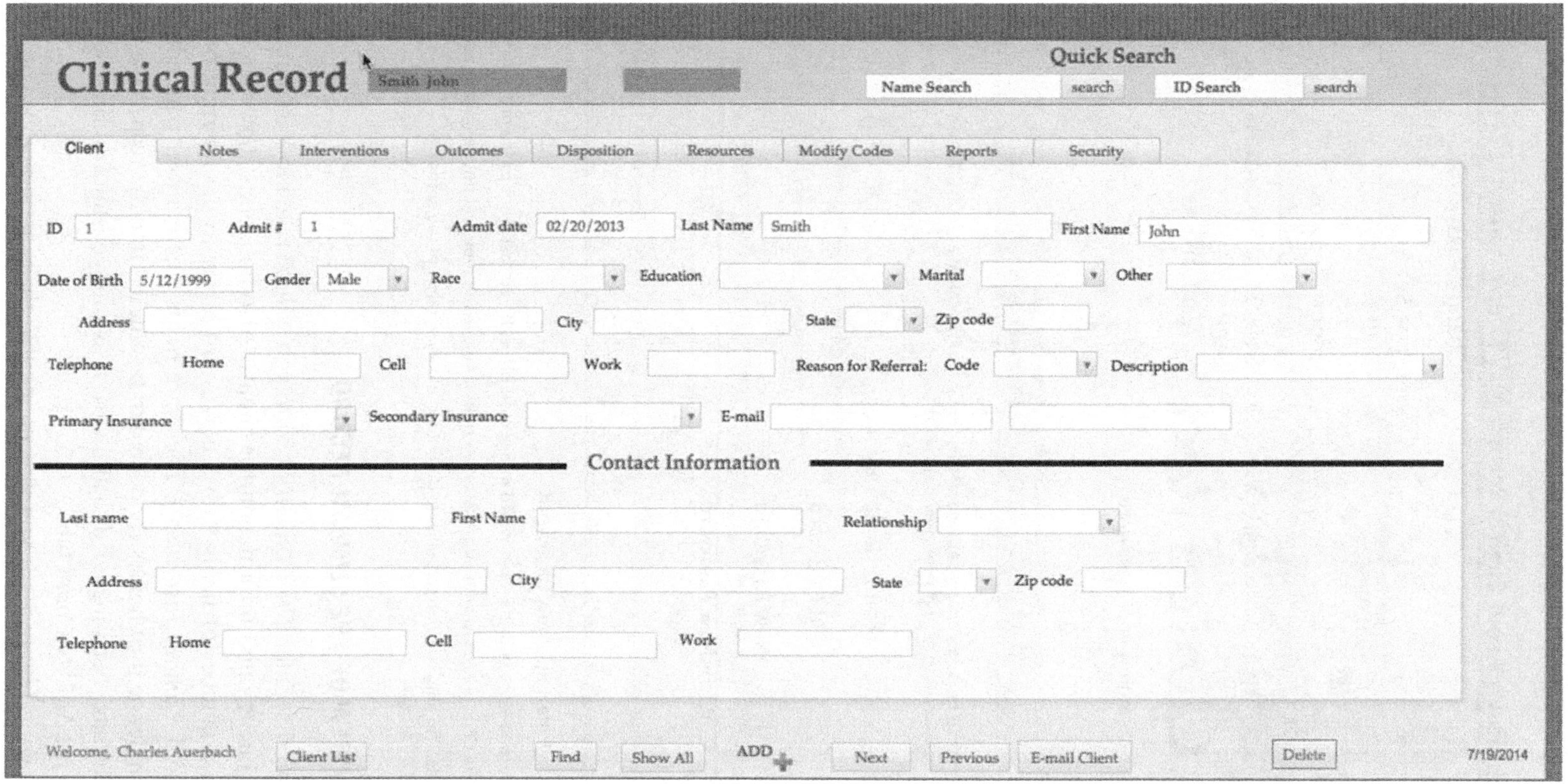

FIGURE 10.3 Client background data screen.

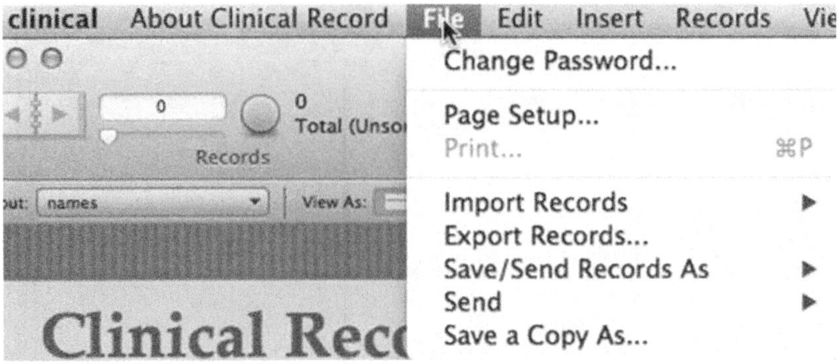

FIGURE 10.4 Changing your password.

FIGURE 10.5 Entering a new password.

NOTE: Be sure to store your new password in a secure place. If you lose your password, you will not be able to access *The Clinical Record* with administrative rights. As a result, you will not be able to add new users or modify fields. The only solution to this is to download a new version of the software.

AN OVERVIEW OF *THE CLINICAL RECORD*

When you first enter *The Clinical Record*, you will be taken to the *Client* tab, which contains background information for clients. Also notice, as shown in Figure 10.3, there are a number of fields with a downward arrow to the far right of field (e.g., *Gender* and *Primary Insurance*). These are fields where a user with administrative rights can define the choices (or codes) to be entered into the respective field. These field codes have been included to allow for maximum customization, and this can be done via the *Modify Codes* tab.

In viewing Figure 10.3, you will notice that there are a number of tabs: *Notes, Interventions, Client, Outcomes, Dispositions, Resources, Modify Codes, Reports,* and *Security.* Clicking on a tab opens a new screen. You first need to enter background data on a client in order to access the other tabs.

THE CLIENT TAB

Adding a Client

To get started, you can begin by entering the partial client data displayed in Figure 10.3 or data for an actual client. At the bottom of this screen, you will see the following figure: +. Click on the plus sign and you will be able to enter the record. Table 10.1 describes each of the fields on this screen and notes for each of these.

Removing a Client

A record can be removed by clicking the Delete button at the bottom right of the window. If you do this, the dialogue shown in Figure 10.6 will be displayed. Be certain you want to do this, because doing so will remove all of the client's information stored in *The Clinical Record.* **There will be no way to undo this.**

There are a number of fields in the client background database that are required—that is, if you do not enter any one of these, you will be prompted to do so.

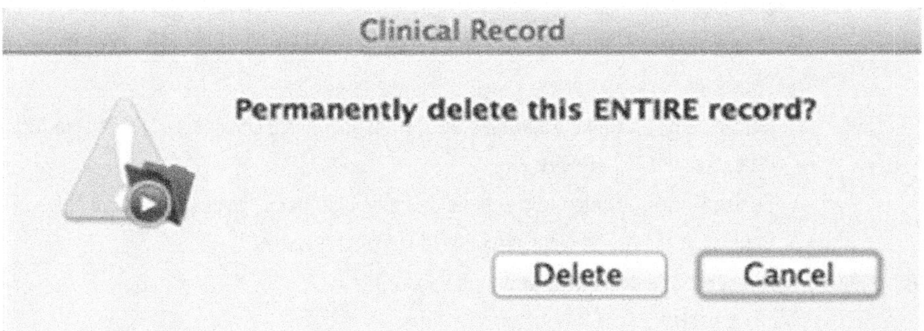

FIGURE 10.6 Deleting a record.

FIGURE 10.7 Missing information warning.

TABLE 10.1 *Client* Background Fields

Field	Type of Field	Description and Notes
ID	Direct entry Numeric	A unique numeric ID given to each client. An error message is issued if there is an attempt to enter a duplicate ID. **Once an ID is given to an individual client, it cannot be changed.**
Admit #	Direct entry Numeric	A client can have more than one admission. The first admission would be 1.
Admit Date	Direct entry/ Date	The date of admission. This field cannot be empty. An error message is issued if it is empty.
Last Name	Direct entry/ Character	Client's last name
First Name	Direct entry/ Character	Client's first name
Date of Birth	Direct entry/ Date	Client's date of birth. This field cannot be empty. An error message is issued if it is empty.
Gender	Choice field/ Character	Client's gender. Drop down field choices are defined via modify codes.
Race	Choice field/ character	Client's race. Drop down field choices are defined via *Modify Codes.*
Education	Choice field/ Character	Client's education. Drop down field choices are defined via *Modify Codes.*
Marital	Choice field/ Character	Client's marital status. Drop down field choices are defined via *Modify Codes.*
Other	Choice field/ Character	Option to create field of administrator's choice. Drop down field choices are defined via *Modify Codes.*
Address	Direct entry/ Character	Client's current address
City	Direct entry/ Character	Client's current city of residence
State	Choice field/ Character	Client's state. Choice fields of all US states. Drop down field choices are defined via *Modify Codes.*
Zip code	Direct entry Numeric	Zip code
Telephone	Direct entry	Three different telephone numbers can be added: Home, Cell, and Work.
Reason for Referral Code	Choice field/ Number	Provides number code associated with a description of the reason for referral. Drop down field choices are defined via *Modify Codes.*
Reason for Referral Description	Choice field/ Character	Gives description of reason for referral. Drop down field choices are defined via *Modify Codes.*

(continued)

TABLE 10.1 Continued

Field	Type of Field	Description and Notes
Primary Insurance	Choice field/ Character	Client's primary insurance. Drop down field choices are defined via *Modify Codes.*
Secondary Insurance	Choice field / Character	Client's secondary insurance. Drop down field choices are defined via *Modify Codes.*
E-mail	Direct entry/ Character	Client's e-mail address
Contact Last Name	Direct entry/ Character	Contact person's last name
Contact First Name	Direct entry/ Character	Contact person's first name
Contact Relationship	Choice field/ Character	Contact person's relationship to client. Drop down field choices are defined via *Modify Codes.*
Contact Address	Direct entry/ Character	Contact person's address
Contact City	Direct entry/ Character	Contact's city
Contact State	Direct entry / Character	Choice fields of all US states. Drop down field choices are defined via *Modify Codes.*
Contact Zip code	Direct entry Numeric	Zip code
Contact Telephone		Contact person's telephone numbers

Required fields are ID, Admit #, Admit Date, and Date of Birth. If any one of these fields is left blank, you will receive the prompt displayed in Figure 10.7, and you will need to respond to the prompt. Click *Yes* to enter the data into the requested field. Once you enter an ID for a client, it will be associated with interventions, outcomes, and disposition. **Do not change the ID, otherwise these links will be removed and you will not have accurate information about your client.**

Locating a Client

There are several ways to find a particular client. You will want to do this in order to view information about a specific individual or to add information to that client's record.

One easy way to locate a client is to click on the *Client List* button located at the bottom of each screen. Figure 10.8 displays an example of a list of clients. Notice

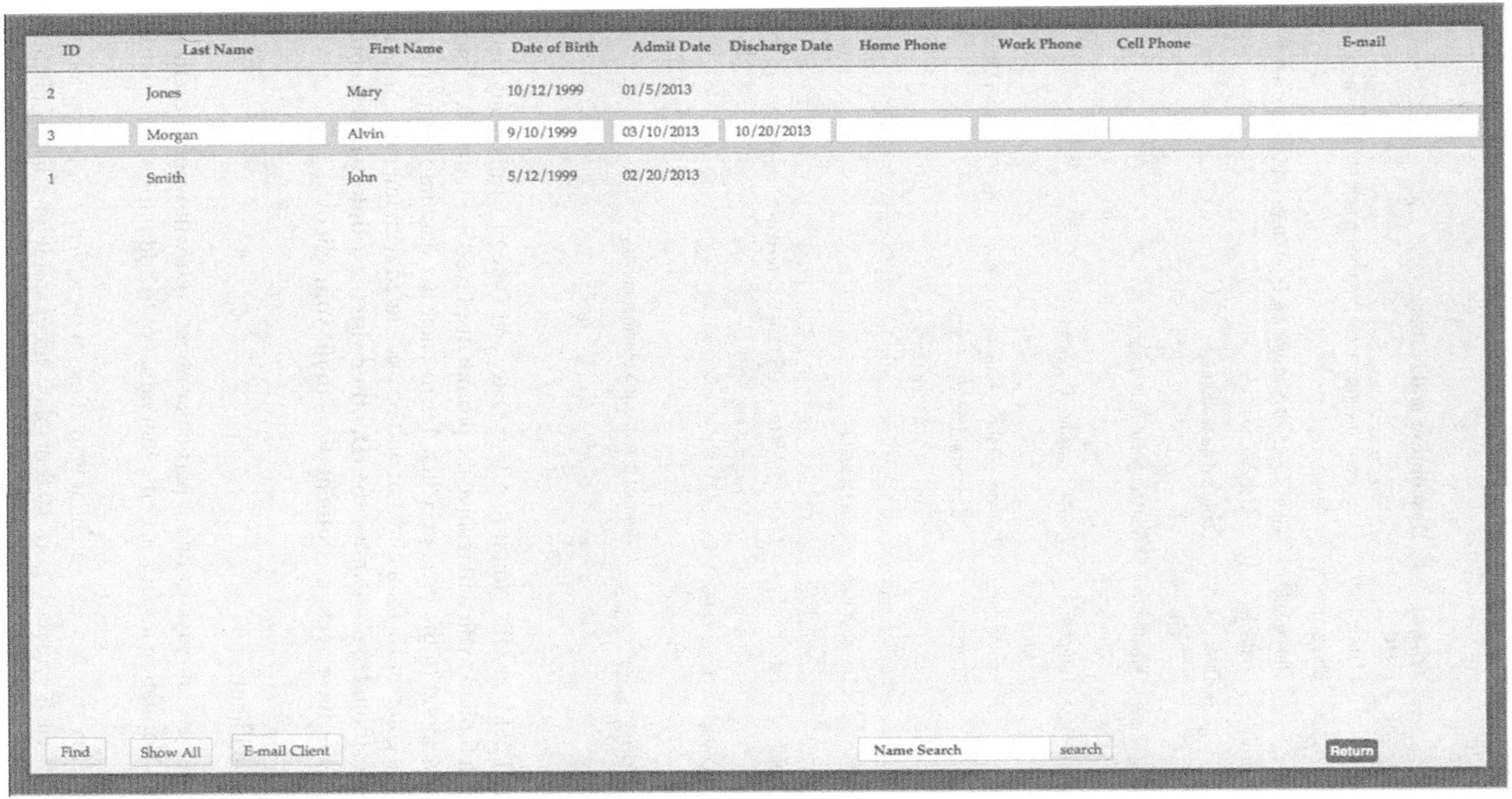

FIGURE 10.8 Locating a client.

FIGURE 10.9 *Quick Search.*

that the list is in alphabetical order. Highlight the client you want, and select the "Return" button at the bottom right corner of the screen to take you to the *Client* screen for that client.

Another way to locate a client is through a *Quick Search,* which is displayed in Figure 10.9. *Quick Search* is located at the top of *The Clinical Record* and is easily viewable from any tab in the application.

You can search for a client either by "Name" or "ID." This is done by entering a last name or ID in the appropriate box and then clicking *search*. For a name search, if there is a unique last name, the record will be retrieved immediately. If there is more than once instance of the last name, a list similar to the one presented in Figure 10.10 will appear.

The tabular listing displays the client's name, date of birth, admit date, and discharge date. Select the desired client and click the Return button at the bottom left of the screen to retrieve the record.

You can also click on the *Client List* button Client List at the bottom left of any screen to produce a tabular list of all clients in the database. Selecting a client and clicking the Return button at the bottom right of this screen will retrieve the record.

Clicking on the find button Find in any screen places *The Clinical Record* into find mode. Here, you will see a blank screen with a magnifying glass symbol in each field, as displayed in Figure 10.11 on pg. 229.

From here, you can enter search criteria in any combinations of fields. Pressing the RETURN key initiates the search. If a record is found matching all specified criteria, it will be displayed immediately. If no matching record is found, the dialogue displayed in Figure 10.12 will be shown on pg. 230. At this point, you can choose to cancel the search or change your search criteria.

MODIFY CODES TAB

Earlier in this chapter, we told you that you could modify codes for the fields with drop down arrows. You do this from the *Modify Codes* tab.

Click on the *Modify Codes* tab, and you will be presented with the screen shown in Figure 10.13 on pg. 231. Clicking on a button opens a screen where you can enter and modify choices for a selected field.

Try this by clicking on the *Reasons* button, which will allow you to add, modify, or delete codes for reasons for referral to the organization. As shown in Figure 10.14 on pg. 232, there are already two reasons entered. Notice that there are fields for both a code and a description. Depending on the type of code you want to work with, you will

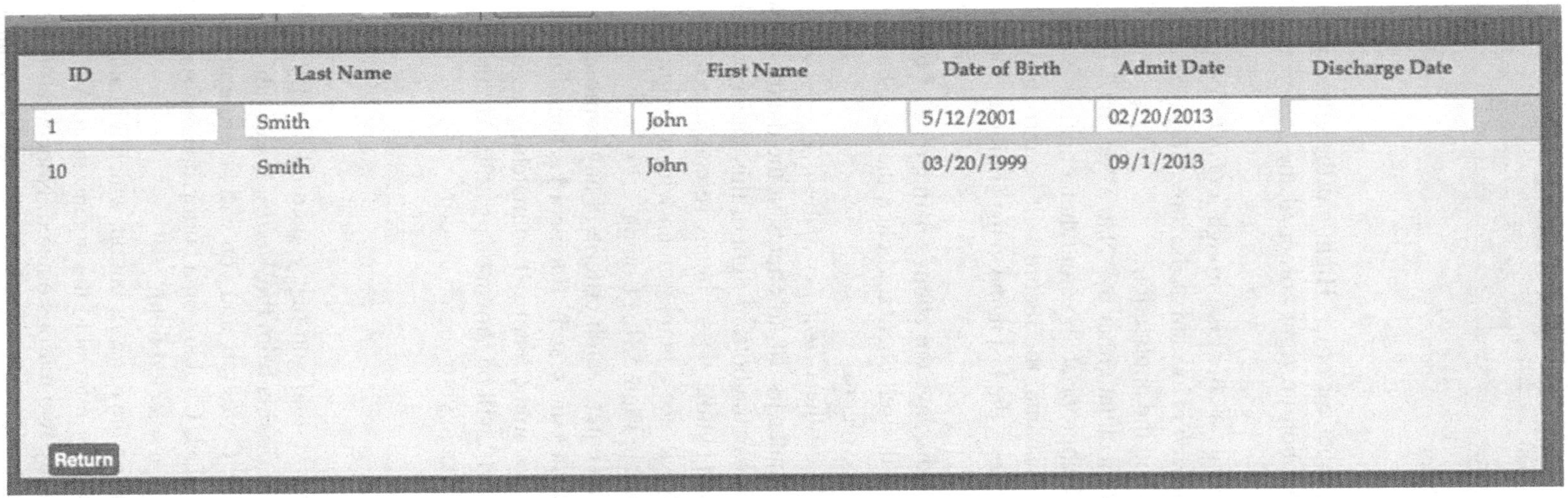

FIGURE 10.10 Example of multiple names returned from a *Quick Search*.

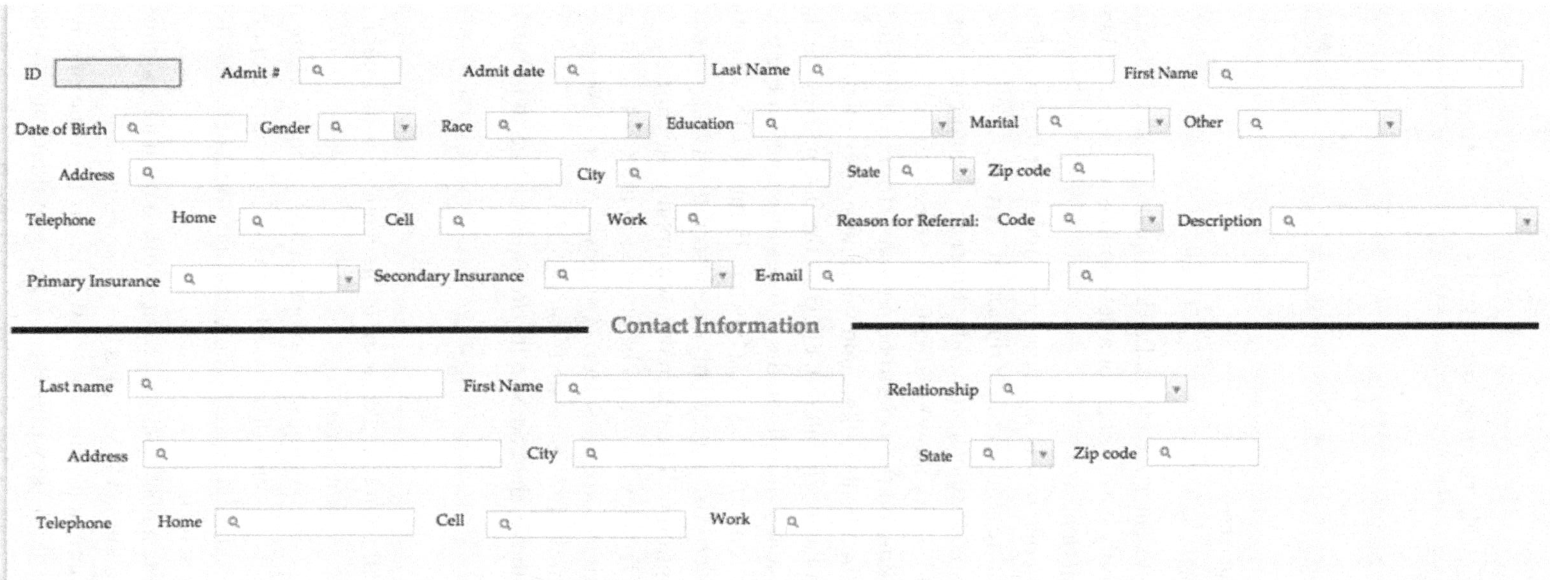

FIGURE 10.11 Search screen from *Client* tab.

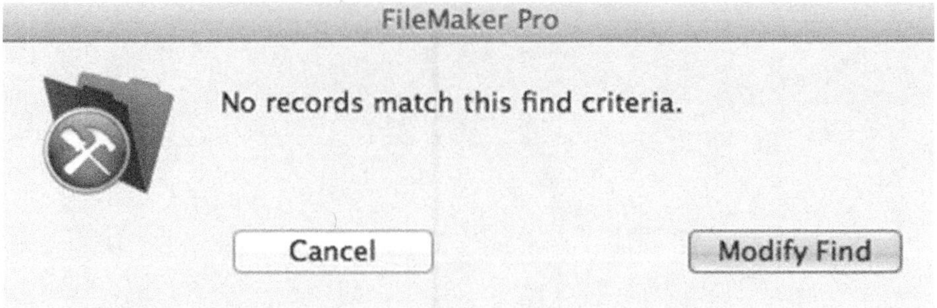

FIGURE 10.12 *Not found* screen.

be given a choice to enter a code and a description, or just a description. Fields like *Gender* and *Race* only have a field for a description, while *DX* allows you to enter both a code and a description.

You can add a code by clicking the plus sign at the top of this screen. To add Code 3 with the corresponding description of "Truancy," click the plus sign and an empty yellow box is displayed for code. Enter a "3" and click on the empty box to the right (it should turn yellow) and enter the description "Truancy." A choice can be deleted by clicking on the field to be removed, followed by clicking the Delete button. To return to the client background window simply click the Return button. Once client information has been entered, click on the down arrow to the right of *Reason for Referral Code* and you will see the choices presented in Figure 10.15 on pg. 232, including the addition of truancy. As shown in Figure 10.15, all options are displayed in alphabetical order. Also notice only the description is displayed. The code associated with a description will be entered based upon your choice.

If you select "Truancy," a 3 will be entered in the *Code* field, as this is the value associated with truancy. Now, select "Truancy" under *Description* so that the two fields match, as shown in Figure 10.16 on pg. 232.

As described above, the codes in the *Reasons* choice field can be removed.

NOTES TAB

Very often, you will want to make notes about a client or an interaction with a client. This could include session notes.

To do this, click on the *Notes* tab to open a text window where notes can be written. Clicking on this tab will display all notes written on the client whose information is displayed in the *Client* tab. The first time you enter notes for a client, all you will see is a blank screen.

When you create a note, you will want to insert the date and time. If you are using a Mac, press the "command" key plus the "-" key simultaneously to insert the current date. Pressing "command" plus the ";" will insert the time of day. If you are using a PC, pressing the "Ctrl" key plus the "–" key simultaneously will insert the current date. Similarly, pressing "Ctrl" plus the ";" will insert the time of day.

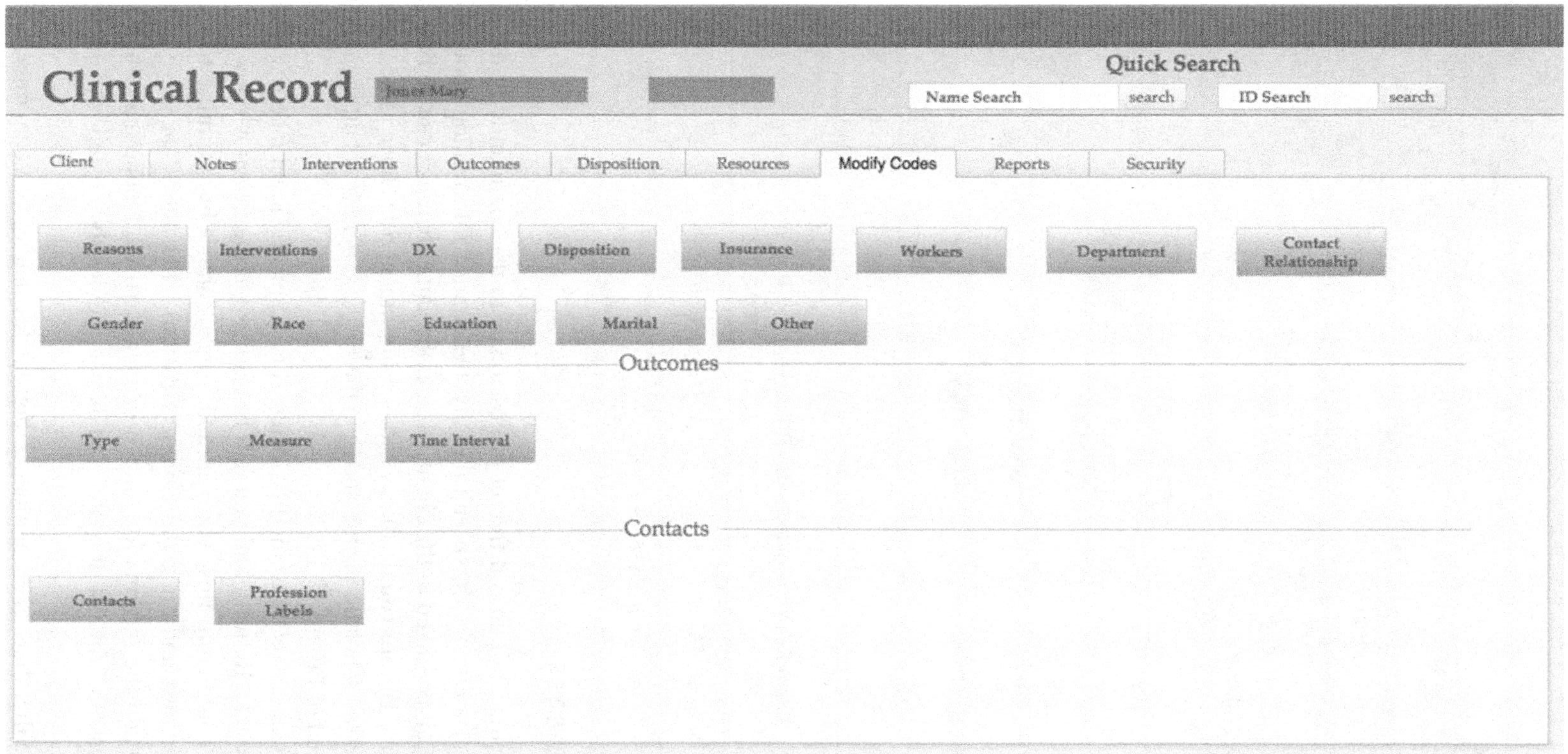

FIGURE 10.13 *Modify Codes* screen.

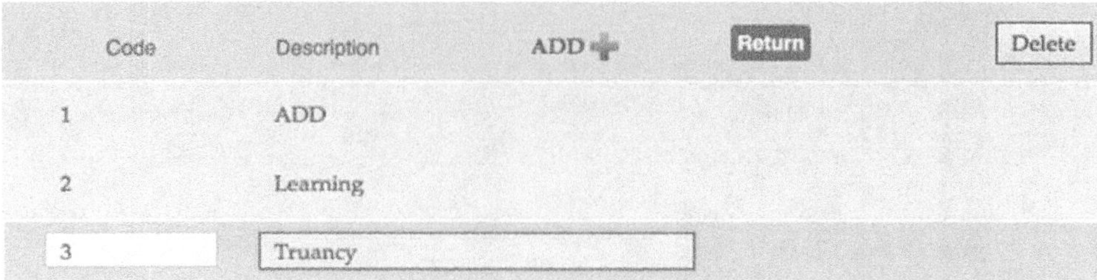

FIGURE 10.14 Adding a code.

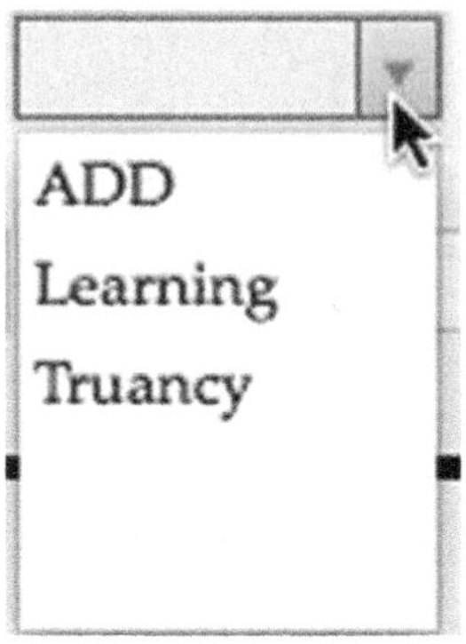

FIGURE 10.15 Example of a choice field.

FIGURE 10.16 Entering reason for referral.

RESOURCES TAB

The Resources tab links different professionals in the community to the client. For example, if a client is in speech therapy, the contact information about the speech therapist can be linked to the client. In fact, the same therapist can be linked to multiple clients. Before you do this, various professional titles have to be defined using *Modify Codes*. Click on the tab and then the *Profession Labels* button in the tab. This is displayed in Figure 10.17.

Now you are ready to modify, delete, or add professional labels. When you are finished, click "Return," and you will be returned to the *Client* window.

After completing this, you can add a new contact by returning to the *Modify Codes* window, and click the *Contacts* button. Click the at the bottom of the screen to add the information shown in Figure 10.18. Notice that when you click on "Profession," the list of professionals you previously created is displayed on the screen.

Notice that there are a number of buttons for managing your contacts. The *Find* button performs searches to locate a contact on any field displayed in Figure 10.18.

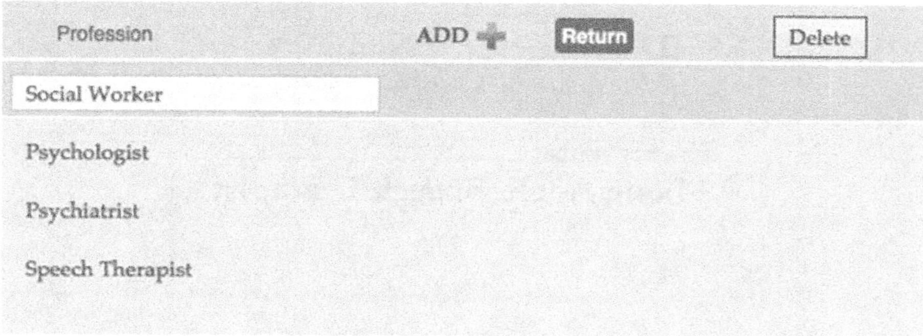

FIGURE 10.17 Example of professional titles.

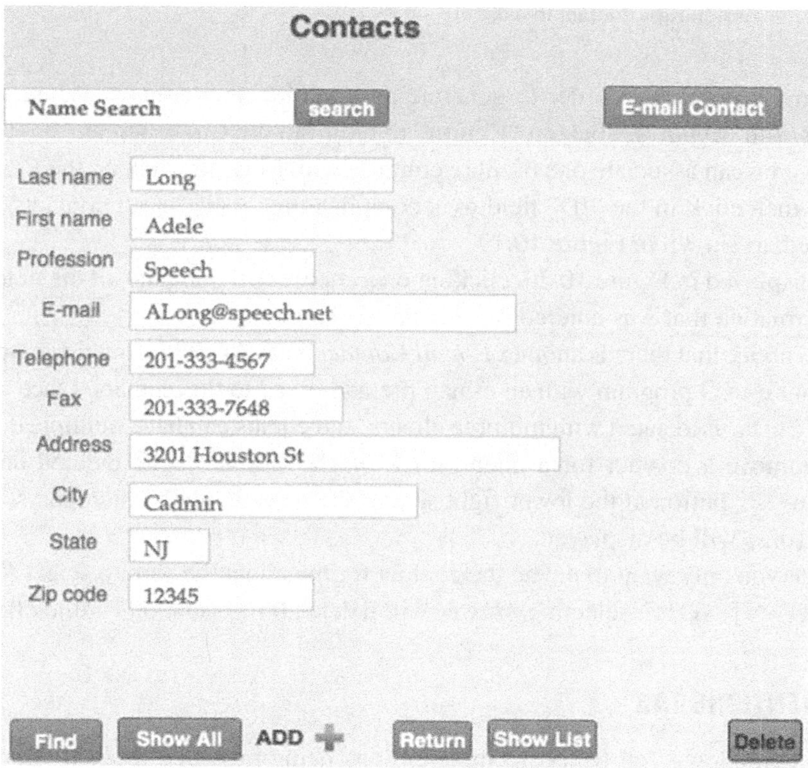

FIGURE 10.18 Contact data entry screen.

In this way, you could, for example, search your contacts for all psychiatrists to make a referral to a client. The *Show All* button closes find mode and will return you to the primary *Contacts* screen, illustrated in Figure 10.18. The *Show List* button displays a tabular alphabetical list of all our contacts. By highlighting a desired contact and clicking "Return," you will be able to modify existing contacts. Also notice that there is an *E-mail Contact* button in the main *Contacts* screen. Clicking on this will open

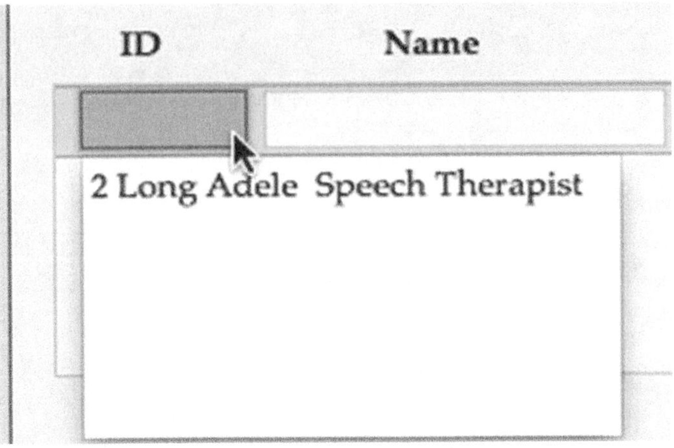

FIGURE 10.19 Assigning a contact to a client.

your e-mail program in order to generate an e-mail to that contact. When you are finished with *Contacts*, click on "Return" to return to the *Client* screen.

Now you can associate one or more contacts with a client. Click on the *Resources* tab and then click in the "ID" field to accomplish this. A list of all contacts will be displayed, as shown in Figure 10.19.

As displayed in Figure 10.20, clicking on a choice will populate all the fields with the information that was entered for that particular contact.

Also notice that there is another *E-mail Contact* button. Clicking on this button will open your e-mail program with an e-mail pre-addressed to this contact. Once again, a contact can be associated with multiple clients, and clients can have multiple contacts.

To remove a contact for a client, click on the contact to be deleted and then click the Delete button at the lower right side of the screen and the dialogue shown in Figure 10.21 will be displayed.

Since you only want to delete the contact for the client, be sure to select *Related*. IMPORTANT NOTE: selecting *Master* will delete all information for the client.

INTERVENTIONS TAB

This screen allows you to record interventions being provided to each client. This makes it easy to quickly review the progress of a case. Table 10.2 describes each of the fields displayed on this screen (see pg. 236).

Before you can begin entering interventions, the choice fields described in Table 10.2 need to be defined by selecting the *Modify Codes* screen (see pg. 236). Choices for each field type are defined in a similar manner and are described in detail in this section.

You can view and modify the choice of "Workers" in the *Modify Codes* screen. Click on the tab and then the *Workers* button in the tab. A screen similar to that shown in Figure 10.22 will be displayed on pg. 237. To enter workers' names, click the + and

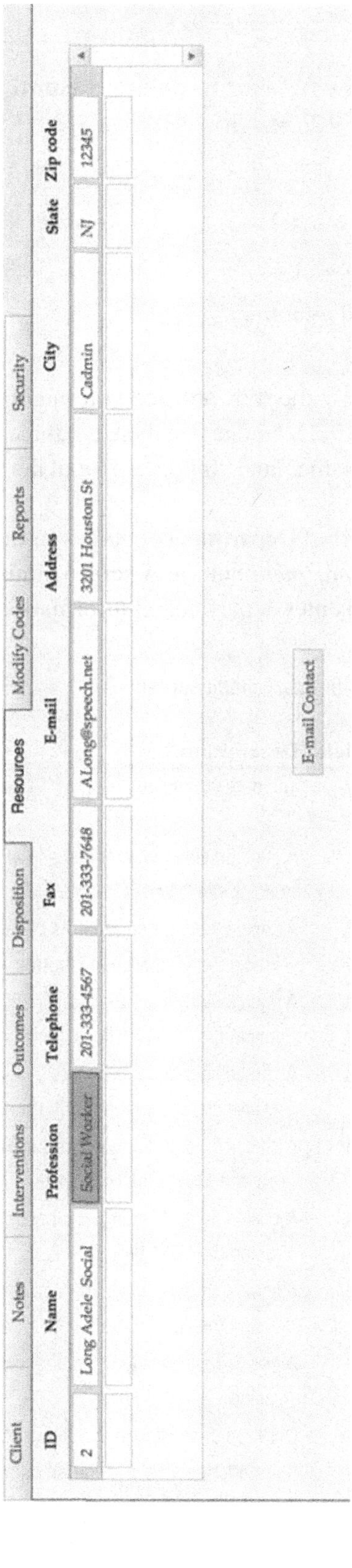

FIGURE 10.20 Example of contact associated with a client.

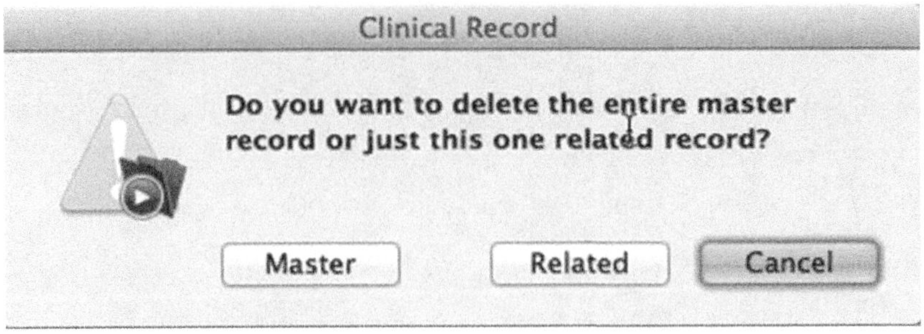

FIGURE 10.21 Deleting a related record.

you can enter an employee name. For practice you might want to enter the fictitious names displayed in Figure 10.22. Notice that there are three fields that need to be populated: "First Name," "Last Name," and "Initials." To exit the worker screen, simply click the button.

You can view and modify "Department" choices in the *Modify Codes* tab. Click on the tab and then the *Department* button. A screen similar to that shown in Figure 10.23 will be displayed. To enter departmental information, click the . For practice

TABLE 10.2 Definition of Fields in *Intervention* Screen

Field	Type of Field	Description
Date	Direct entry/ Date	The date of service
Worker	Choice field/ Character	A choice field of worker names defined in the *Modify Codes* screen using the "Worker" button
Department	Choice field/ Character	A choice field of departments defined in the *Modify Codes* screen using the "Department" button
Intervention Code	Choice field/ Number	A choice field of interventions defined in the *Modify Codes* screen using the "Interventions" button
Intervention Description	Choice field/ Character	A choice field of departments defined in the *Modify Codes* screen using the "Interventions" button
Primary DX code	Choice field/ Number	A choice field of diagnosis codes defined in the *Modify Codes* screen using the "DX" button
Primary DX Description	Choice field/ Character	A choice field of diagnosis label defined in the *Modify Codes* screen using the "DX" button
Secondary DX code	Choice field/ Number	A choice field of diagnosis code defined in the *Modify Codes* screen using the "DX" button
Secondary DX Description	Choice field/ Character	A choice field of diagnosis label defined in the *Modify Codes* screen using the "DX" button
Duration	Direct entry	Duration of session in minutes
Rate	Direct entry	Charge for service in dollar amount

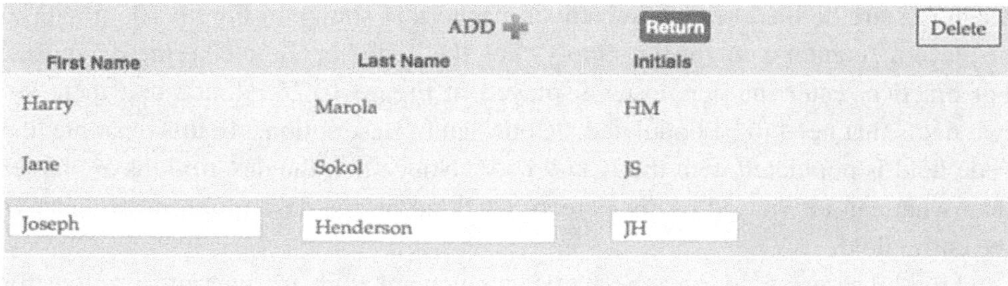

FIGURE 10.22 Entering employee names.

FIGURE 10.23 Entering departmental codes.

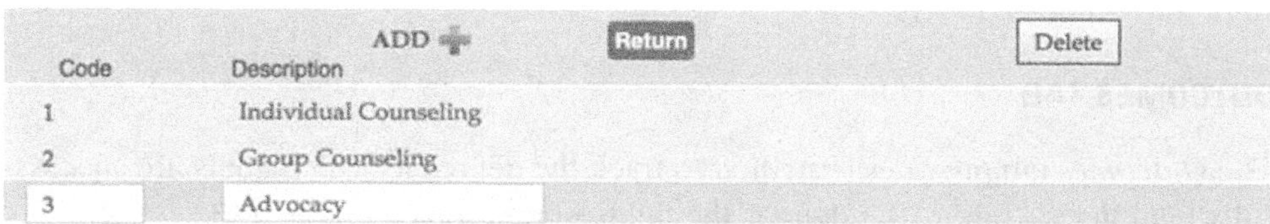

FIGURE 10.24 Entering interventions.

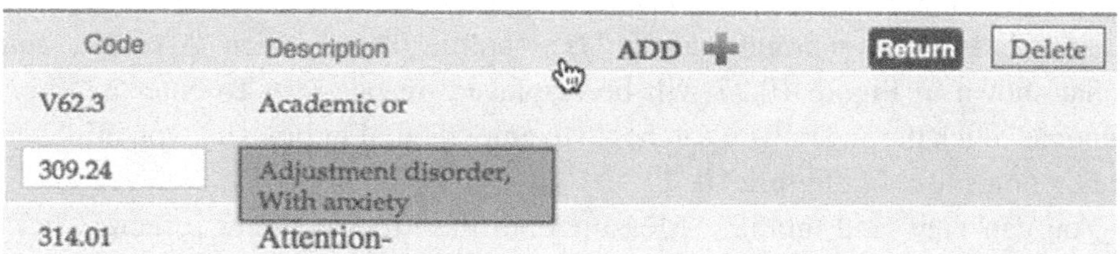

FIGURE 10.25 Entering a diagnosis (DX).

you might want to enter the fictitious departments displayed in Figure 10.23. Notice that there are two fields that need to be populated: "Abbreviation" and "Full Title."

You can view and modify "Interventions" in the *Modify Codes* tab. Click on the tab and then the *Interventions* button in the tab. A screen similar to that shown in Figure 10.24 will be displayed. To enter an intervention click the ✚. For practice, enter the interventions listed in Figure 10.24. Notice that there are two fields that need to be populated: "Code" and "Description."

You can view and modify diagnosis choices in the *Modify Codes* tab. Click on the tab and then the *DX* button in the tab. The codes for both primary and secondary diagnoses are defined here. A screen similar to that shown in Figure 10.25 will be displayed. To enter a diagnosis, simply click the + and begin to entering diagnoses. For practice, enter the diagnoses displayed in Figure 10.25. Notice that there are two fields that need to be populated: "Code" and "Description." In this example, the code field is populated with the ICD-9 code. Notice that the descriptions are larger than what can be viewed on the screen. Clicking on the description itself displays the entire field.

After all choice fields have been updated, you are ready to enter interventions for any client entered into the system. To enter an intervention for a client, you will need to first select the client's record. Follow the instructions for locating client records, described earlier in this chapter.

To add an intervention for a selected client, click on the *Interventions* tab. Figure 10.26 presents an example of an intervention for a client. Interventions will always be listed in order of date conducted. Also notice that clicking on a choice field will provide a full description.

To delete an intervention, click on the date to be deleted and then click the Delete button at the lower right side of the screen, and the dialogue shown in Figure 10.6 will be displayed on pg. 223.

OUTCOMES TAB

The *Outcomes* tab provides a method to track the degree to which goals are successfully completed. Table 10.3 defines the fields in this screen on pg. 240.

Before you can begin entering outcomes, the choice fields mentioned in Table 10.3 need to be defined using the *Modify Codes* screen.

You can view and modify choices for "Type of Outcome" in the *Modify Codes* screen. Click on the tab and then the *Type* button in the screen. A screen similar to that shown in Figure 10.27 will be displayed on pg. 240. To enter a "Type of Outcome" click the + and you can begin to enter them. For practice, you might enter the outcomes listed in Figure 10. 27.

You can view and modify "Measures" in the *Modify Codes* screen. Click on the tab and then the *Measure* button in the screen. A screen similar to that shown in Figure 10.28 will be displayed. To enter a "Measure" click the + and enter all outcome measures, one at a time. For practice, enter the measures displayed in Figure 10.28 on pg. 240.

You can view and modify "Time Interval" in the *Modify Codes* screen. Click on the tab and then the *Time Interval* button in the tab. A screen similar to that shown in Figure 10.29 will be displayed on pg. 241. To enter a "Time Interval " click the +, and you can enter them. For practice, enter the time intervals shown in Figure 10.29.

If desired, numerical intervals, such as 1, 2, 3, and so on, can be directly entered into the outcomes time interval field instead of using one of the options from the drop down arrows.

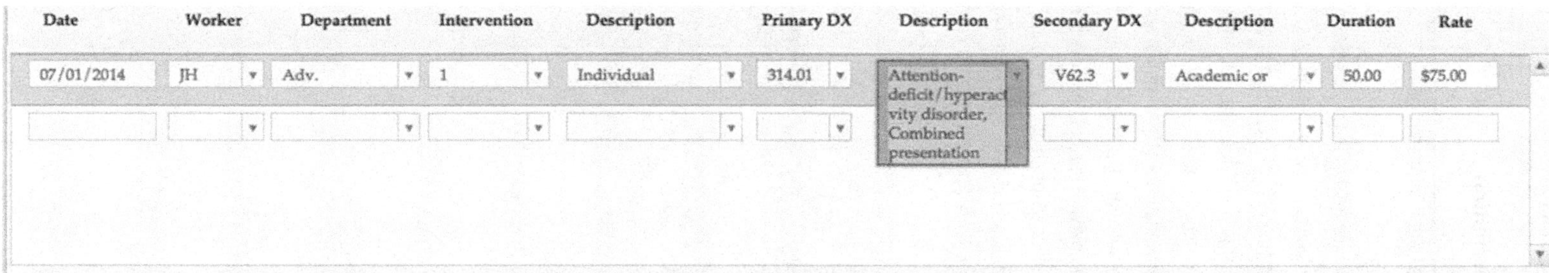

FIGURE 10.26 Example of intervention screen.

TABLE 10.3 Definition of Fields in the *Outcomes* Screen

Field	Type of Field	Description
Date	Direct entry / Date	The date of outcome measure
Type of Outcome	Choice field/ Character	A choice field of outcome types as defined in the *Modify Codes* screen using the "Type" button
Measure	Choice field/ Character	A choice field of measurements as defined in the *Modify Codes* screen using the "Measure" button
Score	Number Field	An outcome score. Can be used to record scores on standardized scales like the Beck Depression Inventory.
Outcome Status	Choice field/ Character	The outcome is a task that must be completed. The choices are: Fully Achieved, Partially Achieved, or Not Achieved.
Goal Description	Edit Field	A full description of your goal can be entered here.
Time Interval Description	Choice field/ Character	A choice field defining the intervals between measurements defined in the *Modify Codes* screen using the "Time Interval" button

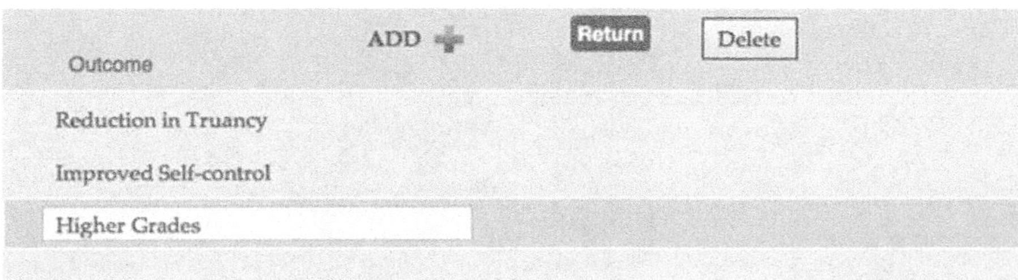

FIGURE 10.27 Example of entering outcome codes.

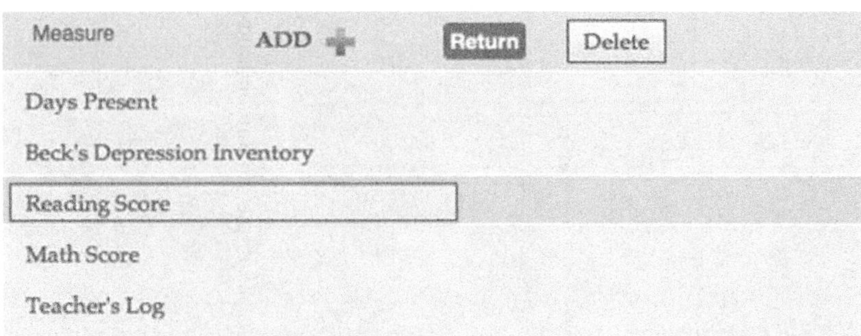

FIGURE 10.28 Example of entering measures.

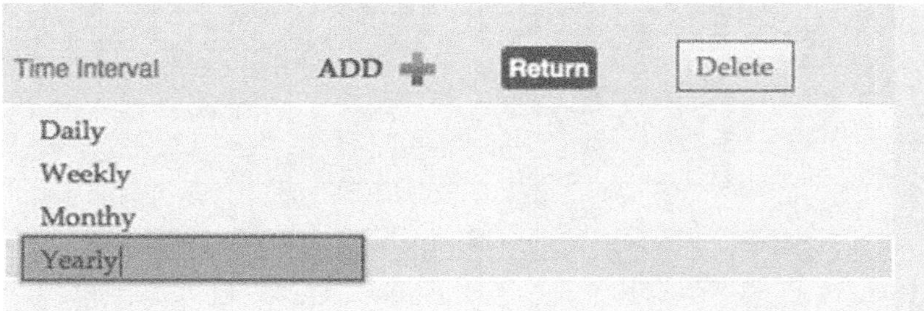

FIGURE 10.29 Entering time interval codes.

Figure 10.30 displays an example of some possible outcomes for a school-aged client. Notice that for the first three outcomes measured, a numeric value was entered in the *Time Interval* field.

DISPOSITION TAB

The *Disposition* tab is where information about a client's termination of services is recorded. Table 10.4 displays on pg. 243 and defines the fields in this screen.

Before you can begin entering disposition information, the choice fields mentioned in Table 10.4 need to be defined in the *Modify Codes* screen. Figure 10.31 displays an example of entering codes. For more specifics on how to do this, refer to the instructions described in previous sections of this chapter.

Figure 10.32 displays on pg. 244 an example of a completed *Disposition* screen. Once you enter a discharge date, "closed" will appear next to the client's name at the top middle of the screen. If you remove the date, "closed" will be replaced with "open." If the client returns, this event remains closed and a new record is created with a new "Admit #." For more information, see the section on "Multiple Admissions."

REPORTS TAB

There are three reports available in *The Clinical Record: Intervention Report, Worker by Intervention Report,* and *Department by Intervention Report.* To access these reports, click on the *Reports* tab, and the screen illustrated in Figure 10.33 will be displayed on pg. 245.

All the reports are based upon a time interval, so when a report button is clicked, the dialogue in Figure 10.34 will be displayed. A begin date and end date must be entered to complete the report. Clicking on "OK" will generate the report with the date range entered in Figure 10.34 on pg. 246.

To preview or print the report, click on the preview button: Preview.

If you want an *Intervention Report*, a screen similar the one in Figure 10.35 will be displayed. To print the report, click on the print icon Print. Notice that the report is divided by type of intervention. The number of interventions by date will be listed

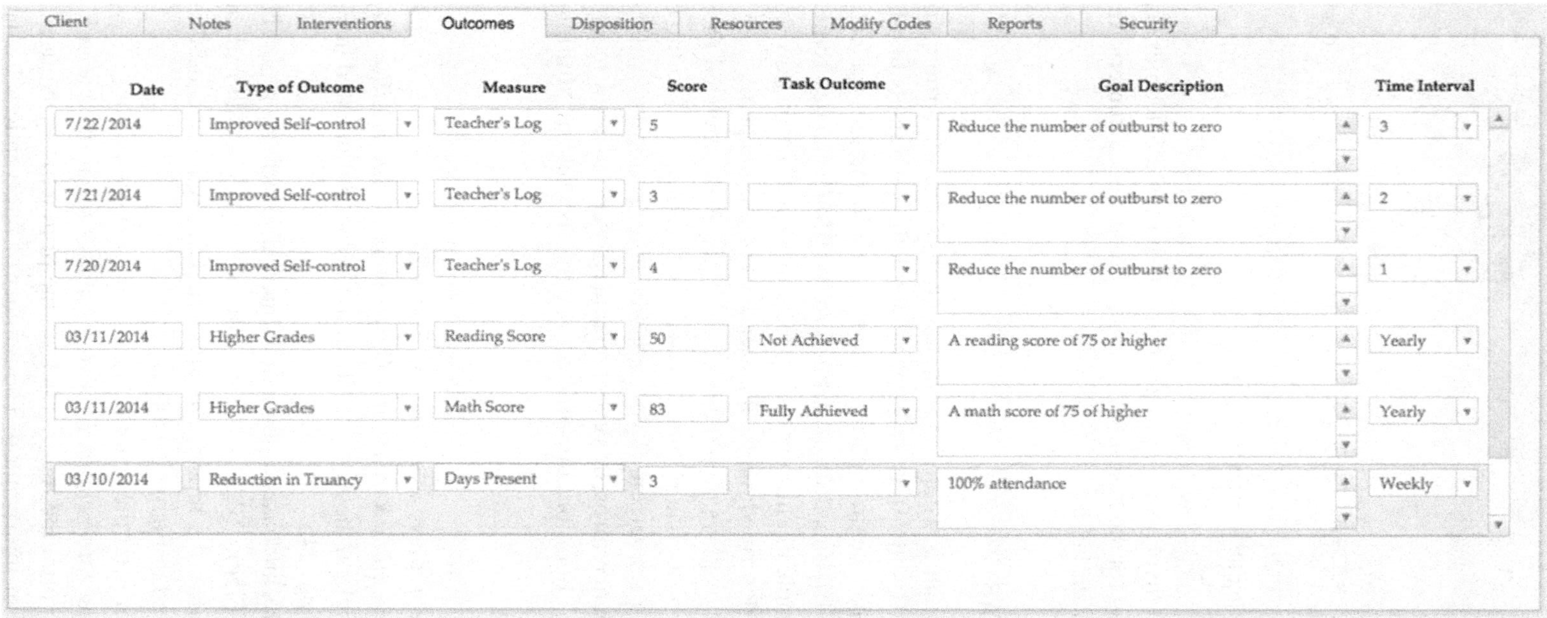

FIGURE 10.30 Example of *Outcomes* screen.

TABLE 10.4 Definition of Fields in the *Disposition* Screen

Field	Type of Field	Description
Admit #	Direct entry of numeric value	A client can have multiple admissions and discharges. A new record needs to be created for every admission and discharge.
Date	Direct entry/ Date	The date of discharge for this event
Discharge Code	Choice field/ Number	A choice field of types of discharge defined in the *Modify Codes* screen using the "Disposition" button
Discharge	Choice field/ Character	A choice field of types of discharge defined in the *Modify Codes* screen using the "Disposition" button
Final DX code	Choice field/ Number	A choice field of DX defined in the *Modify Codes* screen using the "DX" button
Final DX	Choice field/ Character	A choice field of DX defined in the *Modify Codes* screen using the "DX" button
Comment	Edit Field	A lengthy description of discharge issues can be entered.

with totals. To return to the main *Client* screen, click on the *Exit Preview* button Exit Preview and then *Return* Return .

Creating the other two reports follows the same process. Figure 10.36 displays an example of the *Worker by Intervention Report*. This report provides information on the number and type of interventions by employee.

Figure 10.37 provides an example of the *Department by Intervention Report*. This report lists the types of interventions recorded for department during the specified time period.

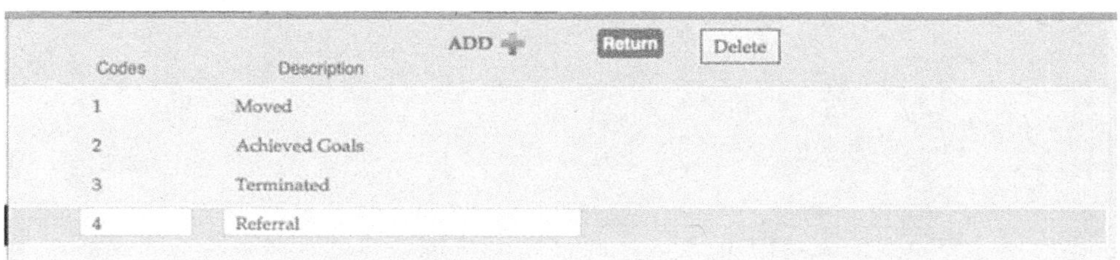

FIGURE 10.31 Entering codes for dispositions.

SECURITY TAB

Many times, when a computer application has multiple users, an administrator may choose to limit access for certain users. For instance, an employee may need to view and enter client records, but should not have the ability to download all client records. The *Security* tab provides a method for allowing control over various aspects of *The Clinical Record*. To begin, however, you need to enter each person who will be using *The Clinical Record*.

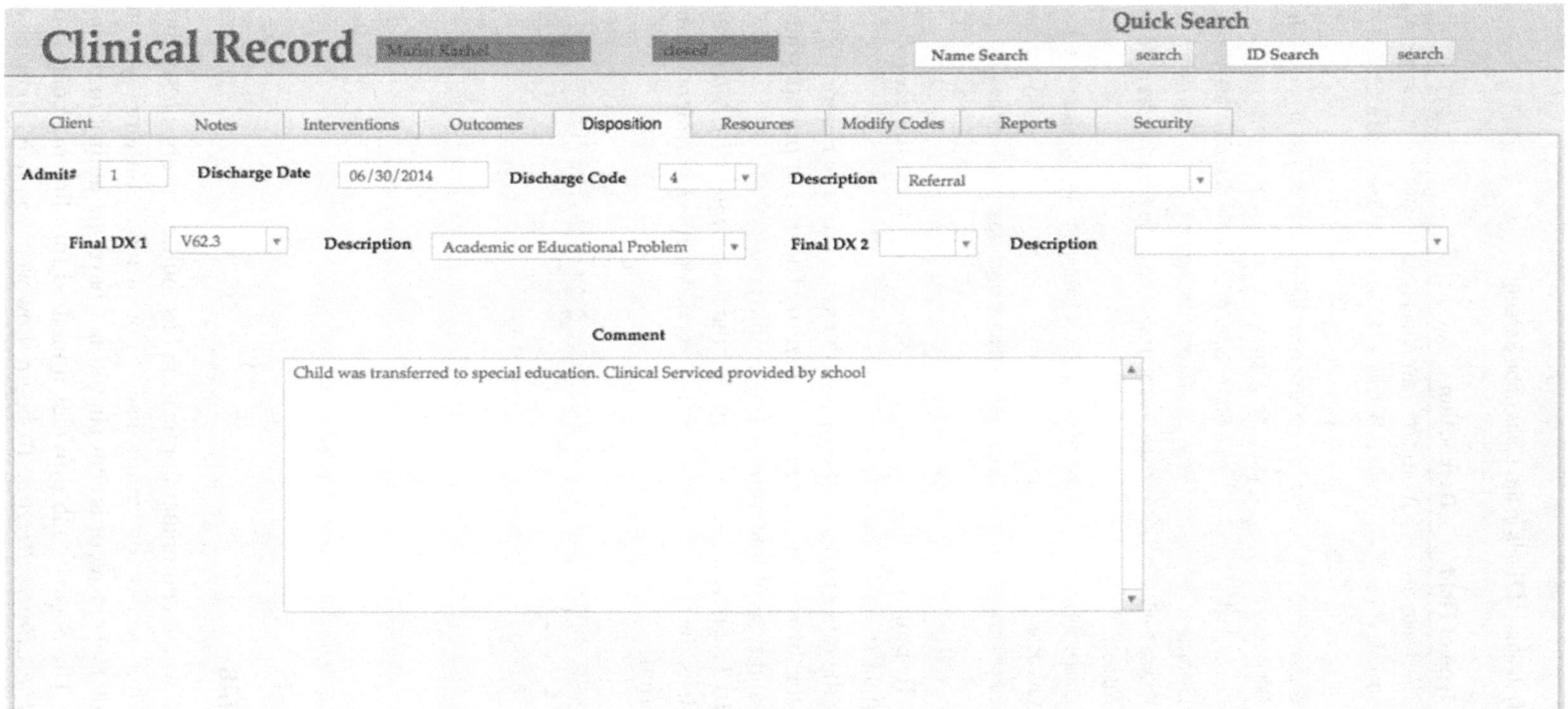

FIGURE 10.32 Example of *Disposition* screen.

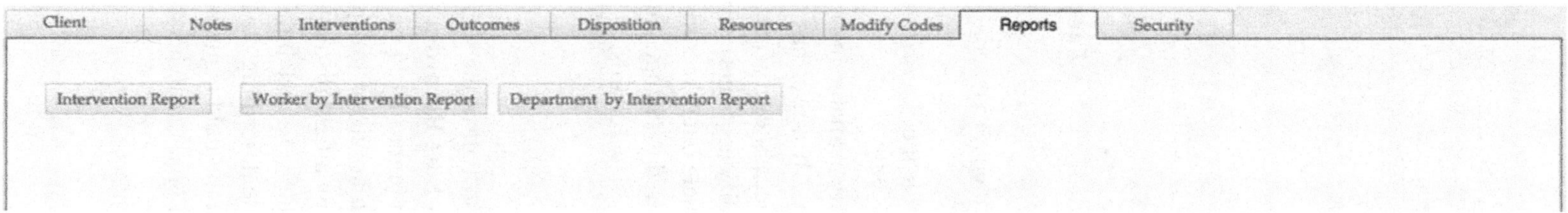

FIGURE 10.33 *Report* screen.

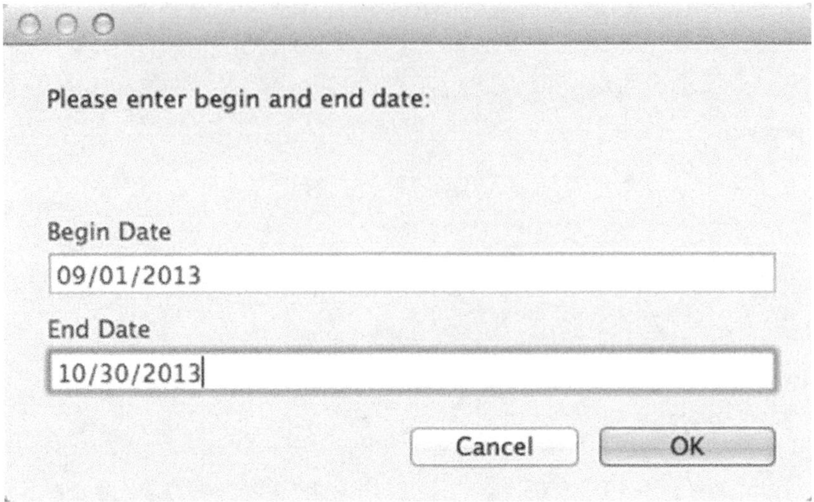

FIGURE 10.34 Entering a date range to produce a report.

To add a user, simply click on the *Security* tab and the screen displayed in Figure 10.38 will be shown on pg. 249.

There are three levels of security available in *The Clinical Record*: "Full Access," "Partial Access," and "Read Only." If a user has "Full Access," he or she has full administrative rights, and can access every part of the program. With "Partial Access," a user cannot add or modify accounts or import or export records; however, he or she can add, modify, and delete client records and do similar tasks. Users with "Partial Access" will also be required to change their password every 30 days. Users with "Read Only" rights can only view records.

SORTING RECORDS

In some cases, you may want to sort all of the records in your database. To do this, in the menu bar, select **Records / Sort Records**. You will then be presented with a screen similar to that displayed in Figure 10.39 on pg. 250.

The fields in the *Client* screen are listed in alphabetical order in the box to the left. Each of these fields represents a field displayed in the *Client* screen; however, it does not have the same exact name. To match these, a complete description of the fields can be found in the first table describing the *Names Table* in Appendix D.

Double clicking a field moves the field name into the box on the right. Multiple fields can be entered into the sort box. Once the sort criteria have been established, click on the "Sort" button.

REOPENING A CASE

Clients whose cases have been closed often return at some point in the future. It is important that the details of previous admissions be retained. When a client returns,

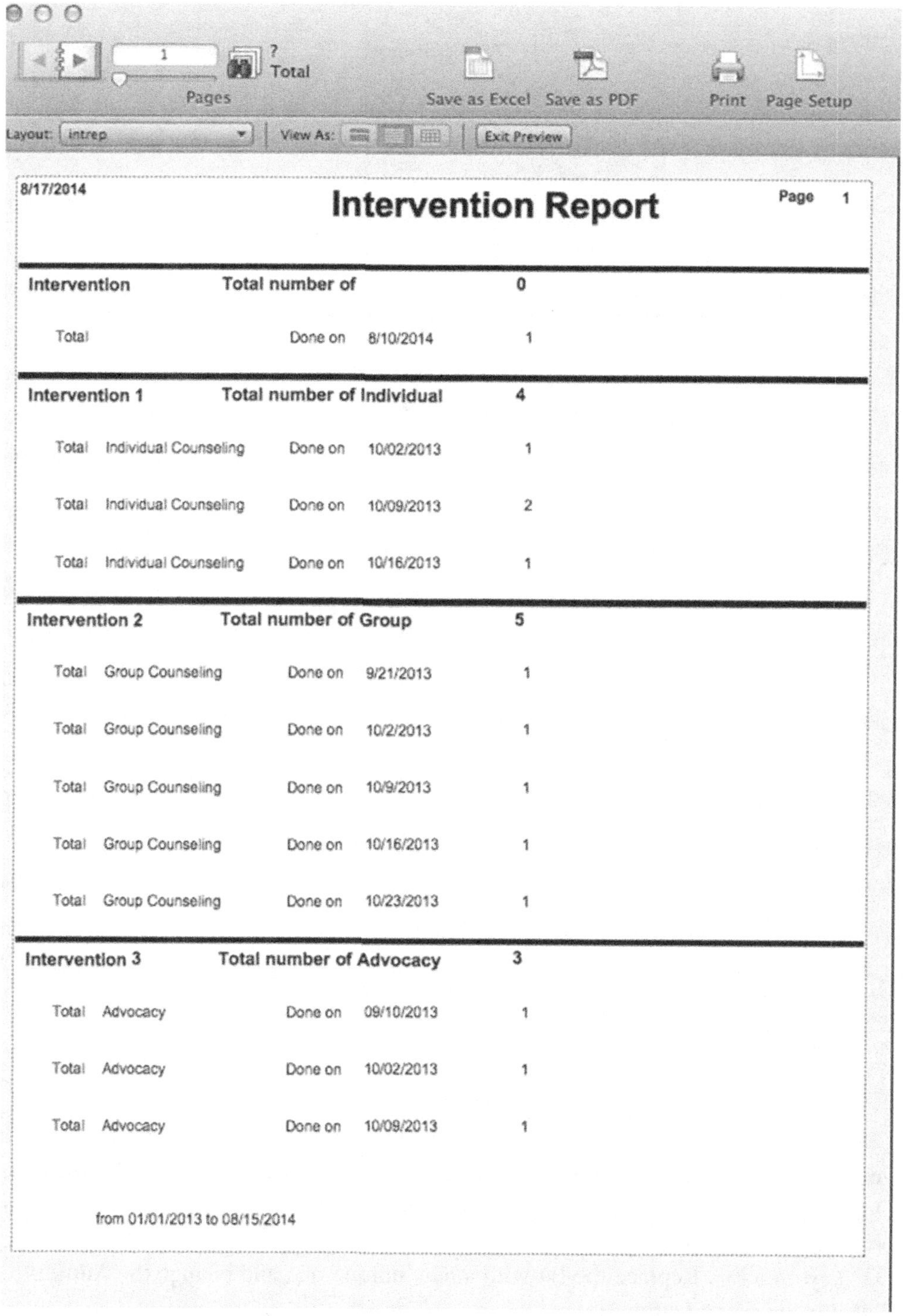

8/17/2014

Intervention Report

Page 1

Intervention	**Total number of**			**0**
Total		Done on	8/10/2014	1
Intervention 1	**Total number of Individual**			**4**
Total	Individual Counseling	Done on	10/02/2013	1
Total	Individual Counseling	Done on	10/09/2013	2
Total	Individual Counseling	Done on	10/16/2013	1
Intervention 2	**Total number of Group**			**5**
Total	Group Counseling	Done on	9/21/2013	1
Total	Group Counseling	Done on	10/2/2013	1
Total	Group Counseling	Done on	10/9/2013	1
Total	Group Counseling	Done on	10/16/2013	1
Total	Group Counseling	Done on	10/23/2013	1
Intervention 3	**Total number of Advocacy**			**3**
Total	Advocacy	Done on	09/10/2013	1
Total	Advocacy	Done on	10/02/2013	1
Total	Advocacy	Done on	10/09/2013	1

from 01/01/2013 to 08/15/2014

FIGURE 10.35 Example of an *Intervention Report*.

7/24/2014

Worker Report **Page** 1

HM		**Harry Marola**	
	1	Individual	**Total** 4
	2	Group Counseling	**Total** 5
Total for **Harry Marola**		9	
JS		**Jane Sokol**	
	1	Individual	**Total** 1
	2	Group Counseling	**Total** 1
	3	Advocacy	**Total** 3
Total for **Jane Sokol**		5	
	Total for All Workers	14	

from 09/01/2013 to 10/30/2013

FIGURE 10.36 Example of *Worker by Intervention Report*.

you can use the search features described earlier to locate previous admissions. Once background information (e.g., name, address, date of birth) is located, it can be duplicated by pressing "command" plus the "D" key on a Mac or "Ctrl" plus the "D" key on a PC. Replace the ID with a new unique one and change the Admit# to 2, if it is the second admission.

EXITING *THE CLINICAL RECORD*

To exit the application, as shown in Figure 10.40 on pg. 250, click on **Clinical Record** in the menu bar to the top left and click **Quit Clinical Record**. On a Mac,

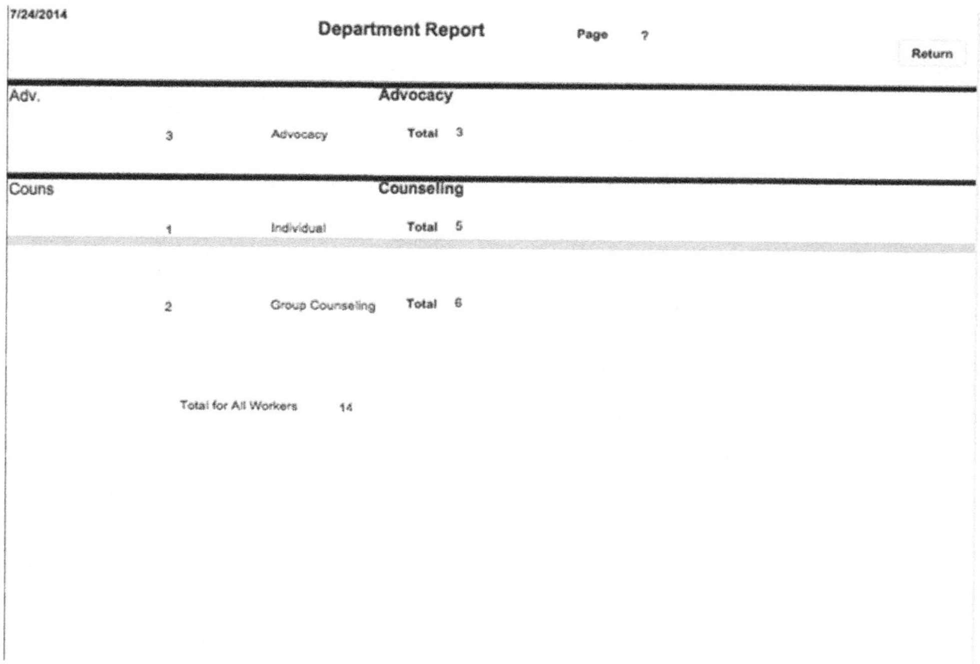

FIGURE 10.37 Example of *Department by Intervention Report.*

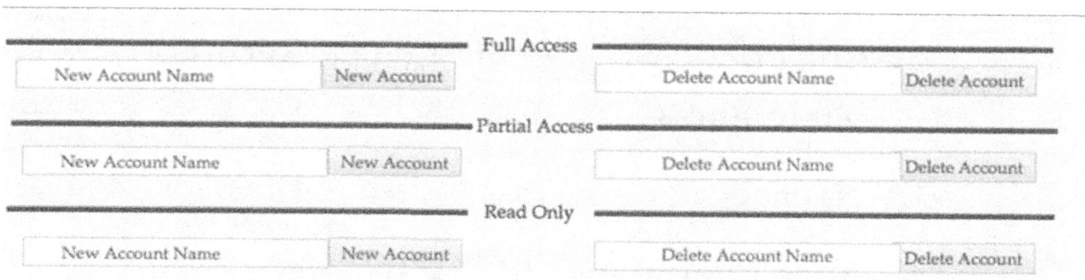

FIGURE 10.38 *Security* screen.

you can use "command" plus the "Q" key as a shortcut. On a PC, "Ctrl" plus "Q" can be used to exit.

EXPORTING DATA FROM *THE CLINICAL RECORD* TO *R* AND A FINAL CASE STUDY

One of the major benefits of using *The Clinical Record* is that you will be able to export records for further analysis. In this section we will discuss how client information you collect using *The Clinical Record* can be exported to *R* for analysis.

In this section, we will demonstrate how to do this by using an example of data retrieved from the Community Reception Center located in Greenbush. The Community Reception Center has been using *The Clinical Record* to record and store client data. The Center is interested in evaluating a pilot program called School

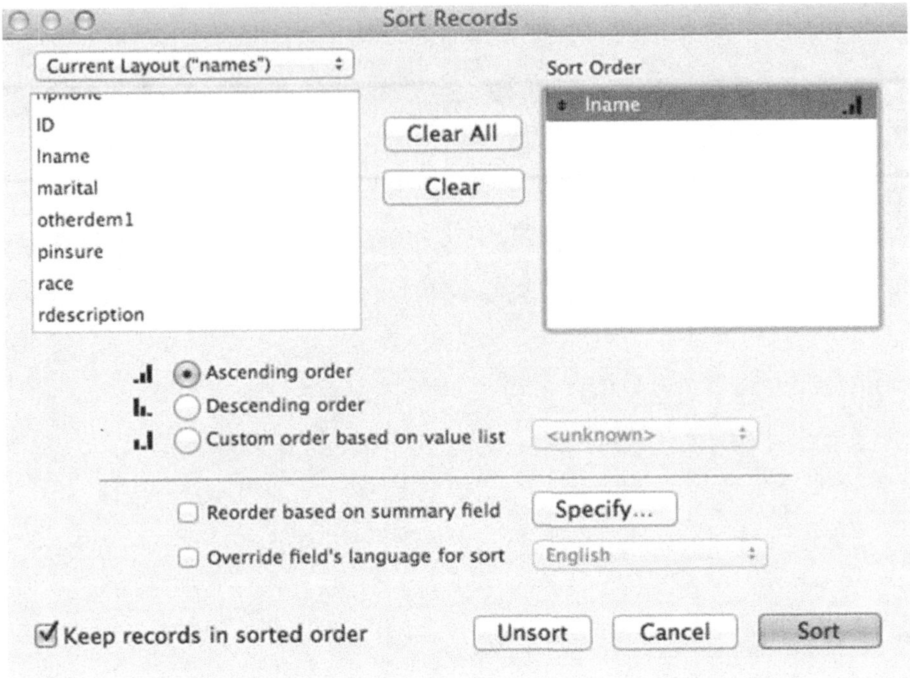

FIGURE 10.39 Sort screen.

FIGURE 10.40 Exiting *The Clinical Record.*

Matters that was designed to reduce truancy in a small group of clients who were referred by Greenbush High School. The Center would like to expand the program and is seeking funding from the school district. Students were referred to the program if they had 10 or more absences in the previous semester. In order to get additional funding,the Community Reception Center would like to determine the extent to which School Matters is effective in improving school attendance for the referred clients.

The first step in exporting this data from *The Clinical Record* is to click **File** from the menu bar and then **Export Records**, as displayed in Figure 10.41.

After completing this, the menu in Figure 10.42 will appear. You need to replace "Untitled" with a file name and then choose an appropriate file "Type." There are a number of types you can choose, but we recommend using "Tab-Separated Text." Then click the *Save* button.

Figure 10.43 displays the field selection menu.

You can select fields from any or all of the tables in *The Clinical Record* (i.e., names, intervention, outcomes, or disposition) by selecting the table and then the desired fields. A complete description of the fields and the tables in which they are found is listed in Appendix D.

You can move individual fields from a table by highlighting them and then clicking the *Move* button. Alternatively, you can select ALL the fields in a table by clicking the "Move All" button.

You will be able to move between the various tables in *The Clinical Record* to select desired fields, which will become variables once they are imported into *R*. To do this, simply select the desired tables, one at a time, using the drop down choices at the top of the large box on the left. For example, in Figure 10.43, the fields in the *outcomes* table are displayed. Again, we refer you to Appendix D for a complete description of the fields stored in each table of *The Clinical Record*.

As you select the type of data to export, you may want to include background items, such as gender and age, in addition to specific fields of interest, such as outcomes.

At the Community Reception Center, administrators want to extract the data described in Table 10.5 on pg. 253.

If you accidentally select a field to export and want to eliminate it, simply highlight it in the "Field export order" box and then click the "Clear" button.

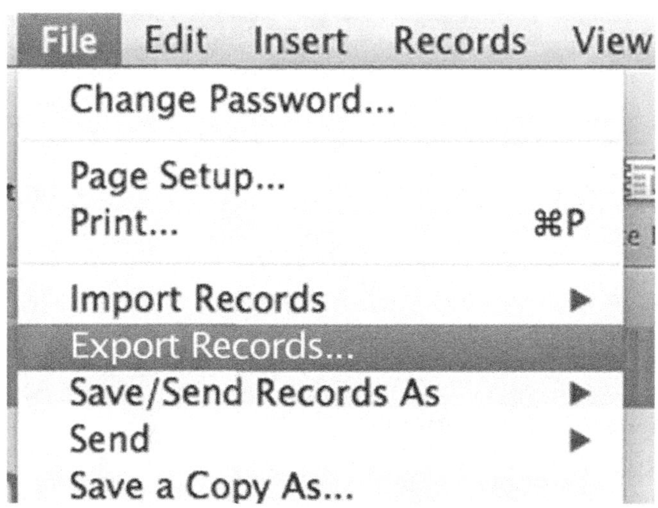

FIGURE 10.41 Export menu.

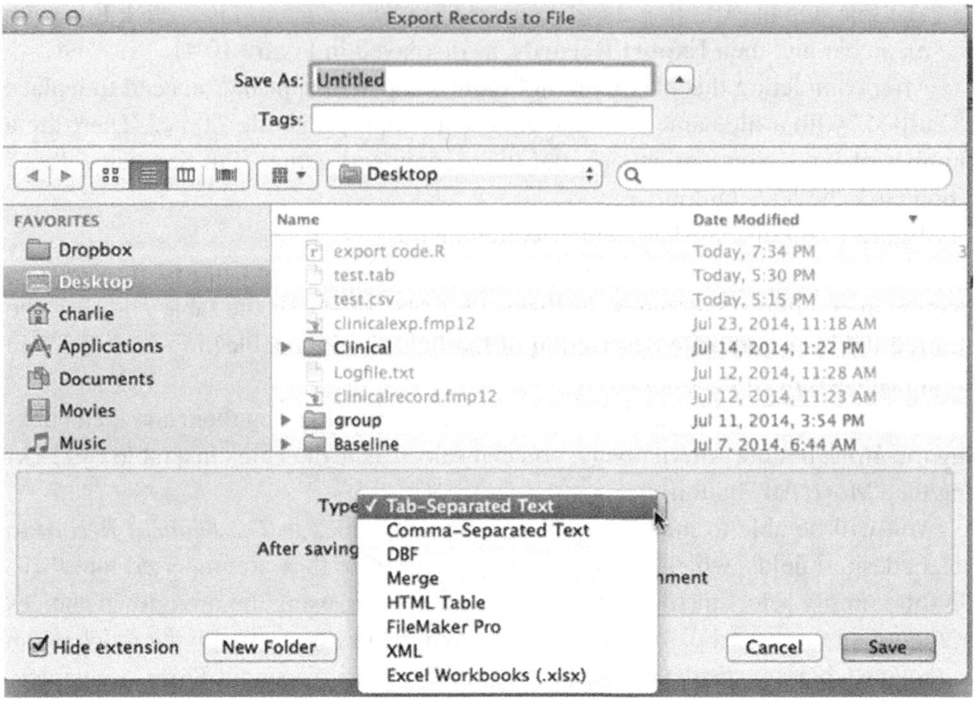

FIGURE 10.42 Selecting an export file type.

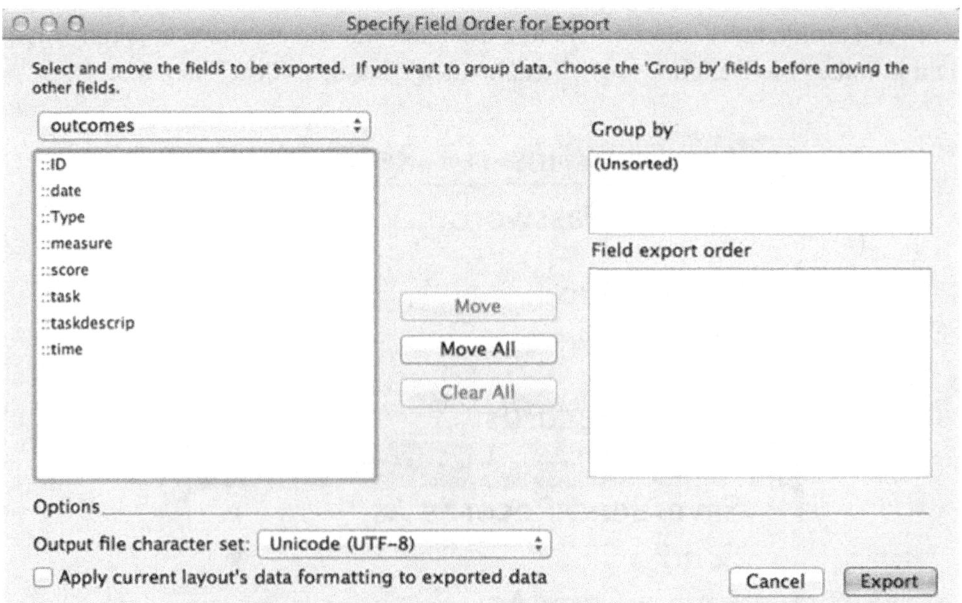

FIGURE 10.43 Selecting fields from the *Outcomes* table.

TABLE 10.5 Description of Fields to Be Exported From the Community Reception Center

Clinical Record table:field	Description of Field	Measurement Description
ID	Client's unique identification number	Actual ID assigned
outcomes:date	Date the measurement was taken	This is an actual date in mm/dd/yyyy format.
outcomes: Type	The type of outcome being measured	For all of these clients, we are measuring "Reduction in Truancy."
outcomes: measure	What is actually being measured	We are measuring days absent during the time period—in this case, semesters.
outcomes:task	The degree to which the client met his or her goals between entering the program and the end of the school year	The client could be rated as: not achieved, partially achieved or fully achieved.
outcomes:taskdescrip	An open notes field in which the social worker could add any comments	
outcomes: time	Two measurements were taken: one after the fall semester when the client was referred to the program and another after the end of the program ended	"1" denotes the measure was taken prior to entering the program; "2" denotes the measure was taken at the conclusion of the program.
gender	Field taken from the *names* table denoting the gender of the client	Possible responses include: male or female

Once you select all the fields you wish to export, you can put them in the desired order by dragging them up and down in the "Field export order" box.

Now you are ready to export the file by clicking the "Export button" at the bottom right of the "Specify Field Order for Export" dialogue. Take careful note of the order and names of the fields, as this will be needed to accurately import the file into *R*.

Once this is accomplished, you can exit *The Clinical Record*.

IMPORTING DATA INTO *R*

The file created in the previous section can be downloaded from the authors' website at www.ssdanalyis.com. It is called *truancy.tab* and it is located in the Datasets tab. To begin analyzing this data, you will need to enter *RStudio*.

As shown in the following, the first step in importing this data is to create a vector containing the field names that were downloaded.

```
>names=c("id","date","type","measure","score",
"target","goal",
"time","gender")
```

The next step is to read the file into a vector using the following statement:

```
>out<-
read.table(file.choose(),header=F,sep="\t",col.
names=names)
```

Once the file is read into R, you can modify, analyze, and save it, as described in previous chapters.

DOES *SCHOOL MATTERS* WORK?

To evaluate this pilot program, the administrators at the Community Reception Center want to compare clients' absences prior to starting School Matters to their absences at the conclusion of the program.

Begin by creating a table of *time*, which is a time interval for the measure score (i.e., days absent). As displayed in Table 10.5, a value of "1" was entered for the fall semester, prior to the beginning of the intervention, and a "2" was entered to denote the follow-up period, upon the conclusion of the program. Using the **table()** function as follows shows 17 measures each at Time 1 and Time 2.

```
>table(out$time)
 1  2
17 17
```

To compare the students' mean number of absences from Time 1 to Time 2, load the *psych* package and run the **describeBy()** function as displayed here.

```
>describeBy(out$score,out$time)
```

The output from the command is displayed in Figure 10.44, which shows a large decrease in the average number of days absent between the first (mean = 10.65) and second measures (mean = 5.18). There is also an increase in the amount of variation in Time 2 (sd = 3.84) compared to Time 1 (sd = 1.9).

The decrease in the average number of days absent can also be displayed graphically using the *ggplot2* package. First, attach the package and create the

```
group: 1
  vars  n  mean  sd median trimmed  mad min max range skew kurtosis   se
1    1 17 10.65 1.9     10   10.53 1.48   9  14     5 0.74    -1.03 0.46
---------------------------------------------------------------------------
group: 2
  vars  n mean   sd median trimmed  mad min max range skew kurtosis   se
1    1 17 5.18 3.84      4    4.93 2.97   0  14    14 0.81    -0.35 0.93
```

FIGURE 10.44 Comparison of mean absences by time.

vector *scoremean,* which is a vector containing the mean number of absences at Time 1 (before the intervention) and Time 2 (after intervention), using the following code. Notice the use of the **factor()** function, which communicates to *R* to treat *time* as a categorical, or factor, variable (i.e., 1 and 2 should not be considered numeric).

```
>scoremean<-
aggregate(out$score,by=list(factor(out$time)),FUN=mea
n,na.rm=T)
```

Now the graph can be drawn using the following syntax. The syntax is similar to that described in Chapter 5. The results are displayed in Figure 10.45.

```
>ggplot(scoremean,aes(x=Group.1,y=x)) +
  geom_bar(stat="identity",fill="gray") +
  geom_text(aes(label=paste(format(x,digits=3))),vj
 ust=1.5,
  colour="black",size=6) +
  labs(x="Time Period",y="mean days absent") +
 theme_bw()
```

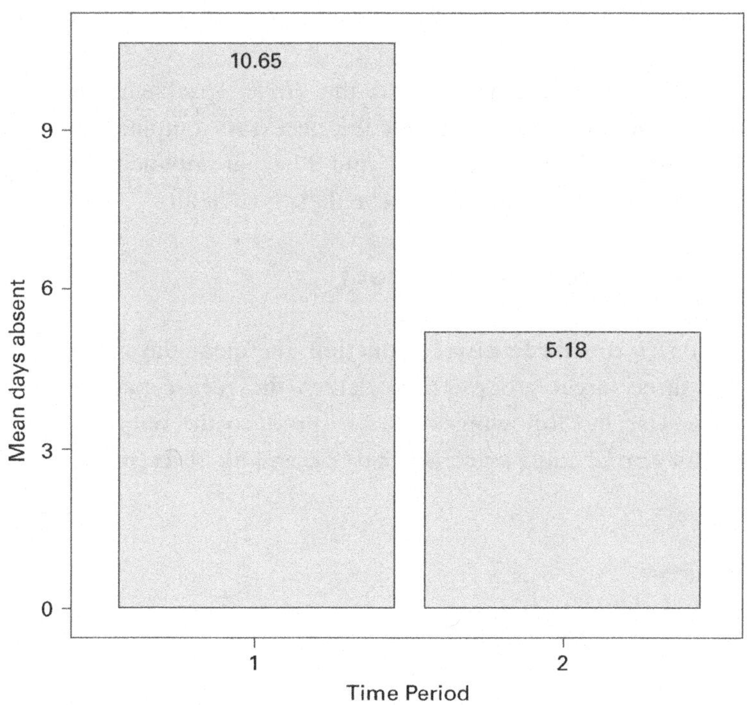

FIGURE 10.45 Bar chart comparing absences before and after intervention.

The next step in the analysis is to test for Type I error. Since we have a numeric dependent variable, number of absences (contained in the variable *score*), this means the difference between Times 1 and 2 can be compared.

In order to do this, we will need to create subsets for Time 1 and Time 2. To accomplish this, the two lines of syntax displayed below are needed. All the data for Time 1 are copied into the vector *t1*, and all the data for Time 2 are copied into the vector *t2*.

```
>t1<-subset(out,time==1)
>t2<-subset(out,time==2)
```

Next, the number of days absent for each student at Time 1 is copied into the vector *score1* and the days absent for Time 2 into the vector *score2*.

```
>score1<-t1$score
>score2<-t2$score
```

We can now create a data frame using the following syntax:

```
>outcome<-data.frame(score1,score2,t2$target,t2$gender)
```

The variable *target* contains information on the degree to which the goals have been met. Since this exists only for Time 2, we created the data frame with this data.

Detach the *psych* package and load the *Hmisc* package. Using the *Hmisc* **describe()** function below produces the necessary output. Almost half of the students (47%) fully achieved their goal, and 29% partially achieved it (see Figure 10.46). Four students (24%) did not achieve their goal at all.

```
>describe(outcome$t2.target)
```

Using the *psych* **describeBy()** function, the mean days absent can be compared for the three target groups. First detach the *Hmisc* package and load the *psych* package. Use the following syntax to produce the output in Figure 10.47: **>describeBy(outcome$score2,outcome$t2.target)**

```
outcome$t2.target
      n missing  unique
     17       0       3

Fully Achieved (8, 47%), Not Achieved  (4, 24%), Partially Achieved (5, 29%)
```

FIGURE 10.46 Descriptive for variable target.

```
------------------------------------------------------------------------
group: Fully Achieved
  vars n mean   sd median trimmed  mad min max range skew kurtosis   se
1    1 8 2.25 1.28    2.5    2.25 0.74   0   4     4 -0.4    -1.22 0.45
------------------------------------------------------------------------
group: Not Achieved
  vars n  mean   sd median trimmed  mad min max range skew kurtosis   se
1    1 4 10.75 2.75   10.5   10.75 2.97   8  14     6 0.12    -2.21 1.38
------------------------------------------------------------------------
group: Partially Achieved
  vars n mean   sd median trimmed  mad min max range skew kurtosis   se
1    1 5  5.4 1.52      5     5.4 1.48   4   7     3 0.15    -2.21 0.68
```

FIGURE 10.47 Comparison of mean days absent pre- and post-intervention.

The mean number of days absent for the "Fully Achieved " group is 2.25 days, compared to 5.4 days for the "Partially Achieved" group and 10.75 days absent for the "Not Achieved" group.

To test for differences between gender and degree of goal achievement, the function **CrossTable()** in the *gmodels* package can be utilized. We can use this function because both *gender* and *target* are factor variables. The following syntax includes the **chisq=T** option, which calculates a chi-square:

```
>CrossTable(outcome$t2.gender,outcome$t2.target,chisq=T)
```

The results are presented in Figure 10.48. Here we see no difference in the degree of goal achievement between male and female clients. The chi-square is nonsignificant ($X^2 = 0.1416667$; $p = 0.9316171$).

Notice, however, the small cell sizes. In this case, then, Fisher's Exact is preferable to X^2 so we will continue our analysis by entering the following in the Console:

```
> fisher.test(outcome$t2.target, outcome$t2.gender)

      Fisher's Exact Test for Count Data

data:  outcome$t2.target and outcome$t2.gender
p-value = 1
alternative hypothesis: two.sided
```

The *p*-value from the Fisher's Exact confirms the fact that we cannot reject null hypothesis, as was observed in the chi-square test.

To test for Type I error in the mean days absent between Time 1 and Time 2, we will use a paired-sample *t*-test. The null hypothesis would be that the difference

```
   Cell Contents
|-------------------------|
|                       N |
| Chi-square contribution |
|           N / Row Total |
|           N / Col Total |
|         N / Table Total |
|-------------------------|


Total Observations in Table:  17


                 | outcome$t2.target 
outcome$t2.gender |    Fully Achieved |      Not Achieved | Partially Achieved |         Row Total |
-----------------|-------------------|-------------------|--------------------|-------------------|
          Female |                 4 |                 2 |                  3 |                 9 |
                 |             0.013 |             0.007 |              0.047 |                   |
                 |             0.444 |             0.222 |              0.333 |             0.529 |
                 |             0.500 |             0.500 |              0.600 |                   |
                 |             0.235 |             0.118 |              0.176 |                   |
-----------------|-------------------|-------------------|--------------------|-------------------|
            Male |                 4 |                 2 |                  2 |                 8 |
                 |             0.015 |             0.007 |              0.053 |                   |
                 |             0.500 |             0.250 |              0.250 |             0.471 |
                 |             0.500 |             0.500 |              0.400 |                   |
                 |             0.235 |             0.118 |              0.118 |                   |
-----------------|-------------------|-------------------|--------------------|-------------------|
    Column Total |                 8 |                 4 |                  5 |                17 |
                 |             0.471 |             0.235 |              0.294 |                   |
-----------------|-------------------|-------------------|--------------------|-------------------|


Statistics for All Table Factors


Pearson's Chi-squared test 
------------------------------------------------------------
Chi^2 =  0.1416667     d.f. =  2     p =  0.9316171
```

FIGURE 10.48 Contingency table and chi-square comparing gender and degree of achievement.

```
	Paired t-test

data:  outcome$score1 and outcome$score2
t = 5.6809, df = 16, p-value = 3.409e-05
alternative hypothesis: true difference in means is not equal to 0
95 percent confidence interval:
 3.429156 7.512020
sample estimates:
mean of the differences 
               5.470588 
```

FIGURE 10.49 Paired t-test comparing pre- and post-intervention scores.

```
d estimate: 1.803744 (large)
95 percent confidence interval:
      inf       sup 
0.9419186 2.6655688 
```

FIGURE 10.50 Output of effect size between *score1* and *score2*.

between the mean of Time 1 and Time 2 is equal to zero. To run the *t*-test, use the following code:

```
>t.test(outcome$score1, outcome$score2, paired=TRUE)
```

The results of this test are displayed in Figure 10.49. The *p*-value of 3.406e-05 displayed in scientific notation is below the criteria of 0.05 for rejecting the null hypothesis. Although we cannot make any causal conclusions, it is likely that the decrease in days absent did not occur as a result of chance.

As stated earlier, it is often helpful to quantify how much change occurs, particularly in intervention research. Cohen's *d*, a measure of effect size, can be calculated with the *effsize* package's function **cohen.d()**. The syntax is as follows, and the results are displayed in Figure 10.50:

```
>cohen.d(score1, score2, na.rm=T)
```

The effect size produced by the command is 1.803744, indicating a large degree of change between the pre-intervention and post-intervention scores. The 95% confidence interval is also displayed indicating that it is likely that the true value ranges between 0.9419186 and 2.6655688. As previously stated, the interpretation of Cohen's *d* is based upon *z*-scores. The score then represents the degree of average improvement in the post-intervention period over the pre-intervention period. An effect size of 1.8 denotes an almost two standard deviation improvement in the post-intervention scores over the pre-intervention scores. An effect size of 0 shows no improvement, while an effect size of 1 indicates a 34.13% increase in improvement in the post-intervention phase over the pre-intervention phase (Bloom et al., 2009). The degree of change can be expressed as a percentage by using the following syntax:

```
>dchange=(pnorm(1.804377)-.5)*100
```

Typing **dchange** yields a percentage of 46.44139. This indicates a 46.4% improvement in attendance. The **pnorm()** function provides the area under the normal curve based upon a *z*-score/effect size.

CONCLUSION

The results of this analysis provide evidence that the School Matters program is related to the reduction of truancy among the clients referred to the program. There was a statistically significant decrease in the number of days absent prior to referral compared to after the conclusion of the program. The means days absent decreased from 10.65 to 5.18, for an average reduction of 5.47 days. Presenting this information to the school district helps make the case for the expansion of this program.

APPENDIX A

RESOURCES FOR RESEARCH METHODS

This appendix is broken into five sections. The first two contain texts about research methods, in general, and, more specifically, about conducting agency-based research. We highly recommend these texts, and they are often used in graduate programs as required or recommended textbooks. The third section contains texts that are good references for gaining more in-depth knowledge about *R*. The last two sections contain freely available resources. These vary in scope and content, but have been developed and utilized in a variety of settings. Resources in these two sections can be accessed by the provided hyperlinks. To better help you select resources that may be appropriate for your specific needs, we have annotated each citation.

BASIC TEXTS ON RESEARCH METHODS IN THE SOCIAL SCIENCES

Hamilton, L. C. (1991). *Regression with graphics: A second course in applied statistics*. Pacific Grove, CA: Cengage Learning.

This text demonstrates how computing power has expanded the role of graphics in analyzing, exploring, and experimenting with raw data. It is primarily intended for students whose research requires more than an introductory statistics course, but who may not have an extensive background in rigorous mathematics. It is also suitable for courses with students of varying mathematical abilities.

Royse, D. (2010). *Research methods in social work* (6th ed.). Independence, KY: Cengage Learning.

This how-to book includes simplified, step-by-step instructions using real-world data and scenarios. In addition, it comes with updated tools that show you how to create a research project and write a thesis proposal. Every chapter comes with self-assessment sections so you can see how you are doing and prepare effectively for the test.

Rubin, A., & Babbie, E. R. (2013). *Research methods for social work* (8th ed.). Belmont, CA: Brooks/Cole Publishing.

This text combines a rigorous, comprehensive presentation of all aspects of the research endeavor with a thoroughly reader-friendly approach that helps students overcome the "fear factor" often associated with this course. Allen Rubin and Earl R. Babbie's classic bestseller is acclaimed for its depth and breadth of coverage, clear and often humorous writing style, student-friendly examples, and ideal balance of quantitative and qualitative research techniques—illustrating how the two methods complement one another.

Thyer, B. (Ed.). (2009). *The handbook of social work research methods* (2nd ed.). Thousand Oaks, CA: SAGE Publications.

This text covers all the major topics that are relevant for social work research methods. Edited by Bruce Thyer and containing contributions by leading authorities, this handbook covers both qualitative and quantitative approaches as well as a section that delves into more general issues such as evidence-based practice, ethics, gender, ethnicity, international issues, integrating both approaches, and applying for grants.

Whittaker, A. (2012). *Research skills for social work* (2nd ed.). Thousand Oaks, CA: SAGE Publications.

This book presents research skill concepts in an accessible and user-friendly way. Key skills and methods such as literature reviews, interviews, and questionnaires are explored in detail, while the underlying ethical reasons for doing good research underpin the text. For this second edition, new material on ethnography has been added.

TEXTS ON CONDUCTING AGENCY-BASED RESEARCH

Auerbach, C., & Zeitlin, W. (2014). *SSD for R: An R package for analyzing single-subject data*. New York: Oxford University Press.

Single-subject research designs have been used to build evidence for the effective treatment of problems across various disciplines, including social work, psychology, psychiatry, medicine, allied health fields, juvenile justice, and special education. This book serves as a guide for those desiring to conduct single-subject data analysis. The aim of this text is to introduce readers to the various functions available in *SSD for R*, a new, free, and innovative software package written in *R*, the open-source statistical programming language, by the book's authors.

Corcoran, J., & Secret, M. (2013). *Social work research skills workbook: A step-by-step guide to conducting agency-based research.* New York: Oxford University Press.

With the move toward greater accountability and evidence-informed practice, students must be well equipped to be not only consumers but also producers of research. This text is a hands-on practical guide that shows students how to apply what they learn about research methods and analysis to the research projects that they develop in their internships, field placements, or employment settings.

Epstein, I. (2010). *Clinical data-mining: Integrating practice and research.* New York: Oxford University Press.

Clinical Data-Mining (CDM) involves the conceptualization, extraction, analysis, and interpretation of available clinical data for practice knowledge-building, clinical decision-making, and practitioner reflection. Depending upon the type of data mined, CDM can be qualitative or quantitative; it is generally retrospective, but may be meaningfully combined with original data collection. This pocket guide, from a seasoned practice-based researcher, covers all the basics of conducting practitioner-initiated CDM studies or CDM doctoral dissertations, drawing extensively on published CDM studies and completed CDM dissertations from multiple social work settings in the United States, Australia, Israel, Hong Kong, and the United Kingdom. In addition, it describes consulting principles for researchers interested in forging collaborative university-agency CDM partnerships, making it a practical tool for novice practitioner-researchers and veteran academic-researchers alike.

Fraser, M. W., Richman, J. M., Galinsky, M. J., & Day, S. H. (2009). *Intervention research: Developing social programs.* New York: Oxford University Press.

When social workers draw on experience, theory, or data in order to develop new strategies or enhance existing ones, they are conducting intervention research. This relatively new field involves program design, implementation, and evaluation and requires a theory-based, systematic approach. The five-step strategy described in this brief but thorough book ushers the reader from an idea's germination through the process of writing a treatment manual, assessing program efficacy and effectiveness, and disseminating findings. Rich with examples drawn from child welfare, school-based prevention, medicine, and juvenile justice, *Intervention Research* relates each step of the process to current social work practice. It also explains how to adapt interventions for new contexts, and provides extensive examples of intervention research in fields such as child welfare, school-based prevention, medicine, and juvenile justice, and offers insights about changes and challenges in the field.

Grinnell, R. M., Gabor, P., & Unrau, Y. A. (2012). *Program evaluation for social workers: Foundations of evidence-based programs.* New York: Oxford University Press.

This popular student-friendly introduction to program evaluation provides social workers with a sound conceptual understanding of how to use basic evaluation techniques in the evaluation of their cases (case-level) and programs (program-level).Eminently approachable, straightforward, and practical, this edition includes the fundamental tools that are needed in order for social workers to fully appreciate and understand how case- and program-level evaluations will help them to increase their effectiveness as contemporary data-driven practitioners.

ADDITIONAL *R* RESOURCES

Burn, D. A. (1993). Designing effective statistical graphs. In *Handbook of statistics* (Computational Statistics, Volume 9). Amsterdam, The Netherlands: Elsevier.

An effective statistical graph is a work of art and science. To make an effective statistical graph, we need to understand the art of graphic design and the science of statistics. The principles for designing an effective graph combine these two points of view. By applying these principles, we can make better, more informed decisions in how we represent data. And the resulting picture should be the more perfect "mental vision" and the more "certain touch" of a "true artist."

Chang, W. (2012). *R graphics cookbook.* Sebastopol, CA: O'Reilly Media.

This practical guide provides more than 150 recipes to help you generate high-quality graphs quickly, without having to comb through all the details of *R*'s graphing systems. Each recipe tackles a specific problem with a solution you can apply to your own project, and includes a discussion of how and why the recipe works.Most of the recipes use the *ggplot2* package, a powerful and flexible way to make graphs in *R*. If you have a basic understanding of the *R* language, you're ready to get started.

De Vries, A., & Meys, J. (2012). *R For dummies.* Chichester, UK: For Dummies.

The quick, easy way to master all the *R* you'll ever need. Requiring no prior programming experience and packed with practical examples, easy, step-by-step exercises, and sample code, this extremely accessible guide is the ideal introduction to *R* for complete beginners. It also covers many concepts that intermediate-level programmers will find extremely useful.

Faraway, J. J. (2004). *Linear models with R.* Boca Raton, FL: Chapman and Hall/CRC.

This book focuses on the practice of regression and analysis of variance. It clearly demonstrates the different methods available and, more important, the situations in which each one applies. It covers all of the standard topics, from the basics of estimation to missing data, factorial designs, and block designs. It also discusses topics, such as model uncertainty, rarely addressed in books of this type. The presentation incorporates numerous examples that clarify both the use of each technique and the conclusions one can draw from the results. All of the data sets used in the book are available for download.

Fox, J., Weisberg, S., & Fox, J. (2011). *An R companion to applied regression.* Thousand Oaks, CA: SAGE Publications.

The authors provide a step-by-step guide to using the high-quality free statistical software *R*, an emphasis on integrating statistical computing in *R* with the practice of data analysis, coverage of generalized linear models, enhanced coverage of *R* graphics and programming, and substantial web-based support materials.

Kabacoff, R. (2011). *R in action: Data analysis and graphics with R.* Shelter Island, NY; London: Manning; Pearson Education.

R in Action is the first book to present both the R system and the use cases that make it such a compelling package for business developers. The book begins by introducing the *R* language, including the development environment. Focusing on practical solutions, the book also offers a crash course in practical statistics and covers elegant methods for dealing with messy and incomplete data using features of *R*.

Keen, K. J. (2010). *Graphics for statistics and data analysis with R.* Boca Raton, FL: Chapman & Hall/CRC.

This book presents the basic principles of sound graphical design and applies these principles to engaging examples using the graphical functions available in R. It offers a wide array of graphical displays for the presentation of data, including modern tools for data visualization and representation.

Lander, J. P. (2014). *R for everyone: Advanced analytics and graphics.* New York: Addison-Wesley.

Using the open source *R* language, you can build powerful statistical models to answer many of your most challenging questions. *R* has traditionally been difficult for non-statisticians to learn, and most *R* books assume far too much knowledge to be of help. *R for Everyone* is the solution.

Teetor, P. (2011). *R Cookbook.* Sebastopol, CA: O'Reilly Media.

With more than 200 practical recipes, this book helps you perform data analysis with R quickly and efficiently. The R language provides everything you need to do statistical work, but its structure can be difficult to master. This collection of concise, task-oriented recipes makes you productive with *R* immediately, with solutions ranging from basic tasks to input and output, general statistics, graphics, and linear regression.

Verzani, J. (2004). *Using R for introductory statistics* (1st ed.). Boca Raton, FL: Chapman & Hall/CRC.

This book makes *R* accessible to the introductory student. The author presents a self-contained treatment of statistical topics and the intricacies of the *R* software. The pacing is such that students are able to master data manipulation and exploration before diving into more advanced statistical concepts. The book treats exploratory data analysis with more attention than is typical, includes a chapter on simulation, and provides a unified approach to linear models.This text lays the foundation for further study and development in statistics using *R*. Appendices cover installation, graphical user interfaces, and teaching with *R*, as well as information on writing functions and producing graphics. This is an ideal text for integrating the study of statistics with a powerful computational tool.

Wickham, H. (2009). *Ggplot2 elegant graphics for data analysis*. New York: Springer.

This book will be useful to everyone who has struggled with displaying their data in an informative and attractive way. You will need some basic knowledge of *R* (i.e., you should be able to get your data into *R*), but *ggplot2* is a mini-language specifically tailored for producing graphics, and you will learn everything you need in the book. After reading this book you will be able to produce graphics customized precisely for your problems, and you will find it easy to get graphics out of your head and onto the screen or page.

FREELY AVAILABLE RESOURCES FOR CONDUCTING OUTCOME EVALUATIONS

Administration for Children and Families. (2010). *The program manager's guide to evaluation* (2nd ed.). Washington, DC: US Department of Health and Human Services, Children's Bureau. http://www.acf.hhs.gov/sites/default/files/opre/program_managers_guide_to_eval2010.pdf.

This text explains what program evaluation is, why evaluation is important, how to conduct an evaluation and understand the results, how to report evaluation findings, and how to use evaluation results to improve programs that benefit children and families. It also contains tips, samples, and a thoroughly updated appendix containing a comprehensive list of evaluation resources.

Bond, S. L., Boyd, S. E., & Rapp, K. A. (1997). *Taking stock: A practical guide to evaluating your own programs*. Chapel Hill, NC: Horizon Research. http://www.horizon-research.com/publications/stock.pdf.

This guide is unique in that it assumes that community-based organizations are conducting their own evaluations without support from an outside evaluator or consultant. The guide discusses the usefulness of evaluations, documentation needs, data collection. It also provides tips for organizing, interpreting, and reporting findings.

Centers for Disease Control and Prevention. (2011). *Developing an effective evaluation plan*. Atlanta, GA: Centers for Disease Control and Prevention, National Center for Chronic Disease Prevention and Health Promotion, Office on Smoking and Health; Division of Nutrition, Physical Activity and Obesity. http://www.cdc.gov/tobacco/tobacco_control_programs/surveillance_evaluation/evaluation_plan/pdfs/developing_eval_plan.pdf.

This workbook applies the CDC Framework for Program Evaluation in Public Health (www.cdc.gov/eval). The Framework lays out a six-step process for the decisions and activities involved in conducting an evaluation.

European Monitoring Centre for Drugs and Drug Addiction. (2000). *Tools for evaluating practices: Workbooks on evaluation of psychoactive substance use disorder treatment*. http://www.emcdda.europa.eu/themes/best-practice/tools.

This series of eight workbooks provides the guidance necessary to conduct a variety of evaluations. While specifically designed for substance use programs, principles taught in these workbooks can be applied to other types of social service programs. These workbooks were developed in collaboration with the World Health Organization and the United Nations International Drug Control Programme.

Substance Abuse and Mental Health Services Administration National Registry of Evidence-Based Programs and Practices. (2012). *Non-researcher's guide to evidence-based program evaluation*. Rockville, MD: Author. http://www.nrepp.samhsa.gov/Courses/ProgramEvaluation/resources/NREPP_Evaluation_course.pdf.

This freely available course (which can be accessed online or downloaded) provides a guide for conducting evaluations. Many of the topics discussed in the early chapters of this book are included in this course; however, additional topics are included (e.g., hiring external evaluators, managing evaluation projects).

Van Marris, B., & King, B. (2007). *Evaluating health promotion programs*. Toronto, Ontario: Centre for Health Promotion, University of Toronto. http://www.thcu.ca/resource_db/pubs/107465116.pdf.

This workbook uses a logical 10-step model to provide an overview of key concepts and methods to assist health promotion practitioners in the development and implementation of program evaluations.

W. K. Kellogg Foundation. (2004). *W. K. Kellogg Foundation evaluation handbook*. Battle Creek, MI: Author. http://www.wkkf.org/resource-directory/resource/2010/w-k-kellogg-foundation-evaluation-handbook.

This handbook provides a framework for thinking about evaluation and outlines a blueprint for designing and conducting evaluations, either independently or with the support of an external evaluator/consultant. Written and freely distributed by the W. K. Kellogg Foundation.

FREELY AVAILABLE RESOURCES FOR CREATING LOGIC MODELS

Barkman, S. (n.d.). *Utilizing the logic model for program design and evaluation*. West Lafayette, IN: Purdue University. http://www.humanserviceresearch.com/youthlifeskillsevaluation/LogicModel.pdf.

This resource provides a good description of logic models, provides examples, templates, and terminology. This is an excellent starting point if you want to develop your own logic model.

Child Welfare Information Gateway. (n.d.). *Logic model builders*. Washington, DC: US Department of Health and Human Services, Administration for Children & Families. https://toolkit.childwelfare.gov/toolkit/.

This interactive tool can be used to develop logic models for programs related to family support and child welfare. You must establish an account; however, there is no charge for this. Logic models can be displayed in a variety of formats and saved as a Word document.

Openshaw, L. L., Lewellen, A., & Harr, C. (2011). A logic model for program planning and evaluation applied to a rural social work department. *Contemporary Rural Social Work, 3*, 40–49. http://journal.und.edu/crsw/article/view/386/129.

This article discusses the uses and advantages of logic models in program planning and evaluation. A comprehensive example is provided, as is a template for creating a logic model.

Taylor-Powell, E., Jones, L., & Henert, E. (2003). *Enhancing program performance with logic models*. Madison: University of Wisconsin-Extension, Cooperative Extension. http://www.uwex.edu/ces/pdande/evaluation/pdf/lmcourseall.pdf.

This pdf is a course that provides an approach to planning and evaluating education and outreach programs. It helps program practitioners use and apply logic models—a framework and way of thinking to help us improve our work and be accountable for results. You will learn what a logic model is and how to use one for planning, implementation, evaluation, or communicating about your program. An interactive online version of the course can be accessed at http://www.uwex.edu/ces/lmcourse/#.

W. K. Kellogg Foundation. (2004). *Using logic models to bring together planning, evaluation, and action: Logic model development guide*. Battle Creek, MI: Author. http://www.wkkf.org/resource-directory/resource/2010/w-k-kellogg-foundation-evaluation-handbook.

This is a freely available and thorough curriculum on how to build and utilize logic models for evaluation purposes. It comes with examples, exercises, and checklists. Written and distributed by the W. K. Kellogg Foundation.

World Health Organization. (2000). *Workbook 1: Planning evaluations*. Geneva, Switzerland: Author.

This is one of eight workbooks produced in conjunction with the European Monitoring Centre for Drugs and Drug Addiction. It contains a host of information, but also specific information on developing logic models.

APPENDIX B

TERMINOLOGY USED IN THIS BOOK

Alternate hypothesis—Denoted as H_1 or H_A, the hypothesis that there is a relationship between the variables. This hypothesis can be directional (e.g., there is an improvement) or non-directional (e.g., there is a relationship, but the direction of the change is unimportant).

Character variable—Character, or string variables, are non-mathematical; they are commonly used in data analysis (for example, using "f" and "m" to represent female and males).

Command—In *R* there are hundreds of different commands to produce various statistical calculations. For example, the **table( )** command provides frequencies on the categories of a categorical variable.

Constant/*y*-intercept—The predicted value of *Y* when all independent variables are zero.

Cross-sectional research design—a research design that involves measuring variables at only one point in time. Causality cannot be determined with cross-sectional designs, as it is impossible to determine the nature of the relationship between variables.

Dependent variable—The dependent variable is affected by a change in the independent. It is sometimes referred to as the outcome variable.

Effect size—A method to quantify how large a difference exists between two groups means. Cohen's *d*, a measure of effect size, can be calculated with the *effsize* package's function, **cohen.d( )**.

Factor variable—A factor variable is a type of categorical variable that can be represented as a string or a number. Converting categorical variables to factors in *R* has a number of advantages, especially when tables and graphics are used in data analysis.

Function—An *R* function is a collection *R* code and commands to perform a particular task.

Heteroscedasticity/homoscedasticity—The concept of the degree of variability of an independent variable around a dependent variable across a range of values. Heteroscedasticty suggests unequal variability, while homoscedasticity suggest equal variability. Parametric statistical modeling assumes homoscedasticity of residuals, and heteroscedasticity suggests that a developed model may not be a good fit.

Independent variable—A variable that is not dependent on another but is thought to produce a change in the dependent variable. Also called a predictor.

Interaction—This means that one predictor variable's relationship with the outcome variable is dependent on its relationship with another independent variable.

Level of measurement—A level of measurement is the mathematical characteristic of a variable. Variables with higher levels of measurement (e.g., ratio) have more precision than those with lower levels of measurement (e.g., nominal).

Log-odds—The log of the probability of success divided by the probability of failure.

Logistic regression—Logistic regression is included within the class of structure of the generalized linear model (GLM), which is appropriate to use in predicting different types of dependent variables from a set of independent variables. Logistic regression focuses on the chances of an event occurring versus not occurring.

Longitudinal research design—A research design that takes place with repeated measures. In these designs the same variables are observed repeatedly to see the degree to which change takes place.

Missing data—This is information about an observation that has been omitted. This usually occurs when a subject or respondent elects not to answer a particular question. In *R* "NA" represents missing data, and when instructed, *R* will not include the observation in its calculations.

Multicollinearity—The phenomenon where two or more independent variables are highly correlated. This suggests high overlap between what is being measured in these variables. One of the simplest ways to deal with multicollinearity is to eliminate the variable from the equation that is most highly correlated to the others.

Multiple regression—Multiple linear regression is an extension of simple regression with the inclusion of multiple independent variables. Because there are multiple independent variables, the interpretation of the coefficients is more complex.

Null hypothesis—The hypothesis of no change, often notated as H_0. The null hypothesis states that there is no relationship between the independent variable(s) and the dependent variable.

Odds ratio—The odds of an event occurring divided by the odds of it not occurring.

Package—A package is a collection of *R* functions and code to perform a specific type of statistical analysis. These have been written by *R* users, and many packages can be downloaded directly from the Comprehensive R Archive Network, or CRAN.

Recode—A method used to combine, collapse, or correct data.

Residual—A residual is the difference between what is actually observed from what a statistical model predicts.

Simple regression—The most basic type of regression would be an equation predicting a single dependent variable from a single independent variable. Often referred to as ordinary least squares, or OLS.

Slope—The degree of change in Y (the outcome variable) for each unit increase in X (the predictor variable).

Type I error—This is the probability of making an incorrect decision by rejecting the null hypothesis and accepting the alternate when, in fact, the null is correct. In the social sciences, findings are typically considered statistically significant if p, or the probability of making a Type I error, is 0.05 (5%).

Variable—A variable is anything that can differ from observation to observation. The following are examples of variables: gender, household income, and number of children. This is in direct contrast to a constant, which is held stable between observations.

Vector—A vector is a collection of elements that can be stored as a variable. Vectors can be numbers, characters, dates, or any combination of these. Applying a function to a vector in *R* affects each element in the vector.

APPENDIX C

R PACKAGES REFERRED TO IN THIS BOOK

Package	Short Name	Description of Package on CRAN
aod	Analysis of Overdispersed Data	This package provides a set of functions to analyze overdispersed counts or proportions. Most of the methods are already available elsewhere but are scattered in different packages. The proposed functions should be considered as complements to more sophisticated methods such as generalized estimating equations (GEE) or generalized linear mixed effect models (GLMM).
car	Companion to Applied Regression	This package accompanies J. Fox and S. Weisberg, *An R companion to applied regression* (2nd ed.), Sage, 2011.
effects	Effect Displays for Linear, Generalized Linear, Multinomial-Logit, Proportional-Odds Logit Models a	Graphical and tabular effect displays, e.g., of interactions, for various statistical models with linear predictors.
effsize	Efficient Effect Size Computation	This package contains the functions to compute the standardized effect sizes for experiments (Cohen *d*, Hedges *g*, Cliff delta, Vargha and Delaney A). The computation algorithms have been optimized to allow efficient computation, even with very large data sets.

(continued)

Package	Short Name	Description of Package on CRAN
foreign	Read Data Stored by Minitab, S, SAS, SPSS, Stata, Systat, Weka, dBase,. . .	Functions for reading and writing data stored by some versions of Epi Info, Minitab, S, SAS, SPSS, Stata, Systat, and Weka and for reading and writing some dBase files.
ggplot2	An implementation of the Grammar of Graphics	An implementation of the grammar of graphics in *R*. It combines the advantages of both base and lattice graphics: conditioning and shared axes are handled automatically, and you can still build up a plot step by step from multiple data sources. It also implements a sophisticated multidimensional conditioning system and a consistent interface to map data to aesthetic attributes. See the *ggplot2* website for more information, documentation, and examples.
gmodels	Various R programming tools for model fitting	Various R programming tools for model fitting
Hmisc	Harrell Miscellaneous	The Hmisc package contains many functions useful for data analysis, high-level graphics, utility operations, functions for computing sample size and power, importing datasets, imputing missing values, advanced table making, variable clustering, character string manipulation, conversion of R objects to LaTeX code, and recoding variables.
memisc	Tools for Management of Survey Data, Graphics, Programming, Statistics, and Simulation	One of the aims of this package is to make life easier for users who deal with survey data sets. It provides an infrastructure for the management of survey data including value labels, definable missing values, recoding of variables, production of code books, and import of (subsets of) SPSS and Stata files. Further, it provides functionality to produce tables and data frames of arbitrary descriptive statistics and (almost) publication-ready tables of regression model estimates. Also some convenience tools for graphics, programming, and simulation are provided.

(continued)

Package	Short Name	Description of Package on CRAN
psych	Procedures for Psychological, Psychometric, and Personality	A number of routines for personality, psychometrics, and experimental psychology. Functions are primarily for scale construction using factor analysis, cluster analysis, and reliability analysis, although others provide basic descriptive statistics. Item Response Theory is done using factor analysis of tetrachoric and polychoric correlations. Functions for simulating particular item and test structures are included. Several functions serve as a useful front end for structural equation modeling. Graphical displays of path diagrams, factor analysis, and structural equation models are created using basic graphics. Some of the functions are written to support a book on psychometrics as well as publications in personality research. For more information, see the personality-project.org/r webpage.
SSDforR	SSD for R to analyze single system data	Package to visually and statistically analyze single system data
Resource-Selection	Resource Selection (Probability) Functions for Use-Availability Data	Resource Selection (Probability) Functions for use-availability wildlife data as described in Lele and Keim (2006, *Ecology, 87*, 3021–3028), and Lele (2009, *J. Wildlife Management,* 73, 122–127).

APPENDIX D

CLINICAL RECORD/FILEMAKER FIELD NAMES

NAMES TABLE

Field Name	Label/Description
ID	ID
admitnum	Admit #
status	Status Closed or Open Case
admit	Admit Date
lname	Last Name
fnmae	First Name
gender	Gender
dob	Date of Birth
race	Race
education	Education
marital	Marital
otherdem1	Other Demographic
reason	Reason for Referral Code
rdescription	Reason for Referral Description
Address	Client Address
City	Client City
State	Client State
zip	Client Zip
hphone	Home Telephone
cphone	Cell Number
wphone	Work Telephone
notes	Clinical noted
email1	Primary e-mail

email2	Secondary e-mail
clname	Contact Last Name
cfname	Contact First Name
crelationship	Contact Relationship
caddress	Contact Address
ccity	Contact City
cstate	Contact State
czip	Contact Zip
cphone	Contact Home Telephone
cwphone	Contact Work Telephone
ccelphone	Contact Cell Number
pinsure	Primary Insurance
sinsure	Secondary Insurance

INTERVENTIONS TABLE

Field Name	Label / Description
ID	ID
Date	Date
worker	Worker
department	Department
Intervention	Intervention
Description	Description
DX1	Primary DX
Dx1_description	Description of Primary DX
DX2	Secondary DX
DX2_description	Description of Secondary DX
duration	Duration
fees	Rate

DISPOSITION TABLE

Field Name	Label / Description
ID	ID
admitnum	Admit #
disdate	Discharge Date
discode	Discharge Code
description	Description
finaldx1	Final DX 1
dxdescription1	Description of Final Diagnosis 1
finaldx2	Final DX 2
dxdescription2	Description of Final Diagnosis 2
comment	Comment

OUTCOMES TABLE

Field Name	Label / Description
ID	ID
Date	Date
Type	Type of Outcome
measure	Measure
score	Score
task	Outcome Status
taskdescrip	Goal Description
time	Time Interval

REFERENCES

Administration for Children and Families. (2010). *The program manager's guide to evaluation* (2nd ed.). Washington, DC: US Department of Health and Human Services, Children's Bureau. Retrieved from http://www.acf.hhs.gov/sites/default/files/opre/program_managers_guide_to_eval2010.pdf.

Allen, A. O. (1990). *Probability, statistics, and queueing theory: With computer science applications* (2nd ed.). San Diego, CA: Academic Press, Inc. Retrieved from http://books.google.com/books?hl=en&lr=&id=PMMUbHvr-7sC&oi=fnd&pg=PR11&dq=arnold,+1990+%2B+statistics&ots=ANCEXzLEBV&sig=42rSmNpMCJm0b3e04gsF3ZZKEIQ.

American Speech-Language-Hearing Association. (2008). *Loss to follow-up in early hearing detection and intervention [Technical Report]*. Rockville, MD: Author. Retrieved from http://www.asha.org/policy/TR2008-00302.htm.

Auerbach, C., & Mason, S. E. (2010). The value of the presence of social work in emergency departments. *Social Work in Health Care, 49*(4), 314–326.

Auerbach, C., Mason, S. E., & Laporte, H. H. (2007). Evidence that supports the value of social work in hospitals. *Social Work in Health Care, 44*(4), 17–32.

Auerbach, C., Mason, S. E., Zeitlin Schudrich, W., Spivak, L., & Sokol, H. (2013). Public health, prevention and social work: The case of infant hearing loss. *Families in Society, 94*(3), 175–181.

Auerbach, C., Rock, B. D., Goldstein, M., Kaminsky, P., & Heft-Laporte, H. (2001). A department of social work uses data to prove its case (88–99B). *Social Work in Health Care, 32*(1), 9–23.

Auerbach, C., & Schudrich, W. Z. (2013). SSD for R: A comprehensive statistical package to analyze single-system data. *Research on Social Work Practice, 23*(3), 346–353. doi: 10.1177/1049731513477213.

Auerbach, C., & Zeitlin, W. (2014). *SSD for R: An R package for analyzing single-subject data*. New York: Oxford University Press.

Auerbach, C., Zeitlin, W., Augsberger, A., McGowan, B. G., Claiborne, N., & Lawrence, C. K. (2014). Societal factors impacting child welfare: Validating the Perceptions of Child Welfare Scale. *Research on Social Work Practice*, 1049731514530001. doi: 10.1177/1049731514530001.

Becker, S., Bryman, A., & Ferguson, H. (Eds.). (2012). *Understanding research for social policy and social work: Themes, methods and approaches*. Chicago: Policy Press/University of Chicago Press.

Bloom, M., Fischer, J., & Orme, J. G. (2009). *Evaluating practice: Guidelines for the accountable professional* (6th ed.). New York: Pearson.

Bloom, M., & Orme, J. (1994). Ethics and the single-system design. *Journal of Social Service Research, 18*(1–2), 161–180.

Bond, S. L., Boyd, S. E., & Rapp, K. A. (1997). *Taking stock: A practical guide to evaluating your own programs*. Chapel Hill, NC: Horizon Research. Retrieved from http://www.horizon-research.com/publications/stock.pdf.

Burn, D. A. (1993). 22 Designing effective statistical graphs. In *Handbook of statistics* (Vol. 9, pp. 745–773). Elsevier. Retrieved from http://www.sciencedirect.com/science/article/pii/S0169716105801464.

Casella, G., & Berger, R. L. (1990). *Statistical inference* (Vol. 70). Belmont, CA: Duxbury Press. Retrieved from http://departments.columbian.gwu.edu/statistics/sites/default/files/u20/Syllabus%206202-Spring%202013-%20Li.pdf.

Centers for Disease Control and Prevention. (2011). *Developing an effective evaluation plan*. Atlanta, GA: Centers for Disease Control and Prevention, National Center for Chronic Disease Prevention and Health Promotion, Office on Smoking and Health; Division of Nutrition, Physical Activity and Obesity. Retrieved from http://www.cdc.gov/tobacco/tobacco_control_programs/surveillance_evaluation/evaluation_plan/pdfs/developing_eval_plan.pdf.

Chang, W. (2012). *R graphics cookbook*. Sebastopol, CA: O'Reilly Media.

Cherry, S. (1998). Statistical tests in publications of The Wildlife Society. *Wildlife Society Bulletin, 26*(4), 947–953.

Corcoran, J., & Secret, M. (2013). *Social work research skills workbook: A step-by-step guide to conducting agency-based research*. New York: Oxford University Press.

Council on Social Work Education (CSWE). (2008). *Educational policy and accreditation standards*. Alexandria, VA: Author.

Epstein, I. (2010). *Clinical data-mining: Integrating practice and research*. New York: Oxford University Press. Retrieved from http://resourcecenter.ovid.com/site/catalog/Book/6059.pdf.

Faraway, J. J. (2004). *Linear models with R* (1st edition.). Boca Raton, FL: Chapman & Hall/CRC.

Fox, J., Weisberg, S., & Fox, J. (2011). *An R companion to applied regression*. Thousand Oaks, CA: SAGE Publications.

Fraser, M. W., Richman, J. M., Galinsky, M. J., & Day, S. H. (2009). *Intervention research: Developing social programs*. New York: Oxford University Press.

Freedman, D., & Diaconis, P. (1981). On the histogram as a density estimator: L 2 theory. *Zeitschrift Für Wahrscheinlichkeitstheorie Und Verwandte Gebiete, 57*(4), 453–476. doi: 10.1007/BF01025868.

Grinnell, R. M., Gabor, P., & Unrau, Y. A. (2012). *Program evaluation for social workers: Foundations of evidence-based programs*. New York: Oxford University Press.

Hamilton, L. C. (1991). *Regression with graphics: A second course in applied statistics*. Pacific Grove, CA: Cengage Learning.

Holosko, M. J., Thyer, B. A., & Danner, J. E. H. (2009). Ethical guidelines for designing and conducting evaluations of social work practice. *Journal of Evidence-Based Social Work, 6*(4), 348–360.

Kaufman-Levy, D., & Poulin, M. (2003). *Evaluability assessment: Examining the readiness of a program for evaluation*. Juvenile Justice Evaluation Center, Justice Research and Statistics Association. Retrieved from http://www.ncjrs.gov/App/abstractdb/AbstractDBDetails.aspx?id=209590.

Keen, K. J. (2010). *Graphics for statistics and data analysis with R*. Boca Raton, FL: Chapman & Hall/CRC.

Kirk, S., & Reid, W. J. (2002). *Science and social work: A critical appraisal*. New York: Columbia University Press.

Moore, D. S., & McCabe, G. P. (1989). *Introduction to the Practice of Statistics*. New York: W. H. Freeman.

Morris, L. L., Fitz-Gibbon, C. T., & Freeman, M. E. (1987). *How to communicate evaluation findings*. Thousand Oaks, CA: SAGE Publications.

National Association of Social Workers. (2008). *Code of ethics*. Washington, DC: Author.

National Coalition on Care Coordination. (n.d.). *Policy brief: Implementing care coordination in the Patient Protection and Affordable Care Act*. New York: Author.

Rock, B. D., Auerbach, C., Kaminsky, P., & Goldstein, M. (1993). Integration of computer and social work culture: A developmental model. In B. Glastonbury (Ed.), *Human welfare and technology: Papers from the Husita 3 Conference on IT and the quality of life and services*. Maastricht, The Netherlands: Van Gorcum, Assen.

Rock, B. D., Goldstein, M., Harris, M., Kaminsky, P., Quitkin, E., Auerbach, C., & Beckerman, N. L. (1996). A biopsychosocial approach to predicting resource utilization in hospital care of the frail elderly. *Social Work in Health Care, 22*(3), 21–37. doi: 10.1300/J010v22n03_02.

Rubin, A., & Bellamy, J. (2012). *Practitioner's guide to using research for evidence-based practice* (2nd ed.). Hoboken, NJ: John Wiley & Sons. Retrieved from http://books.google.com/books?hl=en&lr=&id=feknT9iqmSYC&oi=fnd&pg=PR3&dq=practitioner%27s+guide+to+using+research+for+evidence+based+&ots=FCS4JCqFVj&sig=VU82VwGkC4aYxoXpYrkH2-SSvP8.

Samuels, J., Schudrich, W., & Altschul, D. (2008). *Toolkit for modifying evidence-based practices to increase cultural competence*. Orangeburg, NY: The Nathan Kline Institute.

Schudrich, W. (2012). Implementing a modified version of Parent Management Training (PMT) with an intellectually disabled client in a special education setting. *Journal of Evidence-Based Social Work, 9*(5), 421–423.

Spivak, L., Sokol, H., Auerbach, C., & Gershkovich, S. (2009). Newborn hearing screening follow-up: Factors affecting hearing aid fitting by 6 months of age. *American Journal of Audiology, 18*(1), 24–33.

Substance Abuse and Mental Health Services Administration National Registry of Evidence-Based Programs and Practices. (2012). *Non-researcher's guide to evidence-based program evaluation*. Rockville, MD: Author. Retrieved from http://www.nrepp.samhsa.gov/Courses/ProgramEvaluation/resources/NREPP_Evaluation_course.pdf.

The R Project for Statistical Computing. (n.d.). *What Is R?* Retrieved from http://www.r-project.org/about.html.

Van Marris, B., & King, B. (2007). *Evaluating health promotion programs*. Toronto, Ontario: Centre for Health Promotion, University of Toronto. Retrieved from http://www.thcu.ca/resource_db/pubs/107465116.pdf.

Weisberg, S., & Fox, J. (2010). *An R companion to applied regression* (2nd ed.). Thousand Oaks, CA: Sage Publications.

Whitaker, T. R. (2012). Professional social workers in the child welfare workforce: Findings from NASW. *Journal of Family Strengths, 12*(1), 8.

Wickham, H. (2009). *Ggplot2 elegant graphics for data analysis*. Dordrecht; New York: Springer.

W. K. Kellogg Foundation. (2004). *W. K. Kellogg Foundation evaluation handbook*. Battle Creek, MI: Auth. Retrieved from http://www.wkkf.org/resource-directory/resource/2010/w-k-kellogg-foundation-evaluation-handbook.

INDEX

R FUNCTIONS INDEX

Made in the USA
Middletown, DE
04 June 2024

55265632R00170